GEORGIA CEMETERIES

VOLUME I
FULTON COUNTY

Penny Westfall

HERITAGE BOOKS
2008

HERITAGE BOOKS

AN IMPRINT OF HERITAGE BOOKS, INC.

Books, CDs, and more—Worldwide

For our listing of thousands of titles see our website
at
www.HeritageBooks.com

Published 2008 by
HERITAGE BOOKS, INC.
Publishing Division
100 Railroad Ave. #104
Westminster, Maryland 21157

International Standard Book Numbers
Paperbound: 978-0-7884-1342-1
Clothbound: 978-0-7884-7212-1

Table of Contents

Introduction

Fulton County encompasses Georgia's largest city, Atlanta, plus the vicinity to the north-west of the city – a county rich with Civil War history. Atlanta, the capital of Georgia, is also the seat of Fulton County.

Genealogical researchers of Georgia families will want to add this volume to their library. This volume concentrates on historical cemeteries, comprising thousands of names gathered from a dozen Fulton County cemeteries to create a valuable research tool. The majority of the readings are dated within the eighteen and nineteen hundreds.

Readings are grouped by cemetery, including: Pleasant Hill, Founders, Old Roswell, Mt. Pisgah, Maxwell, Mt. Oliver, Pleasant Hill Historical, Resthaven, Providence Baptist, Union Hill Baptist, Hopewell Baptist Church, and Greenlawn. Surname headings for each cemetery are listed alphabetically with individual entries alphabetized under each heading. Entries include (as available) given name, birth date and death date. Relationship information, such as spouse or sibling, has been listed whenever possible.

Anderson
> Mary 18 Sept 1842-4 Jan 1903

Ashley
> Kate L.w/o Robert A;1870-1964
> Robert A. h/o Kate L;1870-1946

Baker
> Annie Nelson 1 Dec 1864-18 Mar 1891
> Evelyn C. d/o Kate N; 26 Mar 1837-25 Dec 1923
> Francis Lorinda w/o John F; 18 Oct 1805-26 Jan 1857
> W.E. 20 Feb 1830-5 Jan 1906

Barrington
> Evelyn 16 Nov 1889-9 Jan 1960

Beall
> C.C. 14 Feb 1883-4 Jun 1911

Betner
> Addie 10 May 1885-12 Jul 1886

Brook
> George William 27 Jul 1924-23 Nov 1979

Brooks
> Pearl 20 May 1915-12 May 1935
> Wylene 18 Jul 1933-12 Apr 1934

Brown
> Sarah Caldwell 31 Jan 1827-21 Sept 1907

Buice
> Olive N. 15 May 1884-3 Sept 1916

Butler
> Frances Stewart h/o Eva B; 7 Feb 1855-13 Jun 1930
> Samuel Irvin 7 Jul 1857-Aug 26, 1912

Caldwell
> Addie 29 Aug 1859-27 Jun 1933
> Thomas 16 Mar 1864-25 Jul 1883
> William 24 Nov 1861-11 Sept 1877

Carton
> Monica 23 May 1910-7 Jul 1992

Clark
> D.W. d: 23 Dec 1895; 38y
> Tranquilla d: 1 April 1904; 12y

Clay

Lena McGinnis w/o Robert Kile; 28 May 1899-18 Aug 1955
Robert Kile h/o Lena M; 12 Jul 1891-8 May 1972

Coleman

Eva 8 Aug 1895-30 Jul 1897
Flora Annis 27 Sept 1872-23 Aug 1892
Maud 25 Jul 1889-10 Aug 1890
Nancy E. w/o W.K.; 16 Oct 1854-29 Aug 1898
Pleasant h/o Sarah E; 9 May 1823-17 Nov 1894
Sarah E w/o Pleasant; 23 Jul 1828-26 Dec 1910

Collins

Alice R. w/o Mark G.; 24 Aug 1922-20 Dec 1972
Mark G. h/o Alice R.; 10 Aug 1914-19 Jan 1995

Conaway

Lillian Arnold w/o William J; 4 Oct 1870-30 Oct 1944
Marie w/o Marcus M. Minor; 31 Mar 1895-26 Dec 1969

Covington

Elias Gilbert 5 Nov 1906-18 Nov 1906
Mary Jane 6 Aug 1911-6 Aug 1911
Willie Oleva 22 Mar 1878-6 Jan 1936

Covongton

Alice Vienna 15 Sept 1904-22 Sept 1904
Ruby May 6 Sept 1902-19 Jun 1903

Crawford

Jeffery Reid 10 Dec 1952-13 Dec 1952

Drake

Annie w/o John W. Rollins; 17 Nov 1871-15 Nov 1966
Henry 1866-1939
John W. h/o Margareta B.; 4 Aug 1824-24 Aug 1892
Margareta B. w/o John W; 20 Dec 1829-20 May 1915

Dunwoody

C.A. 1827-1905
Corinne E. d: 12 Apr 1875; 14y 6m
Edward M. d: 31 May 1873; 16y 6m 14d
Ella Wing w/o John E.; 15 Jan 1859-6 Mar 1962
George H. 12 Nov 1864-2 Oct 1903
Henry M. d: 2 Jul 1863; 37y 3m 19d
Howard M. 27 Jul 1890-16 Aug 1895
John Elliot h/o Ella Wing; 10 Nov 1858-7 Aug 1929
L.A. 1927-1965
Leila d: 26 Oct 1866; 13y 6m 10d

Matilda Elizabeth 26 Jun 1829-24 Jun 1882
Enhull
    Alman G. Hock 28 Apr 1880-13 Jan 1964
Farlain
    Rosina w/o John Minton; d: 4 Oct 1897; 75y
Faulkner
    Carlous Lane 29 Jan 1873-9 Jul 1951
    Charles Wesley h/o Henrietta W. 27 Mar 1832-8 Mar 1903
    Henrietta Whitmore w/o Charles W. 30 Mar 1836-30 Apr 1919
    Ida Isabell 12 Nov 1870-6 Nov 1878
    Thomas Atherton 3 Sep 1875-16 Nov 1878
Feckoury
    Della Singley 1896-1935
    John H. Wing 3 Sept 1890-2 Nov 1949
    Nancy M. 11 Sep 1855-21 Jan 1921
    Phillip E. 13 Jun 1912-8 Mar 1914
    Sarah E. 1 Jun 1889-31 Jan 1855
    Michael F. 10 Mar 1883-7 Nov 1973
Gipson
    John J. h/o Rebecca Ann; 1856-1924
    Rebecca Ann w/o John J.; 1857-1927
    Fannie V. 1896-1966
Greer
    Cordella Robinson 1851-1926
    Turner Atticus d: 28 Jul 1959; 78y
    Turner Goldsmith 1836-1911
Hampton
    Mary E. 5 May 1833-23 Feb 1883
Harris
    Ada Feckoury w/o John L.; 14 May 1920-15 Jan 1988
    John L. h/o Ada Feckoury; 24 Apr 1913-10 Jul 1980
    Rebecca Nancy d: 28 Aug 1953
Hudlow
    Bertie 12 Jul 1896-11 Jun 1911
    Thomas Sherman 1 Jan 1862-27 Aug 1929
James
    William A h/o Sarah; 14 Jul 1897-11 May 1981
Jones
    Susan Jan 1832-29 Jul 1911

King
>Barrington f/o Barrington J.; 9 Mar 1798-17 Jan 1866
>Barrington 31 Mar 1862-26 May 1884
>Barrington J. s/o Barrington; 29 Apr 1853-20 Jul 1899
>Barrington S. s/o B&C.M. ; 17 Oct 1833-10 Mar 1865
>Charles Barrington 1 Mar 1849-5 May 1850
>Charles Clifford 4 Oct 1857-28 Feb 1944
>Inez Morris w/o Norman Prince; 2 Apr 1896-12 Aug 1957
>Margaret E. 18 Feb 1881-2 Apr 1862
>Maria d: 2 Apr 1862; 3m
>Matty 6 Mar 1852-16 Mar 1856
>Norman Prince h/o Inez Morris; 28 Jan 1889-2 Oct 1959
>Thomas Edward 26 Feb 1829-19 Sept 1863

Lang
>John Henry 16 Aug 1862-19 Aug 1886

Leron
>Martha Jane 9 July 1859-7 Dec 1926

Leroy
>B.E. h/o Miranda; 25 Dec 1851-8 May 1921
>Miranda w/o B.E.; 18 Sept 1845-8 May 1921

Lonaway
>Lillian Arnold 4 Oct 1870-30 Oct 1944
>William John 16 Feb 1870-12 May 1939
>Marie 31 Mar 1895-26 Dec 1968

MaGill
>Aurela Isabella 1880-1907
>Helen Zubly 17 Oct 1813-18 Feb 1897

McGinnis
>Robert H 3 Oct 1877-12 Jul 1934

McNeely
>Claud Stewart 3 Aug 1885-12 Jun 1908
>Frances R. 16 Mar 1858-19 Oct 1887
>Mollie L. 15 Apr 1866-1 Jan 1911

Merrill
>Arthur h/o Sarah Harrison; 16 Sept 1908-27 Mar 1990
>Sarah Harrison w/o Arthur; 17 Jun 1912-11 Jul 1983

Minor
>Marcus Marion h/o Marie Conaway; 31 Mar 1895-26 Dec 1968

Minton
>Daisy Dean d/o James D.; 25 Aug 1873-11 Mar 1911
>Edith 16 Apr 1835-29 Jul 1925

James D. h/o Mary D. f/o Daisy D.; 27 Apr 1832-19 Dec 1907
John 1797-1871
Mary D. w/o James D. m/o Daisy D.;23 Apr 1833-2 Apr 1905
Mary W. 1801-17 Jul 1874
Newton
Charles Byrd 3 Jun 1914-20 May 1995
Power
George William 9 Nov 1903-20 Mar 1993
Martha Frances T. w/o Robert J.; d. 20 Apr 1936
Robert Jehue h/o Martha Frances; 20 Dec 1879-1 Sept 1947
Prat
Catherine King w/o Nathaniel Ipheus; 1810-1894
Nathaniel Ipheus h/o Catherine King; 1796-1879
Frances 26 Jan 1857-19 Nov 1857
Frances Lorinda 13 Oct 1835-28 Jan 1877
Horace Alphells 1880-1870
Lilias Logan 27 Aug 1827-11 Dec 1878
Sarah Anna 1844-1937
Price
Mary Allyson 12 Mar 1972-12 Mar 1972
Pruitte
Amellia 15 Nov 1836-31 May 1905
Renland
Anna 11 Nov 1866-12 Jun 1893
Roberts
Isaac M. 28 Feb 1853-15 May 1930
Nannie T. 13 Sept 1869-16 Jun 1924
Sara 20 Oct 1909-24 May 1973
Rogers
John Raymond 25 Sept 1808-2 Sept 1889
Neomie Watson 7 Nov 1875-31 Oct 1899
Rollins
John William h/o Annie Drake; 15 Nov 1868-12 Sept 1932
Rucker
Edith W. w/o George Nap; 1887-1974
George Nap h/o Edith W.; 1884-1970
Rushin
Emmett Raoul 18 Nov 1909-24 Aug 1993
Sherman
Bessie 21 Feb 1888-7 Sept 1908

Ellen Cochran 12 Nov 1850-14 Feb 1939
John D. 1 Dec 1844-1 Dec 1904
Smith
Harold H. 5 Dec 1924-2 Mar 1996
Stewart
Mary J. 3 Sept 1853-11 Sept 1931
Thomson
Alex C. 18 Nov 1929-27 Jan 1983
Tucker
Martha Frances : d. 20 Apr 1926
Tunnell
Katherine Ward Greer 18 Jul 1886-9 Feb 1982
Turner
Atticus Judd Greer d. 28 Jul 1959 : 78y
Wall
Mary Nell 26 Oct 1913-27 May 1928
Watson
Galie 2 Aug 1851-1 Apr 1924
Pashant 2 Aug 1828-20 June 1880
Whitmire
Frances 1799-1880
Frances 15 May 1834-13 Nov 1911
Wing
Ada L. 6 May 1877-29 Aug 1948
Cecile 17 Jul 1890-1 Apr 1906
Eliza W. w/o George W.; 23 Apr 1852-10 May 1947
George 10 Oct 1885-19 Jan 1951
George W. h/o Eliza W.; 15 Sept 1854-7 Mar 1918
Hattie Suddath 17 Dec 1875-10 Oct 1971
Jehile Bartow 20 Sept 1861-7 Nov 1917
Mary Esther 31 Oct 1875-11 Oct 1895
Nicholson Roy 1883-1930
Olive E. 17 Jan 1879-20 Feb 1968
Wood
Annie W. w/o Eugene H.; 1864-1964
Eugene H. h/o Annie W. 1864-1938
Jason S. 1829-1884
Josephine Feckoury 13, Feb 1914-16 Aug 1993

Worake
John B, 4 Aug 1824-24 Aug 1892

Wright
    Isabell Julia 1846-1924

Fulton County
Founders Cemetery

Anderson
    James G. h/o Ela; 3 May 1932-3 Dec 1982
Bullock
    Jane w/o John Dunwoody; Apr 1788-30 Jun 1857
Burney
    James A. 13 Oct 1800-16 Mar 1860
Dunwoody
    John h/o Jane Bullock; 13 Jan 1786-6 Jun 1856
Elliot
    George A 14 Jun 1822-29 Sept 1848
King
    Roswell 3 May 1765-15 Feb 1811

Fulton County
Old Roswell Cemetary

Abercrombie
    Kate B. w/o Tom; 28 Jun 1897-22 Jul 1971
    Tom h/o Kate B.; 18 Mar 1891-21 Aug 1961
Abernathy
    Chessie w/o Ira W.; 24 Jun 1899-6 Feb 1975
    Cody Ford 10 May 1964-11 May 1964
    Ellen w/o Samuel; 1904-1992
    Franklin D. 22 May 1922-20 Feb 1934
    Hattie 5 Jan 1900-13 Jun 1979
    Ira W. h/o Chessie; 5 Apr 1900-26 May 1959
    Lessie C, h/o Tillie; 12 Oct 1904-11 May 1984
    Nora J. d: 9 Aug 1887
    Omer L. 4 Jan 1883-20 Aug 1929

Samuel h/o Ellen; 1901-1967
Tillie E. w/o Lessie C; 6 Feb 1904-28 Jun 1967
William L. 9 Sept 1913-14 Dec 1914
Willie Young 7 Nov 1891-29 Dec 1933
Adams
A.E. Farmer 12 Dec 1890-18 Nov 1914
Almeda E. w/o Robert A; 9 Dec 1877-12 Feb 1970
Amanda J. w/o Edgar J.; 6 Jun 1867-21 May 1955
Bill 28 Oct 1917-11 Mar 197
Clarence R. 8 Jul 1909-16 May 1964
Ed V. 17 Sept 1887-4 Sept 1976
Etta May 17 Dec 1890-12 Apr 1955
Howard H Coleman 1904-1953
J. Silva h/o Lizzie; 8 Dec 1882-29 Dec 1956
Jerry 19 Jan 1937-1 Oct 1983
John Q. 1866-1945
Lizzie w/o J. Silva; 26 Aug 1880-5 Mar 1964
Mary O. 20 Feb 1851-23 Feb 1922
Nancy S. 1864-1946
R.A. 19 Aug 1844-18 Mar 1923
Robert A h/o Almeda E; 4 Mar 1873-11 Apr 1941
Allen
Apelin A 14 Dec 1856-8 Jul 1880
Lorenza D. 12 Jun 1833-14 Feb 1927
Sarah A. 20 Sept 1888-4 May 1966
Allison
Andrew B. 24 Oct 1900-14 May 1935
James P. 10 Oct 1897-14 Nov 1940
Lou Ella 25 Jan 1895-23 Mar 1969
Mary Lee 6 Jul 1917-7 Jul 1976
Sarah d: 12 May 1909; 66y
Anderson
Aubrey 25 Nov 1911-11 May 1972
Carl 21 Dec 1893-7 Aug 1912
Eula B. w/o James Albert ; 9 Jan 1883-6 Feb 1969
Hannah Elizabeth 28 June 1984-30 June 1984
James Albert h/o Eula B.; 4 Jul 1883-9 Jun 1965
Reba C. 4 Oct 1934-28 Apr 1982
Andrews
Larry Leon 10 Sept 1944-26 May 1994

Anglin
 Emma May 7 Apr 1883-10 Dec 1912
 J.W. 6 Aug 1877-28 May 1914
 Maude w/o Paul; 15 Oct 1911-23 Nov 1986
 Paul h/o Maude; 12 Jun 1910-21 Feb 1956
 Roy 1902-1947
Arnold
 D.S. 7 Nov 1830-19 Feb 1908
 Daniel H. 4 Nov 1794-2 May 1868
 Given N. h/o Sarah M.; 1 Sept 1825-13 Sept 1901
 Hattie Bell 27 Oct 1874-16 Jun 1890
 Margaret M. 17 Jul 1823-26 Apr 1886
 Mary A. 21 Jun 1840-6 Jul 1890
 Mary L. 11 May 1800-29 May 1862
 Sarah M. w/o Given N.; 30 Jan 1836-3 Feb 1917
 Sophia T. 1839-1925
Ash
 Martha 1807-Aug 1882
Atcheson
 Jesse W. 1915-1984
 Jesse Willard 18 Nov 1915-1 Jan 1984
Atkinson
 Ora I. 21 Jun 1886-30 Nov 1972
 Robert E. 14 Jan 1876-15 Jun 1938
 Ruby Lee 14 May 1908-17 Aug 1923
Awlings
 Noona 8 Sept 1919-9 June 1974
Baggett
 Cyrell H 13 Feb 1915-20 May 1982
Bagley
 Elder C. h/o Sarah E.; 18 Oct 1892-8 Sept 1960
 Sarah E. w/o Elder C.; 12 Dec 1893-30 Jan 1963
Bagwell
 Ealston 28 Jun 1897-10 Mar 1973
Bailiff
 Alice Mae C. 17 Nov 1886-5 Dec 1988
 Gid T. 11 May 1886-15 Jul 1938
 Harry Alton 20 Feb 1915-22 Oct 1981
Ball
 Bascombe C. h/o Lizzie G.; 17 Nov 1871-22 Nov 1962
 Cora I 8 Sept 1905-25 Sept 1992

Hazel R 28 Mar 1900-6 Sept 1978
Lizzie Gunter w/o Bascombe C.; 24 May 1871-23 May 1958
Martin 3 Nov 1831-13 Jan 1910
Namie Harring 1892-1936
Otis G. 26 Dec 1899-5 Sept 1971
Sophia 7 Apr 1850-1 Nov 1925
Bannister
George Lester h/o Ivy Myrtle; 19 Sept 1878-21 Sept 1920
Ivy Myrtle w/o George Lester; 7 May 1878-8 May 1943
John Lawrence 11 Nov 1855-11 Oct 1923
Lester Pierce 10 Mar 1905-28 May 1931
Maybelle 1 Oct 1954-1 Dec 1925
Barnes
Nancy D. Perkins 1843-1926
Bass
Alvin 13 Aug 1866-24 Sept 1928
Bates
Annis Lee 5 Aug 1946-6 Apr 1949
Homer J. 31 Oct 1918-8 Oct 1992
Beal
Elizabeth 11 May 1920-3 Jul 1920
Bearden
Lemuel Marion 10 Nov 1870-22 Oct 1957
Beebout
Hugh A. 24 Oct 1931-22 Feb 1933
Kate Ramsey 25 Mar 1893-24 Jun 1924
Lewis Edgar 24 May 1930-2 Mar 1931
Luther C. 4 Mar 1933-7 Dec 1933
Robert Emory 27 Mar 1879-23 Mar 1965
Bennett
George R. 7 Sept 1879-14 Sept 1967
Lois B. 25 Jan 1887-1 Mar 1964
Bernhardt
Frances Gunter 18 May 1921-2 Dec 1974
Berry
Charles E. h/o Mary Hood; 1869-1933
Chester C. 1900-1935
Mary Hood w/o Charles E.; 1878-1955
Bibb
Lila 2 Feb 1919-2 Feb 1990

Bishop
    Cora M. 30 Jul 1913-22 May 1987
    Horace B. 11 Apr 1833-12 Mar 1964
    Zola Mae 30 Mar 1890-9 Sept 1960
Blackston
    Glenn R. 5 May 1929-8 Nov 1963
    Mittie F. w/o William R.; 19 Aug 1905-17 Apr 1991
    William R. h/o Mittie F.; 4 Apr 1897-8 Apr 1967
Blackwell
    Jesse H. h/o Maude Rainwater; 1889-1961
    Lizzie A. 1890-1937
    Maude Rainwater w/o Jesse H.; 1889-1925
    Walter Everett 12 Sept 1911-26 May 1914
Blalock
    Bonnie N. w/o James D.; 19 Apr 1923-19 Jan 1987
    James D. h/o Bonnie N.; 29 May 1920-28 Jun 1992
Blook
    Claudie B. 18 May 1887-31 Oct 1922
    Fred W. 3 Oct 1878-29 Mar 1922
Bobbitt
    Jewell G. 14 Aug 1914-30 Oct 1972
Boggs
    Della Apr 1918-24 Jul 1918
    Mary Williams 1882-14 Jul 1918
Booker
    Carl C. 1912-1992
    Frances Elizabeth 1924-1970
    Jaunita Louise d: 7 Nov 1984
    Nolan Jason 23 Jun 1909-26 Jan 1965
Bottoms
    Clara P. w/o Paul W.; 1877-1964
    Gussie E. h/o Zaida; 7 Oct 1901-22 Jan 1977
    Paul W. h/o Clara P.; 1866-1947
    Zaida w/o Gussie E.; 16 Dec 1899-23 Apr 1931
Bowden
    Eugenia M.W. 3 Mar 1876-19 Mar 1956
    William 3 Feb 1875-20 Jan 1941
    William 31 Aug 1903-16 Nov 1883
Bowen
    D.P. 31 Jan 1848-5 May 1926
    Lewis 10 Jun 194-25 Dec 1992

Lydia 3 May 1867-21 Oct 1936
Nancy Jane 16 Feb 1843-23 Nov 1906
Sarey Jane d; 12 Mar 1858
William J. 4 May 1866-9 Jan 1938
Brantley
    Annie P. 20 Oct 1890-2 Nov 1962
    James Levi 5 Nov 1882-16 May 1958
    Louie G. 4 Jun 1904-2 Dec 1904
    Quincy Lucius 25 May 1914-23 May 1939
Braswell
    Julia Aug 1866-Mar 1943
    S.S. 29 Nov 1862-17 Sept 1930
Brimer
    Genie B. w/o Newton L.; 24 Aug 1908-2 Jul 1977
    Newton L. h/o Genie B.; 10 May 1902-22 Feb 1963
Britton
    Joseph F. 6 Mar 1944-13 Mar 1963
    Willie Mae 12 Oct 1924-10 Oct 1994
Broadwell
    Carrie Tally w/o James York; 24 Mar 1892-6 Aug 1957
    Harrison M. 7 Mar 1867-29 Jun 1932
    James York h/o Carrie Tally; d:16 Apr 1940
    Leo 2 Apr 1909-4 Sept 1970
    R. Hugh 17 Jun 1919-4 Feb 1987
Brock
    Ignatius 29 Jul 1901-30 Oct 1984
    Mary Will Weaver 30 Nov 1907-2 May 1994
    Susan 21 Jun 1920-7 Aug 1944
Brooks
    Thomas F. 10 Aug 1940-18 Apr 1995
Brown
    Bertha Dempsey w/o Larkin T.; 1887-1976
    Catherine Weldon 12 Sept 1896-6 Mar 1923
    Cowart O. 1922-1976
    Emory W. 5 Nov 1876-8 Sept 1966
    George Dempsey 29 Jul 1920-20 Jan 1984
    James Harry 18 Nov 1910-29 Jun 1927
    Katie M. 12 Nov 1889-12 Feb 1965
    Katie T. 4 Mar 1910-Aug 26, 1910
    Larkin T. h/o Bertha Dempsey; 1888-1956
    Mary F. Johnson w/o R.B.; 16 Sept 1856-6 Oct 1919

Mary L. 4 Apr 1879-11 Sept 1908
R.B. h/o Mary F. Johnson; 12 Jun 1842-28 Aug 1911
Samuel T. 13 Oct 1882-23 Apr 1910
Wiliam I. 26 Dec 1877-25 Nov 1947

Buice

Ambry A 24 May 1907-22 Oct 1963
Annie R. 29 Jan 1869-25 Oct 1945
H.L. 20 Jun 1860-20 Jan 1928
Hillard 23 Feb 1901-22 Jul 1916
Ralph 1 Oct 1890-16 Jun 1912

Bullard

Fanida H w/o William S.; 1888-1966
Mary L. 5 Feb 1916-23 Apr 1980
William A. 15 Mar 1913-29 Oct 1991
William s. h/o Fanida H.; 1881-1955

Burger

Elizabeth P. w/o William C.; 20 Oct 1911-1977
James L. 6 Jan 1906-8 Apr 1979
Louise 10 Oct 1878-10 May 1963
William C.; h/o Elizabeth P.; 15 Jan 1902-28 Mar 1971

Burrell

Claude J. 1 Oct 1932-3 May 1971
Dewey 25 Jan 1940 25 Dec 1971
Homer B. 4 Sept 1958-25 Dec 1971
Mercedes 22 Jul 1935-11 Oct 1935

Bush

Annie 5 Jan 1869-16 Jun 1892
Asa 18 Jun 1838-29 Oct 1880
Eula Webb 25 Jun 1876-20 Sept 1901
Frances 5 Dec 1833-11 Jan 1889
Frances E. 11 Jan 1910-20 Jan 1983
Harriet V. 13 Aug 1877-7 Sept 1951
Henry E. 22 Oct 1867-4 Feb 1933
Jason 25 Dec 1873-8 May 1919
Malinda 12 Mar 1836-11 Oct 1904
Nancy d: 4 Mar 1873; 70y
Olive M. 20 Mar 1877-12 Feb 1906

Butler

Eva B. w/o Lawrence C. 17 Sept 1881-4 May 1957
Lawrence C. h/o Eva B.; 27 Nov 1871-6 May 1957

Cain
>Ethel Florence 13 Aug 1885-11 Sept 1979
>John 17 Feb 1858-11 Feb 1932
>Newton Carl d: 22 Jan 1936
>Ollie House 18 Nov 1862-11 Apr 1930
>Robert E. 19 Nov 1833-28 Aug 1922

Campbell
>Mary A. 3 Mar 1832-14 May 1894
>N. 30 Sept 1896-21 Oct 1962

Cantrell
>Raymond J. 20 Apr 1921-22 Aug 1976
>Ruby Gunter 17 Oct 1926-23 Aug 1980
>Tom F. 13 Oct 1922-20 Sept 1985

Carden
>Henrey Mathew 7 Sept 1886-11 Nov 1961

Carpenter
>H. Wayne 14 Dec 1866-13 Oct 1936
>Harvey O. Pierce h/o Lillie Reavis; 9 Jun 1883-30 Aug 1939
>John J. h/o Syllvania A. Spruell; 20 Dec 1827-18 Mar 1918
>John Reavis 30 Aug 1911-3 Jan 1914
>Lillie Reavis w/o Harvey; 17 Sept 1882-3 Mar 1972
>Syllvania A Spruell w/o John J.; 7 Apr 1844-25 Aug 1924

Chambers
>G.W. 25 Apr 1825-17 Nov 1898
>Mary M. 1 May 1834-25 Mar 1901

Chamblee
>Curtis 5 Jun 1909-22 Sept 1909
>Georgia Ann 8 Ayg 1910-10 Sept 1910
>Georgia L. w/o William Milledge; 5 Feb 1897-2 Oct 1966
>Joseph Alford 11 Nov 1913-23 Jun 1925
>William Milledge h/o Georgia L.; 17 Jul 1888-23 Mar 1945

Chastain
>Cecil Pyron 1 Aug 1914-18 Apr 1965
>Geanie 14 Apr 1916-6 Oct 1917
>Joseph V. 28 Oct 1911-22 Jul 1933
>Joseph V. h/o Mattie T.; 7 Oct 1879-9 Dec 1928
>Mattie T. w/o Joseph V.; 5 Feb 1880-24 Jan 1972
>Ralph Fred 16 Mar 1918-22 Jun 1959
>William H. 7 Nov 1901-3 Jul 1952

Chester
>Ethel M. w/o George W.; 28 May 1904-31 Dec 1994

George W.; h/o Ethel M.; 1 Jun 1895-26 Nov 1973
Childers
Anna M. 1919-1989
Maggie 16 Oct 1885-29 Mar 1948
Mattie 18 Nov 1912-15 Aug 1937
Nolan F. 1919-1996
Clanton
Eva Dessie 18 Sept 1900-17 Feb 1971
James Clifford 29 Jul 1895-29 Mar 1958
Clayborn
Lillie R.E. 10 May 1903-7 Mar 1953
Clement
Alman B. 23 Apr 1894-10 Nov 1960
Clara P. 17 Mar 1901-20 May 1959
Cline
Cecil R. d: 15 Oct 1918; 27y Buried at Sea
Duncan 11 Dec 1848-16 May 1902
Jefferson D. 7 July 1861-9 Jul 1895
Maggie A d. June 22 1889; 42y
Coats
Floy E. 26 Jul 1915- 7 Apr 1975
Howard Woodrow 9 Sept 1918-8 Dec 1993
Cobb
Annie V. 16 Jun 1902-24 Oct 1977
Buren J. 12 May 1911-19 Sept 1970
Cecil A 22 Aug 1909-22 Mar 1952
Erby W. h/o Onnie V. 20 Nov 1899-21 Mar 1930
Ernest 8 Oct 1918-24 Jan 1967
J. Howell 10 Jul 1887-28 May 1915
J.T. 7 Jan 1849-5 Dec 1916
Minnie I. 9 Jun 1892-13 Apr 1946
Onnie V. w/o Erby W. 16 Jun 1902-24 Oct 1977
Coggans
James l. 17 May 1862-12 Mar 1930
Coker
Annie E. 24 Sept 1875-4 Aug 1906
Bessie Lee 9 Dec 1912-5 Sept 1935
Charlie C. 14 Jan 1886-11 Oct 1887
Daisy d: 17 Jan 1969
Edwin R. d: 3 Mar 1918

Effie d: 6 Dec 1968
Ernest W. 1904-1921
G.E. 28 Jul 1888-6 Nov 1917
George F. 14 Jul 1872-28 Sept 1938
H.S. 3 Sept 1876-23 Sept 1910
Len Andrew 5 Sept 1911-3 Jan 1977
Mary M. d: 11 Oct 1932
Maude P. w/o William E.; 1883-1966
Sarah E. 31 Jul 1876-12 Nov 1968
William E. h/o Maude P.; 1880-1953
Coleman
Anna w/o R.R.; 1785-1857
Arthue T. h/o Willie Mae; 20 May 1897-11 Jul 1964
Bernadine 6 Sept 1897-9 Oct 1929
Bonnie M. w/o James W.; 24 Dec 1905-8 Dec 1964
Cecil 26 May 1909-27 Jan 1982
Charles R. 13 Sept 1935-1 Apr 1988
Charles W. 7 Sept 1925-27 Sept 1990
Debbie H. 2 Sept 1887-15 Feb 1904
E.F. 2 Sept 1868-25 Jul 1923
Ed h/o Ellen; 3 Jul 1888-9 Feb 1973
Effie M. 6 Apr 1888-29 Sept 1979
Eliza E. w/o E.J.; 5 Jul 1848-9 Oct 1916
Ellen E. w/o Ed; 3 Jul 1888-9 Feb 1973
Elsie Mae 27 May 1905-3 Oct 1913
F.J. 3 Oct 1847-23 Jul 1925
Fannie P. w/o George W.; 27 Nov 1883-21 Jan 1925
Genia w/o Horace E.; 11 Apr 1881-20 Jul 1973
George W. h/o Fannie P.; 27 Dec 1880-30 Nov 1961
Gladis 30 Sept 1909-26 Jun 1910
Harold J. 4 Dec 1921-3 Dec 1993
Harry L. 9 Dec 1911-29 Mar 1964
Horace E. h/o Genia; 27 Nov 1874-28 May 1917
Hosea 1 May 1844-28 Mar 1911
Hosea 20 Dec 1883-5 Oct 1920
Hugh W. 1906-1959
Ida 5 Oct 1888-11 Jul 1912
James W. h/o Bonnie M.; 4 Aug 1900-18 Jun 1980
Jesse 30 Jan 1907-11 Feb 1907
Jesse 31 Jul 1873-2 Dec 1967
Ludie Ann 29 Sept 1887-7 Mar 1971

Mae Dickerson w/o William A.; 24 Mar 1888-8 Mar 1965
Marion Reese 26 Dec 1910- 9 May 1911
Martha G. 11 Oct 1854-31 Jun 1941
Martha Luna 2 Apr 1885-15 Nov 1946
Mary 1813-1885
Mary F. 2 Jan 1846-12 Mar 1920
Mary G. 12 Sept 1885-9 Jul 1892
Melvina H. 1813-1885
N.E. 15 Aug 1874-31 Dec 1916
Nancy 7 Mar 1849-10 Nov 1871
Nancy w/o Valentine; 1819-1871
Nettie Merritt 1896-1963
Newton P. 1838-1900
R. Frank 22 Feb 1905-12 Mar 1990
R.M. 1785-1855
R.R. h/o of Anna; 6 Apr 1885-18 Jun 1927
Susan 10 Sept 1856-20 Dec 1914
Thomas V. 9 Jul 1872-14 Jun 1946
Valentine 15 Nov 1876-6 Jul 1957
Valentine h/o Nancy; 7 Jan 1812-30 Jan 1890
Valentine 1812-1890
William 9 May 1852-11 Feb 1915
William A. h/o Mae Dickerson; 15 Sept 1871-29 Aug 1948
Willie Mae w/o Arthur; 11 Apr 1897-5 Mar 1979
Cook
Bobby 16 Sept 1937-30 Apr 1954
Brenda Sue 1949-1967
Irene D. 31 Mar 1918-13 May 1967
Copeland
Robert Lee h/o Sarah Downs; 16 Jun 1867-2 Nov 1950
Sarah Downs w/o Robert Lee; 19 May 1867-2 Nov 1950
Cornette
Era A 7 May 1902-22 Jan 1974
Cowaret
O.J. 23 April 1887-16 Dec 1930
Cowart
Bessie Wright w/o L.B.; 16 Jun 1890-15 Sept 1943
Claudia Mae w/o E. Dexter; 6 Feb 1894-8 Aug 1975
E.Dexter h/o Claudia Mae; 13 Oct 1892-9 Feb 1946
Elsie Smith w/o Leo Clyde; 4 Jun 1909-13 Apr 1969
L.B. h/o Bessie Wright; 14 Aug 1885-22 Sept 1959

Lena Otwell 21 Oct 1892-10 Dec 1980
Leo Clyde h/o Elsie Smith; 25 Mar 1900-17 Aug 1943
Cranshaw
Lenora Ann 14 Mar 1836-3 Feb 1904
Crow
H. d. 21 Feb 1908; 70y
Mary G. d. 8 Apr 1904; 65y
Crowe
Jack R. 10 Jan 1910-9 Dec 1983
James T. h/o Lizzie M.; 24 Mar 1874-11 Mar 1956
Lizzie M. w/o James T.; 8 Mar 1875-13 Jul 1933
Crowley
Elizabeth Jane w/o S.; 12 Mar 1847-3 Jul 1944
Forest Lee 4 Apr 1866-18 Sept 1894
George h/o Margarette Swindall; 27 Feb 1878-19 Mar 1944
John O. 22 Jun 1874-24 Jul 1909
Margarette Swindall w/o George; 23 Sept 1876-25 Oct 1901
S. h/o Elizabeth Jane; 1 Aug 1847-4 Mar 1937
Thomas William s/o George; 16 Oct 1901-18 Mar 1903
William 15 Jan 1865-24 Feb 1893
Willie s/o George 16 Oct 1901-13 Mar 1903
Cunningham
Cleo Blackwell 1908-1995
Curtis
James Henry 8 Jan 1880-17 Feb 1955
N.C. 1892-1955
Newell Lee s/o Lillian; 16 Sept 1931-27 Aug 1982
Cypher
Ross Stone 18 Nov 1903-29 May 1933
Dalton
Maud M. 8 May 1909-10 May 1996
Davis
Alice Elise 20 Dec 1919-3 Jul 1968
Irene Talley 1898-1976
Jane Lyle 1859-1926
John Talley 14 Dec 1928-13 Jul 1978
Dempsey
Bobby 4 Apr 1932-26 Dec 1936
Charles C. 10 Feb 1893-21 Oct 1959
Cleo S. Norton 11 May 1887-7 Dec 1924
Cora J. 8 Apr 1889-25 Oct 1955

Emma L w/o Robert M.; 19 Jul 1863-17 Aug 1941
Etter 1904-1905
Dempsey
Eulala M. 2 Nov 1910-18 Dec 1993
Genia E. w/o Reid J.; 1892-1989
Jack 13 Jul 1921-17 Sept 1993
James D. 23 Jul 1923-12 Dec 1923
James H. 1903-1997
John Wade 28 Sept 1888-21 Jul 1957
Joseph H. 30 Dec 1929-18 Dec 1930
Lelia E. 19 Dec 1907-26 Jun 1908
Lena Hill 22 May 1897-7 Mar 1987
Linnie H. 1885-1984
Nan 7 Mar 1890-16 Mar 1972
O.C. 10 Mar 1884-27 Mar 1955
Ola F. 9 Feb 1898-4 May 1947
Rebecca l. 27 Dec 1946-10 Apr 1952
Reid J. h/o Genia E.; 1892-1954
Robert L. s/o Robert M& Emma L..; 24 Dec 1890-25 Jan 1974
Robert M. f/o Robert L.h/o Emma L.; 10 Jan 1860-1 Oct 1947
Terry 1885-1941
Tressie M. d/o Robert M.&Emma L.; 3 Feb 1897-3 Sept 1911
Violet 1877-1925
Willis J. 22 Sept 1885-6 Jun 1951
Dickerson
Amanda E. 1860-1941
J.J. 8 May 1878-18 May 1936
J.P. 13 Jul 1903-20 Feb 1971
Jennie 4 May 1882-30 Sept 1962
Mildred J. 18 Mar 1920-19 Aug 1995
Savilla w/o Ed Smith; 1883-1908
William M. 1843-1922
Dickey
Myrl Sawyer 2 May 1910-16 Jan 1989

Dodd
Earl h/o Lena M.; 11 Jul 1800-14 Aug 1957
Elizabeth 26 Dec 1931-17 Jan 1996
Everett 4 Jan 1895-3 Jan 1976
J.D. 26 Sept 1926-1 May 1980
Lena M. w/o Earl; 29 Aug 1802-12 Aug 1983

Dorris
>Avarilla A w/o Charlie B.; 30 Jul 1862-13 Dec 1931
>Charlie B. h/o Avarilla A; 20 Aug 1860-10 Apr 1939
>Garrison 11 Dec 1911-11 Nov 1980
>Joseph L. h/o Nellie M.; 1888-1960
>Lillian R. 17 Oct 1890-29 Oct 1977
>Nellie M. w/o Joseph L.; 1891-1978
>Sim N. 9 Aug 1885-27 Apr 1946
>Wallace Eugene 13 Dec 1915-15 Jul 1994

Douglas
>Emma R. w/o William P.; 17 Aug 1868-2 Jan 1917
>William P. h/o Emma R.; 17 Nov 1863-28 Nov 1915

Downs
>J.W. 1830-26 Dec 1908

Drake
>Amanda w/o C.M. Webb; 1855-1916
>Clifton D. 29 Aug 1896-9 Dec 1974
>Ella w/o W.O. Arnold; 28 Nov 1860-12 Nov 1916
>Ernest James 22 May 1896-25 May 1976
>Horace F. h/o Lelia; 11 Jul 1858-20 Nov 1917
>Lelia w/o Horace F.; 4 Jan 1855-17 Jul 1930
>Lellie 31 Jul 1884-19 May 1942

Dreamer
>Anna J. 11 May 1859-31 Dec 1919

Duke
>Evie S. 2 Dec 1901-15 Feb 1977
>Sherman E. 17 Aug 1935-13 Jul 1990

Duncan
>Frances 8 Sept 1896-24 Jul 1973
>Robert O. 4 Jul 1887-13 Nov 1957
>Theron E. 24 Jul 1916-7 Mar 1953

Durham
>Dixie Lucille w/o George Alton; 2 Aug 1915-25 Jul 1977
>George Alton h/o Dixie Lucille; 31 Oct 1907-23 May 1974
>Mary l. Holland 18 Jun 1889-16 Nov 1973

Early
>Alice Hunt 2 Nov 1853-3 Jan 1942
>Mae w/o W.H.; 17 Apr 1881-26 Aug 1928
>W.H. h/o Mae; 13 Dec 1852-14 Apr 1930

Ellington
>Annie V. 6 Mar 1886-4 Dec 1943

Archie Eugene 29 May 1924-23 Feb 1925
Aquilla A. Reeves 15 Dec 1869-18 Nov 1943
Hartwell Rusk 23 Jan 1913-28 Oct 1967
Ida K. 11 May 1895-15 Aug 1981
James G. 15 Jun 1900-24 Dec 1928
John P. h/o Ardilla A. Reeves; 14 Jun 1868-15 Aug 1909
Maggie M. 5 Jun 1891-18 Dec 1959
Mamie Dorris w/o Richard Lee; 12 Jun 1893-26 Jul 1979
Richard Lee h/o Mamie Dorris; 2 Apr 1890-1 Jun 1969
Thomas 25 Jun 1893-18 Feb 1973
William 30 Oct 1885-17 Jul 1959

Elliot
Lucy 1864-1929

Ellis
Daisy 15 Mar 1895-11 Jun 1973
Eugene Christie 10 Jun 1928-25 Jul 1954
John W. 27 Jul 1892-30 Mar 1954
William R. 6 Aug 1920-19 Jan 1986

Englett
Park 27 Jul 1875-16 Mar 1965

Erwin
Emma Lee 24 May 1886-7 May 1909
Glady 11 Nov 1928-24 Jun 1989
Ida Brown 12 Dec 1870-29 Nov 1906
Lilla B. w/o William G.; 1893-1986
Ollie H. 22 Nov 1898-8 Jul 1955
P.N. Hill 11 Aug 1891-25 Jun 1968
Sanford Lee 9 Jul 1861-24 Jan 1944
Talmad B. 16 Dec 1893-26 Dec 1985
William G. h/o Lilla B. 1891-1943
Zannie Groover Hill 27 Mar 1867-29 Nov 1950

Evans
Minnie Lee 29 Sept 1918-15 Jan 1959
Nancy A. 7 Aug 1852-5 Sept 1926
Tina B. 11 Mar 1879-7 Aug 1966
W. Kermit 27 Jan 1910-25 Jan 1978
William L. 5 Feb 1874-31 Dec 1965

Ezzard
Mary Tallulah 6 Dec 1884-17 Jan 1922
Thomas M. 20 Apr 1921-21 Sept 1974
Thomas Mixon 5 May 1882-26 Apr 1970

Farmer
James Goss 1892-1918
Sarah C. 7 Oct 1866-25 Mar 1898
Farr
Ethel d/o Jonathan Davis; 13 Nov 1892-13 Nov 1905
Eva F. 15 Jan 1882-2 Sept 1969
Fannie Brantley 16 May 1891-29 Feb 1932
Givins 5 Aug 1858-20 Jul 1912
H.C. 13 Aug 1885-21 Jun 1964
Ida 12 May 1876-30 Mar 1916
J. 20 Apr 1864-28 Apr 1864
Jonathan Davis h/o Margaret Burks; 17 Jun 1861-1 Oct 1929
Luther D s/o Jonathan Davis; 29 Dec 1884-17 Jan 1907
Margaret Burks w/o Jonathan D.; 22 Aug 1860-19 Oct 1942
Minerva Turner 1861-1936
Nell Smith w/o Paul Dorris; 20 Nov 1912-20 Apr 1979
Paul Dorris 20 Aug 1910-19 Sept 1957
Samuel G. 23 Mar 1867-20 Nov 1887
William K. 15 Aug 1855-19 Mar 1956
Faulkner
Nancy 10 Sept 1895-14 Nov 1924
Finney
May Arnold 27 Feb 1872-11 Apr 1931
Fitch
Fannie M. 29 Nov 1876-31 Jan 1890
Rebecca 3 Sept 1848-10 Sept 1886
Foster
Barbara Rainwater 1936-1992
Charles C. 7 Sept 1871-16 May 1929
Charles Collins 1896-1968
Charles Collins 1932-1991
Clifton L. 10 Oct 1874-22 Feb 1953
Eel Stribling 12 Jul 1888-21 Jan 1933
Era Rainwater 1901-1988
Gussie Lyon 1893-1964
Joseph Douglas 1897-1967
Joseph H. 7 Aug 1889-7 Nov 1954
Margaret d: 22 Jan 1918; 86y
Margaret F. McLard 29 Oct 1903-4 May 1919

Fouler
Corrine Garrett 18 Jul 1904-23 Feb 1996
Founderburg
Annie Douglas 25 Dec 1898-9 Mar 1960
Fouts
Dugan h/o Janie; 21 Oct 1864-24 June 1943
Elmer L. 4 Aug 1909-4 Aug 1966
Flora Lee 20 Mar 1911-9 Nov 1912
Ida B. 29 Mar 1891-16 Jun 1963
J.C. 7 Feb 1909-16 Dec 1909
Janie w/o Dugan; 27 Nov 1867-21 Sept 1941
Jasper A. 12 Oct 1885-18 Apr 1954
John D. 3 Sept 1892-15 Apr 1933
Joseph E. 31 Oct 1926-8 Dec 1940
Robert J. 10 Feb 1918-2 Jun 1961
Stella H. 10 May 1918-31 Jul 1995
Fowler
Claud J. 29 Jan 1882-10 Nov 1932
Edward Guy 22 Apr 1922-25 Mar 1995
Julia W. 2 Sept 1882-30 Apr 1962
Fraser
Nanie Bell w/o W.E.; 9 Sept 1880-21 Jun 1952
W.E. h/o Nanie Bell; 30 Apr 1878-28 Jun 1955
Frasier
Elizabeth w/o James; 13 Jan 1845-23 Feb 1924
Harry 9 Mar 1887-30 Sept 1918
Henry D. 11 Jan 1880-23 Jan 1946
James h/o Elizabeth; 29 Oct 1851-13 Feb 1933
Lessier 27 Sept 1876-7 May 1883
Simon 8 Jul 1801-10 May 1881
Earnest Henry s/o W.E.; 2 Jan 1900-10 Jun 1900
Jimmie d/o W.E.; 10 May 1905-8 Aug 1907
Freeman
W.T. 29 Aug 1841-8 Jun 1886
Gardener
Addie F. 1897-1971
Exa Carpenter w/o William A.; 1873-1937
J. Early 1894-1975
J. Hughes 1917-1934
Norma C. 1931-1932
William A. h/o Exa Carpenter; 1863-1948

Garrison
  Nancy J. 19 Dec 1848-3 Jun 1881
  Texanna G. 28 Sept 1853-8 Mar 1944
  William Lloyd 18 Feb 1884-31 Aug 1934
Gazaway
  Plassie 15 Apr 1917-7 Nov 1989
Gentry
  Carrie Coleman w/o William E.; 24 Sept 1881-13 Jun 1962
  William E. h/o Carrie Coleman; 28 May 1880-11 Sept 1946
Glover
  Ruby Pursley 1 Sept 1901-25 Jul 1981
  Teasley Edwin 12 Sept 1886-13 May 1985
  William Monroe 14 Mar 1881-23 Nov 1961
Goodwin
  Mary Augusta 17 Jun 1921-11 Apr 1984
  Shirley 27 Dec 1914-8 Dec 1974
  Willie M. 5 Sept 1911-15 Feb 1991
Gore
  Alfred 1873-1955
  Laura B. 1870-1960
Grace
  James M. 20 Mar 1932-18 Dec 1962
Graham
  Drucilla 15 Jun 1891-12 Sept 1974
  Eddie C. 18 Nov 1915-24 Feb 1969
  Elizabeth E. 1 Jun 1927-17 Jul 1946
  Hillman 4 Aug 1881-12 Nov 1956
  Lawrence E. 10 Nov 1911-11 Oct 1953
Gray
  Geraldine 25 Jul 1925-24 Oct 1933
  Lucille w/o Will A.; 25 Jun 1905-8 Oct 1994
  Villa 18 Aug 1898-24 Sept 1965
Green
  Henry 6 May 1873-28 May 1937
  Ida w/o Rollie; 1 Dec 1874-16 Jan 1922
  Mattie L. 1910-1997
  Morris 2 May 1904-1 Dec 1970
  Rollie h/o Ida; 5 Sept 1899-20 Jun 1905
Greer
  Elizabeth L. w/o Turner G.; 16 May 1845-3 Feb 1875

Griffin

    B.L. 15 Oct 1907-27 Jun 1951
    Carrie E. 1 Jan 1888-9 Jan 1991
    J.J. (Mrs) 10 Feb 1850-15 Mar 1904
    O.J. 21 May 1850-29 Aug 1918
    Robert P. 17 Feb 1849-12 Mar 1936
    William G. 18 Dec 1886-5 Jan 1967

Grime

    Eliza E. 22 Aug 1817-1 Jun 1900

Grimes

    Newton J. 22 Mar 1833-18 Dec 1914

Grover

    Effie 13 Oct 1875-20 Sept 1958

Gunter

    Bessie Lillian 15 Jul 1892-15 Mar 1982
    Bill 25 Nov 1889-30 Oct 1973
    Daisy 21 Aug 1879-4 Nov 1881
    Ethel 29 May 1897-18 Oct 1974
    Harl E. h/o Clara G. Lewis; 11 Aug 1895-6 Apr 1940
    Hugh A 11 Dec 1917-9 Feb 1969
    James E. 11 Dec 1917-20 Jun 1985
    Jemima G 5 Apr 1838-7 Feb 1902
    Rebecca S. w/o Ulva F.; 25 Nov 1884-6 Jun 1971
    Robert Ernest 27 Apr 1890-25 Mar 1957
    Ulva F. h/o Rebecca S.; 11 Oct 1888-25 Jan 1942
    Zettie Mae 8 Aug 1879-26 Apr 1950

Gutner

    Edgar Augustus 3 Aug 1874-3 Aug 1939

Hackett

    John C. 28 Jul 1870-27 Sept 1951
    Nancy E. 10 Nov 1872-10 Jun 1962

Hagler

    Mary Lou 1863-31 May 1900

Hall

    Katie T. 4 Aug 1900-20 Dec 1928

Hampton

    Ethel Odessa w/o James Cowart; 5 May 1890-12 Jan 1956
    Jack Morris 20 Dec 1916-31 Oct 1917
    James C. 14 Oct 1915-14 Oct 1915
    James Cowart h/o Ethel Odessa; 5 Aug 1885-27 Sept 1967

James H. h/o Sarah Oliver; 19 Mar 1854-9 Jan 1891
Sarah Oliver w/o James H.; 3 Sept 1855-2 Dec 1933
Walter J. 1 Jul 1893-13 Jun 1987
Hamrick
Florence H. O'Neil 17 Jan 1931-11 Jun 1985
William A. 19 Mar 1926-13 Aug 1970
Hancock
Elizabeth C. 21 Nov 1913-8 Jul 1994
R.H. 2 May 1893-4 Aug 1967
Wiley A. 8 Jun 1882-6 Apr 1950
Harden
Howard J. 1922-1954
Harmon
Letha Kirk 1907-1965
Harris
Ann Waters 28 Jul 1880-24 Mar 1955
Hartsfield
Jesse Mae 27 Dec 1881-21 Jan 1928
Hatcher
Charles 31 Dec 1944-26 Jun 1970
Donald Ray 26 Dec 1942-23 Nov 1975
Hawkins
A. Grady 1900-1967
Amanda Cochran w/o Homer Ashbury; 1897-1965
Amy A. 7 Jul 1868-13 Feb 1948
Bertha Mae 1903-1983
Homer Ashbury h/o Amanda Cochran; 1891-1953
J.M. 31 Jul 1914-29 Dec 1914
John M. 19 Aug 1890-2 Sept 1931
Leila M. D: 6 Feb 1989
Mattie E. 17 Apr 1892-2 Sept 1931
Myrtle K. w/o Thomas E.; 1895-1958
Thomas E. h/o Myrtle K.; 1896-1956
Hayes
Grady A. 12 Feb 1916-11 May 1979
Mary Neal 29 Jan 1931-2 Mar 1931
Tony 20 Nov 1959-28 May 1978
Hays
Cephas Fletcher 8 Mar 1908-Mar 1908
Cephas Fletcher 1856-1938
Christopher O. h/o Lila Ellen; 27 Jul 1854-5 Jul 1906

Clinton A. 29 Mar 1880-25 Apr 1912
Elizabeth M. 1872-1936
Lela H. 23 Dec 1855-27 Jul 1890
Lila Ellen w/o Christopher O.; 2 Oct 1859-6 Sept 1947
Lucy P. 17 Jun 1899-28 Jun 1989
Luiaz A. 13 Dec 1824-2 Aug 1892
Mary Adel 30 Apr 1880-6 Dec 1944

Hembree
Maggie Luela w/o Marlon Duaine; 10 Oct 1893-19 Aug 1933
Marlon Duaine h/o Maggie Luela; 30 Dec 1889-15 Mar 1956
Missouri M. 18 Aug 1881-16 Sept 1900
F.M. 9 Jun 1848-9 Dec 1908
Retta Susan 11 Aug 1885-6 Dec 1971

Hill
Home Leroy 20 Sept 1892-4 May 1954

Holifield
Ada Brown 9 Oct 1894-8 Nov 1957
Minnie 8 Aug 1874-24 Jul 1924
William 9 Sept 1895-11 Oct 1968

Holland
Tracy Ann 25 Jan 1965-23 Mar 1969
Willie Mae 17 Sept 1918-6 May 1984

Hollifield
Marie M. w/o Robert M.; 1920-1987
R.H. 23 May 1877-25 Aug 1918
Robert M. h/o Marie M.; 1913-1991
W.H. 14 Feb 1843-9 Dec 1916

Holmes
J. 4 Aug 1884-31 May 1909
Sable Allison 10 Oct 1883-24 Mar 1956

Holt
Ralph F. 5 Mar 1972-3 Nov 1990

Holton
Dora Thompson w/o Thomas Abel; 30 Sept 1900-12 Feb 1965
Ray Malone s/o Dora & Thomas; 1932-1954
Thomas Abel s/o Dora & Thomas; 28 Jun 1924-9 Dec 1938
Thoams Abel h/o Dora Thompson; 21 Apr 1891-9 Dec 1973

Hood
Dora 18 Dec 1884-9 Dec 1917
J.D. 1930-1930
James Cecil 1906-1951

James W. 1875-1952
John W. 1891-1860
Louella 12 May 1860-17 Aug 1941
Marion D. 13 Jul 1846-24 Feb 1917
Ola King 1900-1967
Ollie A. 1885-1970
William Chester 11 Oct 1923-17 Oct 1924
Hook
Elizabeth 27 Sept 1880-27 Jul 1919
Gabriella A. w/o Golson M.; 30 Mar 1836-25 Jan 1891
Golson M. h/o Gabriella A.; 26 Jun 1829-14 May 1904
Linton 31 Dec 1868-13 Feb 1933
Luther A. 15 Oct 1915-23 Mar 1916
Luther T. 14 Jun 1866-28 Feb 1913
Mary G. 12 Sept 1861-13 Nov 1943
Maurice E. 24 Jan 1913-2 Jan 1933
Hopkins
James E. h/o Louella M.; 15 Nov 1874-28 Nov 1949
Louella M. w/o James E.; 30 Nov 1874-Nov 29 1949
Howard
Elizabeth H. 13 Aug 1904-1 Jan 1968
Elsie Echols 21 Nov 1936-5 Aug 1955
Henry G. 27 Jan 1906-9 Nov 1988
Julia E. 23 Mar 1921-10 Sept 1988
Huddleston
Pearl Dempsey 1 Oct 1898-19 Dec 1922
Hudson
Charles Thomas 25 Mar 1921-19 Jul 1981
William A. 6 Apr 1949-11 Aug 1984
Huggins
Augusta Howard w/o John; 11 Sept 1861-12 Feb 1932
Everttem 2 Jan 1913-28 May 1940
J.P. 18 Sept 1883-27 Nov 1965
John h/o Augusta Howard; 26 Jan 1860-5 Oct 1932
Willie R. 17 Sept 1900-17 Mar 1980
Hughes
Cecil C. 7 Feb 1902-22 Apr 1967
Eliza 10 Dec 1844-1 Dec 1912
Gary 14 Jun 1847-24 Feb 1928
Henry Clay 11 Mar 1857-10 Feb 1940

Henry Clifton 16 Mar 1888-7 Jul 1930
Josephine Daniel 19 May 1862-25 Jul 1951
Lula S. 17 May 1870-10 Nov 1950
Pierce 7 Aug 1892-4 Dec 1896
Randall Larry 29 Jun 1941-2 May 1983
Robert A. 23 Sept 1872-23 Mar 1915
Willie Lowe 19 Nov 1890-6 Aug 1993
Hunt
Esther Grice w/o Robert Rivers; 26 Oct 1900-9 Aug 1993
Robert Rivers h/o Esther Grice; 9 Sept 1905-31 Dec 1988
Imes
Agusta B. 19 Oct 1874-30 Mar 1943
James C. 2 Jan 1872-24 Dec 1947
Marvin C. 27 May 1880-9 Sept 1933
Jackson
Ada K. w/o William C.; 21 Oct 1886-21 Oct 1968
Amanda B. w/o Eddie F.; 15 Aug 1912-6 Feb 1989
Eddie C. Graham 18 Nov 1915-24 Feb 1969
Eddie F. h/o Amanda B.; 1 Sept 1910-17 Oct 1989
Elizabeth 8 Mar 1877-25 Jan 1953
Era S. Jett 7 May 1902- 22 Jan 1974
Eunice L. 4 Jan 1918-10 Feb 1990
Frances Eller w/o Joseph Edgar; 23 Dec 1875-16 Jul 1923
George Joseph d: 25 Apr 1983
Hugh Dorsey 26 Feb 1910-7 Feb 1944
Joseph Edgar 26 Nov 1875-13 Mar 1916
Minnie Mae B. 26 Jan 1889-30 Dec 1944
Nancy E. 10 May 1863-27 Jan 1928
Nora Ann Jett 23 Jun 1921-10 Oct 1962
Ralph Kirk 1881-1962
Thomas J. 17 Dec 1855-2 Feb 1933
William C. h/o Ada K.; 12 Oct 1879-1 Sept 1947
William S. 19 Dec 1894-7 Nov 1967
Willie Pearl 9 Sept 1907-1 Mar 1968
Jamerson
William R. 29 Sept 1887-27 Aug 1970
Jameson
Herbert W. 8 May 1906-16 Dec 1951
Morris 3 Aug 1930-8 Dec 1932
Nancy A. w/o Thomas J.; 26 Aug 1865-2 Sept 1945

Thomas J. h/o Nancy A.; 5 Jun 1862-27 Jun 1949
Jarrett
    Jesse 15 Jul 1921-8 Mar 1970
    Joe Marvin 14 Oct 1944-1 Oct 1968
    Katherine L. 24 Jan 1925-27 Mar 1996
Jett
    Nora Ann 23 Jun 1921-10 Oct 1962
Johnson
    Alice 24 Feb 1869-16 Mar 1881
    Ann Marie 1942-1946
    Avirila 11 Mar 1814-21 Jan 1887
    Delia Fouts 16 Jan 1884-30 Sept 1933
    Eloha 23 Feb 1871-21 Apr 1923
    Grady C. 10 Jan 1930-2 Jun 1930
    H. d: 21 Feb 1908; 70y
    H.H. (Mrs) 18 Feb 1883-16 Apr 1928
    J.U. 6 Feb 1851-24 Jun 1915
    Lela 30 Oct 1863-19 Dec 1903
    Martha A. 7 Aug 1835-29 Jun 1912
    Martha E. d: 8 Apr 1904; 65y
    Sallie Cleo 31 Mar 1895-30 Mar 1922
    William Franklin 24 Apr 1859-8 Jul 1924
Johnston
    J.A. h/o L.C.; 18 Apr 1848-1 Nov 1918
    L.C.w/o J.A.; 4 Oct 1854-25 Feb 1922
Jones
    Annie Clyde 28 Jan 1882-20 Jul 1927
    Alexander Campbell h/o Gertrude Garrett; 21 Mar 1869-
    4 Nov 1932
    Alice Gertrude 24 Jul 1920-14 Feb 1921
    Bartow F. 22 Sept 1887-14 Apr 1964
    Clyde N. 7 Jun 1897-15 Nov 1976
    Emmons Walter 9 Jun 1895-20 Jan 1977
    Eugene V. 3 Oct 1897-6 Apr 1924
    Evelyne Frances 26 Oct 1928-27 Apr 1945
    Felton M. h/o Voncile A.; 3 Oct 1900-9 Mar 1981
    Gertrude Garrett w/o Alexander Campbell; 26 Aug 1870-
    14 Feb 1921
    Horace Julian 11 Jul 1919-29 Feb 1920
    Lawrence D. 22 Apr 1917-17 Feb 1972

Lelia B. Polk 1874-1938
Roswell O. 19 Feb 1892-14 Oct 1930
Roy 25 Apr 1896-29 Dec 1928
Samuel Bascom 18 Nov 1870-26 Jun 1922
Thomas F. s/o Clyde N.; 18 Nov 1895-5 Mar 1927
Trude Garrison 26 Aug 1870-31 Dec 1957
Voncile A. w/o Felton M.; 24 Dec 1903-15 Jan 1992
Z.T. (Family Of) d: 1 Dec 1901

Jordan
Hugh Allen 9 Jul 1945-15 Nov 1945

Kelley
J.M. 5 Dec 1846-19 Sept 1925
Jane 27 Feb 1842-12 Jun 1929
Joseph H.P. 7 Apr 1902-Feb 1956

Kelpin
A.B. 6 Dec 1852-30 Dec 1922
Eona D. 12 Dec 1878-25 Jul 1899
Herbert 9 May 1877-12 May 1977
Joseph C. h/o Susan E.; 30 Nov 1850-8 Dec 1926
Mary A. 4 Jun 1826-24 Nov 1887
Miranda S. 14 May 1858-4 Mar 1931
Susan E. w/o Joseph C.; 10 Mar 1852-21 Feb 1928
William 5 Mar 1818-30 Jun 1897

Kirk
A.M. w/o John N.; 10 Jul 1845-23 Apr 1902
Acel C. 27 Dec 1901-4 Aug 1965
Annie H. w/o Thomas J.; 11 May 1856-10 Oct 1940
Annie Mae 1882-1959
Charles 29 Oct 1931-17 Sept 1932
Cornelia L. 4 Jan 1861-26 Aug 1903
Daisy Mae 11 Sept 1888-24 Jun 1975
Daisy R. w/o Gus F.; 23 Jan 1905-6 Jun 1987
Dwight 1896-1948
Estelle w/o Hugh; 20 Mar 1907-11 Oct 1946
Ethel 1897-1948
Eva M. d: 13 May 1892; 2y 8m 23d
Gus F. h/o Daisy R.; 5 Oct 1902-19 Jan 1968
Hattie 18 Sept 1888-15 Sept 1916
Henry d: 1 Mar 1922; 78y
Henry Alice 5 Jun 1917-8 Oct 1992
Henry Franklin 1876-1930

Horace Little 1868-1925
Hugh h/o Estelle; 2 Jun 1903-18 Jun 1964
James T. h/o Sarah F.; 6 May 1886-10 Apr 1925
Jasper Franklin 11 Aug 1890-5 Feb 1896
Jasper Lyrell 14 Aug 1915-16 Aug 1969
John N. h/o A.M.; 12 Apr 1841-13 Jan 1911
Lewis 13 May 1913-26 Jun 1962
Melissa E. w/o James W.; 26 Dec 1852-8 Nov 1905
Nancy I. w/o H.J.; 1847-1908
Nora Samples w/o Cliff Andrew; 1 Nov 1918-28 Oct 1907
Ollie Mae 7 Jan 1909-15 Jun 1981
Ralph H. h/o Leona Tumlin; 14 Aug 1911-24 Mar 1975
Robert 1891-1929
Sarah F. w/o James T.; 22 May 1883-13 Oct 1921
Thomas J. h/o Annie H.; 14 Dec 1850-2 Feb 1935
Viola 11 May 1886-28 Dec 1909
Klein
Florence 8 Mar 1919-8 Nov 1979
Frank 10 Feb 1921-8 Jul 1980
Lackey
Clyde F. 1899-1981
Dennis G. 1896-1968
Lena Mae 1 Aug 1901-26 Nov 1962
Rose E. 1931-1942
Smith L. 29 Oct 1896-10 Feb 1978
Lanar
Mason Phillip 7 Oct 1948-29 Aug 1984
Landers
Rosa R. 18 Aug 1891-16 Jan 1908
Lane
Allen Ray 19 Apr 1954-5 Feb 1955
Bernice M. w/o Warren H.; 16 Aug 1902-8 Nov 1980
Don 15 Jul 1949-22 Jul 1949
Jack N. 15 Jan 1930-25 Aug 1985
Lillie D. 4 Feb 1898-24 Jan 1991
Paul Willis 29 Nov 1895-7 Mar 1965
Warren H. h/o Bernice M.; 27 Sept 1900-20 Mar 1991
Langle
Myrtle Lee 13 Sept 1913-9 Nov 1934

Langley
    Dorothy M. w/o Frank; 24 Sept 1928-6 Jul 1969
    Frank h/o Dorothy M. 25 Jan 1929-9 Feb 1977
    Gladys Faye w/o Johnnie; 2 Mar 1912-29 Oct 1980
    Johnnie h/o Gladys Faye; 16 Mar 1909-10 Nov 1985
Lanier
    Fannie 1895-1918
    Jane 1853-1918
    L.M. 1843-1915
    Red 1890-1891
    Selamer 1870-1895
Latham
    William Lee 4 May 1979-4 May 1979
Lee
    Gordon 4 Nov 1919-11 Dec 1972
    William Louie 1914-1977
Leverette
    Dorothy Davis 7 Mar 1918-26 Oct 1984
Lewis
    Clara Gunter w/o Harl E.; 24 Dec 1898-10 Nov 1957
    Estelle M. 1887-1965
    James W. 1893-1949
Lindsey
    Edna Mae 4 Apr 1913-30 Oct 1930
    Emery R. 9 Feb 1893-21 Jul 1893
    John T. 22 Jan 1867-1 Aug 1928
    Mollie 1856-1893
    Rosie E. 4 Aug 1889-25 1896
Loggins
    Joe B. 10 Jan 1909-2 Jul 1972
    Lee 25 Apr 1902-30 Oct 1971
Long
    Homer P. h/o Roxie T.; 6 Mar 1883-15 Oct 1971
    Larry b/o Mary Geraldine; 7 Nov 1936-20 Nov 1936
    Mary Geraldine s/o Larry; 22 Sept 1935-Sept 1935
    Roxie T. w/o Homer P.; 1 Jan 1884-27 Feb 1972
    Willie I. 21 May 1917-13 Oct 1971
Loudermilk
    Duville Reed 1897-1926
    Vernon P. 1 Aug 1894-6 Nov 1952

Lovorn
    Henry Garland 16 Nov 1897-21 Oct 1964
Lowry
    Claude W. 16 Aug 1897-21 Oct 1964
    O. 16 Jul 1902-10 Feb 1923
    Russell Jones 4 Mar 1853-14 Jul 1935
    Sarah Patterson 21 Dec 1862-28 Sept 1933
    Winnie M. 5 Jul 1900-2 Mar 1925
Lumry
    Edna Jackson 17 Feb 1911-27 Aug 1953
    Theron W. 25 Aug 1901-27 Jan 1968
Lyon
    Ada Paden 1869-1954
    Archie T. h/o Pearl Lyon; 19 Oct 1904-4 Feb 1951
    G.T. 1860-1947
    Harry C. 14 May 1906-27 Dec 1980
    Pat Logan 21 Feb 1901-21 Apr 1931
    Paden 27 Oct 1889-29 Jan 1927
    Pearl B. Huffman w/o Archie T.; 12 Jun 1913 14 Oct 1989
Mabrey
    Peena Carol 13 Oct 1968-13 Aug 1969
Maddox
    Lilian Ball 14 Aug 1902-11 Dec 1969
    William J. 17 Jan 1898-20 Jul 1964
Maloney
    Ernest D. h/o Ola Mae; 1887-1939
    Ola Mae w/o Ernest D. 1887-1969
Mansell
    Annie D. w/o J. Howell; 10 Jun 1881-28 Jul 1965
    Arthur Eugene 23 May 1920-17 May 1923
    Arthur G. 2 Jan 1950-25 Apr 1963
    Billie Sunday 25 Jun 1917-4 Jan 1918
    Etna Moore 8 May 1913-18 Nov 1984
    Gene Lou 16 Jan 1888-12 Mar 1972
    Hazel Susan 1915-1935
    J. Howell 27 Sept 1877-21 Jan 1970
    James Dallas 3 Feb 1912-28 Feb 1912
    Mattie O. 20 Oct 1892-15 Mar 1914
    Maude G. 1883-1931
    Nora B. w/o Robert A.; 25 Aug 1897-17 May 1983

Nora D. 20 Dec 1894-20 Aug 1986
Robert V. 22 Jul 1905-9 Sept 1965
Roscooe 1882-1971
William P. 10 Oct 1885-7 Jan 1972
Mansen
Maud D. 20 Apr 1883-4 Oct 1977
Robert H. 22 Jan 1873-30 Apr 1950
Marion
John 14 Apr 1861-21 Jan 1940
Marler
Eddie O. 2 Sept 1897-2 Sept 1897
Freddie 3 May 1901-27 May 1901
Leonora A 14 Jun 1875-27 Oct 1944
William 30 Apr 1870-21 Mar 1908
William Monroe 30 Apr 1871-26 Mar 1903
Marshall
Alma 25 Jul 1912-11 Dec 1936
Avery C. 31 Jan 1923-4 Jun 1985
Carroll V. 1909-1954
Claude W. 1910-1969
Cora P. w/o Sanford W.; 1882-1958
Sanford W. h/o Cora P.; 1883-1958
Martin
Austin C. h/o Lemina Carpenter; 12 Aug 1869-8 Sept 1911
Christine F. 2 Sept 1933-9 May 1961
Claude H. 17 May 1922-20 May 1973
Flonnie E. 3 Jun 1913-18 Mar 1919
Isla M. 16 Jul 1911-17 Jan 1919
J.Z. 29 May 1867-28 Jun 1923
James L. h/o Martha Reeves; 26 May 1915-7 Dec 1979
James T. 29 Nov 1878-7 Jun 1937
Jerry 25 Aug 1944-13 Mar 1963
John V. 15 Nov 1915-21 Sept 1979
L. Newt 11 Nov 1894-29 Nov 1967
Laura W. 11 Sept 1893-16 Aug 1982
Lemina Carpenter w/o Austin C.; 28 Mar 1869-21 Sept 1943
Lura 6 Mar 1880-18 Sept 1937
Martha Reeves w/o James L.; 24 Sept 1912-1 Nov 1993
R. Dolores 21 Jan 1907-11 Jul 1974
Richard F. 30 May 1902-22 Feb 1929
Sarah H. 15 May 1857-23 Jan 1928

Tomie Lowry 25 Jan 1891-10 Mar 1970
Vada 10 Nov 1880-10 May 1974
W.H. 4 Feb 1835-14 Nov 1913
William Hoyt 10 Apr 1910-30 Jun 1953
William Z. 13 May 1887-24 Jun 1953
Mashburn
    Willene C. 3 Jun 1923-15 Jun 1956
Mason
    Fred B. 24 Apr 1899-24 Aug 1966
    Rayford Dean 9 Aug 1933-20 Aug 1966
Massey
    Edward 9 Mar 1900-2 Nov 1989
    Elizabeth 7 Oct 1916-2 Jan 1992
    Melanie Joy 31 Dec 1972-9 Jul 1978
Mathews
    Elizabeth 7 Oct 1916-2 Jan 1992
    Ethel Mandy 20 Mar 1890-12 Jan 1983
    John A. 19 Sept 1896-12 Aug 1931
Mattison
    Benjamin F. 1858-1940
    Mary E. 1876-1950
    Mattie C. 6 Jan 1897-3 Jul 1973
Mayfield
    James Grier 27 Nov 1906-19 Aug 1965
Mays
    Frances S. w/o William Hartford; 16 Jul 1912-9 Feb 1986
    William Hartford h/o Frances S.; 14 Aug 1912-24 Dec 1986
McArden
    Roy 27 Apr 1915-20 Sept 1957
McClain
    Nancy E. 16 Oct 1879-20 May 1954
McDaniel
    James Lewis 20 Sept 1895-9 Jun 1985
McDerment
    Bertha 23 Dec 1890-26 Oct 1948
    Henry Ralph 27 Dec 1856-14 Jul 1900
McDermond
    Ada Hughes 26 Sept 1891-1 Aug 1919
McFarland
    Jack 28 Aug 1924-6 Nov 1976

McGehee
>Elmer Abner 9 Feb 1907-4 Aug 1953

McGinnis
>Annie K. 22 May 1892-26 Apr 1985
>Baldy h/o Edna L.; 1879-1952
>Edna L. w/o Baldy; 1898-1968
>Kate 18 Sept 1901-26 Apr 1980
>Odus L. 9 Apr 1892-15 May 1964

McNeely
>Annette J. 4 Feb 1885-26 May 1985
>Claud J. 23 Nov 1908-11 Sept 1970
>Edna Lula 11 Sept 1866-9 Jan 1949
>Gladys J. 12 Feb 1919-21 Mar 1991
>Walter B. 23 Feb 1883-13 Jan 1916

McWhorter
>Doyle 10 Dec 1899-16 Jan 1973
>Glenn L. 17 May 1909-19 Feb 1966
>Mamie Worsham 17 Jun 1925-22 Apr 1977
>Rupert 24 May 1901-6 Sept 1957

Medford
>Georgia Duncan 30 Aug 1865-1 Mar 1924

Merritt
>Allen Twiggs 17 May 1971-21 Feb 1957
>Fanny A. 27 Mar 1830-3 Sept 1913
>John H. 22 Oct 1889-18 Jul 1973
>Mae F. 1882-1966
>Maurice P. 1915-1979
>Mollie Taylor 30 May 1867-17 Oct 1955
>Ress H. 1873-1941
>Roy W. h/o Lula L. Rusk; 14 Dec 1897-14 Feb 1993

Minhinnett
>Sarrah W. 8 Nov 1842-8 Apr 1870

Mitchell
>Bernard E. h/o Maggie L.; 1932-1972
>Maggie L.; w/o Bernard E.; 1935-1972

Mitchem
>Roy Inman 14 Jun 1918-12 Aug 1979

Moore
>Sara Chamblee 2 Apr 1917-18 Apr 1973

Morris
>Buena Vista 13 May 1900-23 Jun 1922

Fabian 4 Dec 1860-2 May 1919
Glenn T. 25 Oct 1886-23 Sept 1968
Jack 1946-1977
Jeannette 1915-1969
Mamye J. 30 May 1874-30 May 1916
Mosher
    Maryann Soltan 21 Apr 1944-23 Nov 1987
Moss
    Paul Wayne 28 Apr 1951-22 Mar 1975
Mosteller
    Ethel T. 1901-1966
    Fred C. 27 Dec 1898-5 Jan 1941
    J. Glenn 1894-1975
    Thomas B. 19 Mar 1924-7 Jul 1970
    Zona Mae 17 Jul 1896-3 Oct 1980
Nesbit
    Anne Marion 1875-1951
    Elizabeth Clyde 1887-1944
Norton
    Cloutilue 25 Feb 1914-23 Oct 1960
    Esker L. 22 Feb 1896-27 Feb 1896
    George Ray 11 Jun 1918-14 Nov 1976
    Hugh Frances 8 Mar 1910-20 Dec 1957
    Julie 7 May 1919-7 May 1919
    Lizzie Avis 15 Jul 1885-7 Jul 1886
    Ola Allison Buice 18 Aug 1887-11 Sept 1942
    Syble D. 1890-1971
Oliver
    Alice Martin 9 May 1893-17 Jan 1970
    Peggy Jones 29 Aug 1928-24 Jul 1978
Otwall
    Charlie C. 1866-1936
    Charlie C. 9 Jan 1908-22 Apr 1918
    Clifton 1874-1955
    Paul Lanar 17 Apr 1918-18 Sept 1972
Owen
    Ada L. 28 Nov 1897-5 Nov 1914
    Amanda 20 Nov 1897-21 May 1925
    Julia A. w/o Thomas M.; 24 Jan 1872-22 Jun 1951
    Luther 15 Nov 1888-18 Aug 1941
    Thomas M. h/o Julia A.; 2 Jun 1867-23 Jan 1954

Owens
Ethel w/o W.C.; 29 May 1897-18 Oct 1974
W.C. h/o Ethel ; 25 Nov 1889-20 Oct 1973
Padden
Addie P. 30 Oct 1848-2 Dec 1929
Elija P. 17 Nov 1844-20 Apr 1915
Paden
John T. 1 Sept 1810-6 Sept 1881
R.S. h/o Samantha Tippins; 22 Dec 1886-21 Feb 1976
Pannell
Herbert Thomas 29 Apr 1915-22 Dec 1989
Lucy M. 16 Aug 1895-8 Mar 1970
Robert Thomas 2 Nov 1923-23 Mar 1978
Paris
Louise 24 Jul 1919-19 May 1974
Ernest A. 27 May 1878-31 Mar 1901
Jane 20 Apr 1809-18 May 1993
John 24 Aug 1847-26 Mar 1888
Louella 8 Dec 1849-9 Mar 1880
Bancy M. 21 Sept 1836-18 Jun 1886
Parker
Cary V. 25 May 1905-20 Feb 1956
J.W. 1895-1960
Levie M. 1899-1909
Parks
Coke Bunyan 21 Sept 1893-21 Jan 1965
Patten
Joe 11 Jan 1892-14 Oct 1933
Patterson
Roger K. 5 Dec 1943-21 Dec 1986
Penland
Jacob Marion 11 Apr 1862-11 Mar 1912
Marion w/o William Hoyt; 20 Oct 1895-26 Jun 1980
William Hoyt h/o Marion; 26 Sept 1902-10 Sept 1946
Perkins
Elizabeth O. w/o Turner G.; 30 Aug 1892-14 Feb 1983
Katherine w/o Richard F.; 1 May 1862-15 Apr 1942
Mary 10 Aug 1887-27 Jun 1925
Richard F. h/o Katherine; 13 Feb 1893-15 Dec 1969
Turner G. h/o Elizabeth O.; 11 Feb 1885-15 Mar 1967

Perry

John L. h/o Mary S.; 29 Dec 1953-4 Apr 1916
Lula May 1885-1969
Mary S. w/o John L.; 21 Dec 1869-30 May 1940
Minnie 26 Dec 1896-25 Sept 1899

Phillips

Alfred W. h/o Amanda Maxwell; 6 Sept 1848-10 Oct 1922
Amanda Maxwell w/o Alfred W.; 25 Jan 1850-29 Jan 1926
Daisy Leola 29 Dec 1888-6 Jan 1908
Edna D. w/o Walter C.; 23 Oct 1908-17 Feb 1981
Emily 4 Jul 1843-11 Apr 1915
H. Ingram 18 Jun 1898-29 Jul 1949
Hattie R. 1880-1955
Irene 12 Sept 1907-9 Jan 1982
Mary 18 Aug 1861-30 Jun 1905
Ola Look 9 Feb 1898-27 Jun 1935
Randall E. 26 Feb 1964-14 May 1967
Richard 1870-1946
Richard P. 30 Oct 1850-23 Feb 1929
Walter C. h/o Edna D. 4 Aug 1891-15 May 1979
Walter Gerrett 8 Aug 1929-15 Nov 1981

Pickens

Bertha Crowe 1903-1957
Harley L. 29 Nov 1900-29 Sept 1986

Pittman

Mamie 30 Jun 1902-1995
Pearl Ellington 23 Jan 1906-4 Nov 1970
Silas D. 3 Mar 1897-25 Jan 1962

Pitts

Dorothy E. 4 Mar 1921-10 May 1921
Frances F. 13 Apr 1914-19 Dec 1958
James Stanford 3 Aug 1872 24 Jun 1954
John Thomas 22 Jan 1913-12 Sept 1994
Martha Jane Black 27 Mar 1881-9 Sept 1939
Mary B. 29 Jun 1912-31 May 1981
Mattie S. 7 Jun 1907-11 Mar 1994
Violet M. 20 Jun 1922-1 Mar 1972
Wayne J. 25 Mar 1939-27 Feb 1962
Zelma Lee 16 Feb 1910-28 Jun 1981

Plant

    Forrest h/o Lee Byron; 3 Sept 1894-30 Oct 1953

    Lee Buron w/o Forrest; 18 Dec 1889-14 Oct 1931

Poper

    Anne Mae 14 May 1925-15 Aug 1972

Poss

    Bartow D. 14 Apr 1879-6 Jan 1931

    Howard Lee 28 Oct 1934-15 Aug 1996

    Trina Lynn 5 Jun 1981-6 Jun 1981

Poter

    N.C. 8 May 1864-12 Apr 1890

Powell

    Addie E w/o Chas Sanford; 15 Apr 1895-25 Jan 1971

    Chas Sanford h/o Addie E.; 7 Aug 1890-1 Dec 1945

    William C. 1896-1950

Power

    Charles Geiger 18 Mar 1856-18 Mar 1925

    Elsie Stricklaw w/o Charles E.; 21 May 1905-28 May 1940

    Eva Elder 9 Sept 1868-24 Nov 1947

Preston

    E. 1929-1958

Price

    Marcin R. 19 Jun 1933-18 Jan 1980

Prichard

    Emmett V. 1886-1967

    Gussie Irene Allison 16 Jul 1903-9 Jan 1926

    Harold 1913-1914

    Marjorie 1922-1924

    Mary B. 1890-1983

    Ruby R. 1894-1914

    Thelma 1911-1914

Proudfoot

    Elizabeth Morrison d: 16 Jun 1855; 12y 6m

    Euphemia T. 12 Sept 1911-23 Dec 1976

    Hugh W. 16 Mar 1795-21 Jun 1871

    Rebecca Catherine d: 26 Jun 1816; 1m 3d

Pruett

    Herbert E. 3 Jun 1914-28 Sept 1990

    Robert Earl h/o Thanie Carter; 1887-1956

    Robert Edward 29 Oct 1912-14 Dec 1983

    Thanie Carter w/o Robert Earl; 1891-1986

Pruitt
    Cliff Edward 1915-1963
    Cliff G. h/o Lollie L.; 1889-1962
    Lollie L. w/o Cliff G.; 1898-1971
    Louie James 16 Oct 1922-10 Oct 1960
    Robert H. 6 Dec 1918-26 Dec 1995
Pursley
    James Mason 1878-1953
    Minnie C. 1878-1973
Rabern
    Jeff B. h/o Minnie Bell; 31 Jan 1879-6 Feb 1925
    Minnie Bell w/o Jeff B.; 11 Dec 1890-29 Nov 1956
Rainey
    Floyd A. 21 May 1869-8 Aug 1939
    Glen 8 Aug 1910-11 Aug 1991
    Hattie I 6 Feb 1873-20 Apr 1942
    James Floyd 7 Sept 1914-31 Aug 1958
    Lena A. 3 Nov 1881-24 Jan 1962
Rainwater
    C. 3 Mar 1910-8 Dec 1945
    Guy 1911-1983
    J. Byron 1908-1939
    Lessie W. 1897-1930
    Luther 1885-1943
    Robert W. 8 Sept 1921-20 Aug 1982
    Victor M. 31 Oct 1919-31 Aug 1970
    Willie Lee Eady 1905-1981
Ramsey
    Edith H. 8 Apr 1921-11 Oct 1970
    Mildred d: 1 May 1923
    Seaborn 7 Jul 1808-21 Feb 1892
    Wilda E. 8 Dec 1826-19 May 1894
Ray
    Billy F. 22 Oct 1928-18 Jul 1977
    Elsie Cook 1927-1994
    Linda Irene 12 Jul 1951-17 Jul 1951
Reed
    Charles L. 1928-1967
    Ferbia Mitchell 1860-1927
    Hubert W. 14 Feb 1901-18 May 1973
    Posey Austin 1866-1928

Reese
> Clara C. w/o J. Clarence; 19 May 1897-27 Jan 1979
> Clarence h/o Clara C. 10 Apr 1888-11 Jul 1960

Reeves
> Ardilla A. w/o John P. Ellington; 15 Dec 1869-18 Nov 1945
> Bessie S. w/o Charlie J.; 1906-1977
> Charlie J. h/o Bessie S.; 1907-1989
> Dora E. w/o Mathew W.; 7 Nov 1878-11 Jul 1949
> Estelle 15 Jun 1904-11 Dec 1984
> Eva Corey d: 15 Nov 1907
> Fannie Waters 4 Feb 1891-20 Sept 1967
> Georgia Reece w/o William Homer; 28 Jun 1882-25 Dec 1946
> Harry M. 7 Oct 1914-20 Nov 1995
> Henry L. h/o Louella; 18 May 1896-5 Feb 1952
> Irene K. w/o Montgomery D.; 11 Mar 1912-31 Aug 1988
> J.T. 14 Feb 1898-19 Sept 1983
> Julia G. 13 Nov 1901-4 Apr 1969
> Lewis E. 12 Nov 1906-24 Dec 1928
> Louella w/o Henry L.; 3 Mar 1900-4 Jul 1988
> Mathew W. h/o Dora E.; 22 Mar 1868-7 May 1944
> Montgomery D. h/o Irene K.; 9 Nov 1897-29 Jan 1974
> Pearl 2 Feb 1902-2 Oct 1976
> Posey Dean 14 Nov 1888-1 Mar 1957
> Posey Dean 6 Dec 1911-21 Jun 1921
> Ruth D. w/o Willis R.; 17 Jun 1895-31 Dec 1979
> Thomas W. 11 Oct 1948-21 Jan 1973
> Todd Eric 15 May 1970-21 Jul 1970
> William Homer h/o Georgia Reece; 20 Sept 1879-11 Jan 1965
> Willis R. h/o Ruth D.; 4 Oct 1892-4 Apr 1978

Rexroade
> Noel Daniel 24 Dec 1973-24 Jun 1974

Rhodes
> Mary Lorena 1894-1968

Richards
> Michael W. 21 Jan 1955-28 Jan 1955

Richardson
> Fonnie C. 1 Feb 1897-29 Jul 1974
> Lucy M 9 Dec 1906-27 Dec 1991

Riley
> Arthur 3 Aug 1894-19 Feb 1943
> Jesse F. 17 Aug 1905-22 Mar 1970

John W. 9 Jun 1897-1 Feb 1967
Lena A. w/o Virgil L.; 18 Apr 1894-8 Dec 1946
Margaret 23 Dec 1873-13 Mar 1919
Thomas D. 23 Jul 1900-9 Mar 1984
Virgil L. h/o Lena A.; 8 Dec 1895-10 Aug 1958
Robertson
   Alsey E. 19 Feb 1857-26 Aug 1933
   Elvira C. 25 Dec 1822-16 Feb 1884
   Frances 18 May 1859-31 May 1920
   Mamie D. 3 Jan 1855-13 Nov 1919
   Margaret M. 2 Mar 1850-2 Oct 1872
   Mary B. 5 May 1861-4 Jul 1887
   N.L. 30 Jan 1818-12 Apr 1900
   Nancy E. 26 Oct 1845-14 Feb 1938
Rogers
   Julia U. d: 20 May 1892; 6d
Rollins
   Belle 20 Dec 1886-2 Mar 1916
   John Barrington 13 Oct 1905-21 Feb 1979
   Letha M. 3 Nov 1894-12 May 1973
   M.L. w/o R.B.; 8 Nov 1863-6 Nov 1939
   R.B.h/o M.L.; 1 Jun 1865-31 Oct 1923
Roper
   Effie Viola 19 Apr 1913-10 Mar 1976
   William Floyd 16 Jul 1967-15 Mar 1988
Rowe
   Lottie M. 1908-1956
   Mary 27 Jan 1866-19 Sept 1932
   Walter T. 8 Apr 1859-26 Dec 1942
Rucker
   Howard G. h/o Naomi J.; 28 Nov 1878-2 Jan 1933
   Ida Dorris 29 Mar 1880-3 Apr 1970
   John Wade 5 Jan 1876-7 Apr 1956
   Naomi J.; w/o Howard G.; 25 Sept 1878-10 Feb 1968
Rudolph
   Edwin L. 1899-1966
   Josephine G. 1903-1989
Rusk
   Lula L. w/o Roy W. Merritt; 9 Oct 1899-13 Jul 1984
Sampler
   Emily V, 29 Aug 1846-20 May 1921

Thomas 5 May 1829-17 May 1872
Willie T. 24 May 1900-5 May 1902
Samples
Elbert Clyde 5 Sept 1887-6 Aug 1957
Sanders
Mary J. 1 Oct 1889-7 Jun 1984
Sargent
Anne Monk 8 Oct 1933-7 Nov 1988
James h. 9 Jul 1914-18 Mar 1977
Scott
Charles F. b/o Lois; 7 Jun 1937-12 Nov 1954
Chester Tillery 1875-1924
John A. h/o Lelia E.; 1897-1950
Lelia E. w/o John A.; 1905-1979
Lois s/o Charles F.; 3 Apr 1931-15 Aug 1983
Robert J. 14 Mar 1948-16 Sept 1973
Robert John 5 Jun 1922-18 Dec 1986
W.L. 24 Sept 1873-4 May 1954
Seay
John A. 1871-1943
Mamie Little 12 May 1876-30 Mar 1916
Sewell
Ben L. 8 Dec 1879-2 May 1952
Odessa Hampton 5 Oct 1881-20 Aug 1968
Sherman
Frances 3 Jun 1898-19 Oct 1902
John 10 May 1902-28 Aug 1903
N.L. 18 May 1847-23 Jan 1889
Susan 4 Sept 1847-12 Jun 1893
W.E. 7 Mar 1872-13 Aug 1908
Shufelt
Lynn F. 1912-1978
Silton
Sara G. 1896-1990
Thomas F. 1892-1978
Simmons
Elizabeth H. 1920-1973
Thomas H. 1920-1986
Skelton
Jule B. 14 Dec 1908-15 Jun 1980
Sybil Butler 4 Dec 1909-5 Mar 1971

Slaughter
    Robert Bruce 25 Mar 1920-30 Dec 1983
Sleevenhoek
    Dirk W. 28 Mar 1900-22 Aug 1967
    Homer Reeves 4 Mar 1900-22 Jul 1968
    Marcia DeWitt 24 Apr 1897-5 Jun 1951
    Minnie J. 31 Oct 1873-20 Jun 1968
    Villian D. 26 Jun 1870-10 Apr 1955
Sloan
    Lucius 3 Dec 1901-3 Mar 1967
Smith
    A.F. 3 Dec 1852-10 May 1895
    Amanda 1883-1953
    Aubrey K. 19 May 1918-14 Jun 1992
    Chester Lee 25 Jul 1929-4 Mar 1975
    Chris 14 Dec 1961-15 Dec 1961
    Clee 8 Dec 1895-24 Feb 1976
    Delora H. 10 Aug 1922-26 Nov 1996
    Effie 2 Jun 1890-16 Jan 1925
    Farrel O. 18 May 1901-14 Nov 1978
    Gilbert 1891-1942
    James T. 24 Dec 1849-17 Mar 1917
    James T. 31 Jul 1924-27 May 1945
    John C. h/o Mary L.; 30 Mar 1896-11 Aug 1958
    Julie Scott 21 Feb 1902-17 Sept 1976
    L.E. 23 Feb 1872-2 Aug 1904
    Lavell C. 2 Jul 1931-22 Apr 1972
    Loy Edward 30 Jan 1908-6 May 1979
    Lucy Frazier 2 Dec 1886-30 Nov 1918
    Mamie w/o John J.; 1878-1958
    Mary L. w/o John C.; 15 Mar 1906-4 Apr 1981
    Mary S. 14 Jul 1866-25 Oct 1932
    Maude L. 1890-1952
    Nettie O. 6 Mar 1891-9 Dec 1921
    Ollie T. 9 May 1891-10 Jul 1916
    Roy Wendell 12 Sept 1919-11 Oct 1987
    Samuel 27 Jul 1919-15 Jul 1995
    William 2 Nov 1895-19 Nov 1928
Sneed
    Charles Edward 12 Aug 1922-29 Sept 1987

Southern
   Marshall 19 Feb 1903-1 Mar 1973
Spoenemann
   Lillian 1890-1977
Stahl
   Elbert C. 18 Oct 1929-5 Sept 1995
Standridge
   Annie Lee 1 Apr 1896-26 Nov 1985
   Jolly r. 29 Aug 1897-22 Sept 1956
Stanford
   Horace 1 Nov 1920-27 Feb 1967
   Paul 5 Apr 1934-5 Apr 1934
Stark
   P.J. 4 Mar 1814-17 Jan 1889
Stein
   Auguste (Mrs(9 Feb 1871-31 Jan 1953
   Helene E. 4 Aug 1906-19 Apr 1974
Stephens
   Essie 5 Oct 1895-31 Jan 1954
   Etna 8 Jan 1899-16 Feb 1971
   Frank 7 Sept 1884-7 Apr 1984
Stewart
   James 19 Oct 1819-9 May 1878
   Mary 8 Feb 1826-3 Jun 1891
Still
   Evelyn Montine w/o Ronald; 10 Apr 1942-4 Sept 1942
   Ronald w/o Evelyn Montine; 25 May 1941-25 May 1941
Stone
   Suvilla Massey w/o William Oscar; 30 May 1897-31 Dec 1967
   William Oscar h/o Suvilla Massey; 8 Jan 1900-8 Feb 1963
Storey
   Estelle Oliver 1890-1965
   Frances Sins w/o Otis Gartrell; 1929-1969
   Otis C. h/o Frances Sins; 1882-1965
   Steve 9 Jun 1964-29 Sept 1978
Stover
   Sam 30 Nov 1885-20 Jul 1970
Stow
   Frances 8 Jul 1940-4 Jan 1959
   Walter G. 15 Aug 1912-31 Jan 1979

Stribling
>Asa Bush 28 Aug 1903-23 Nov 1941
>Nannie Bush 18 Oct 1878-1 Jan 1929
>Paul O. 18 Jun 1874-30 Aug 1948
>Paul O. 11 Oct 1900-13 Apr 1962

Stricklan
>William 6 Apr 1929-4 Feb 1936

Strickland
>Alvin J. 29 Oct 1896-30 Dec 1960
>B.F. 17 Mar 1883-16 Mar 1959
>Burean Osten 1900-1917
>Cecil James 11 Aug 1911-24 Jul 1986
>Charlie D. 17 Apr 1898-27 Oct 1969
>Clementine A. w/o John M.; 23 Jun 1875-10 Nov 1957
>Eva 24 Sept 1901-19 Feb 1989
>Florence G. 13 Nov 1904-16 Mar 1995
>Harold H. 22 Mar 1901-21 Jun 1968
>Jerry James 4 Mar 1936-28 Dec 1961
>John M. h/o Clementine A.; 6 Jan 1867-18 Apr 1929
>Joseph Henry 1893-1942
>Maltha 1861-1936
>Mary Nesbit 1864-1961
>Riley J. h/o Sarah Ann;1867-1954
>Robert Hardy 1866-1937
>Sarah Ann w/o Riley J.; 1875-1959

Stroup
>Charlie 20 Jul 1876-1 Jul 1890
>Fannie 9 Jul 1889-14 Oct 1889

Sudduth
>Charlie A 23 Feb 1891-8 Nov 1971

Sullivan
>B. Irene Coleman 7 Aug 1903-12 Jan 1977
>Charles Wesley 14 Sept 1900-29 Mar 1980
>David C. h/o Marie C.; 2 Mar 1913-20 Feb 1972
>Frederick R. 18 Dec 1905-4 Aug 1928
>George W. 27 Mar 1868-28 Nov 1955
>Ida H. w/o Tillman N.; 29 Nov 1876-10 Jan 1945
>Ira Pierce 7 Jun 1898-23 Dec 1969
>Jean D. 9 Sept 1965-13 Dec 1965
>Marie C. w/o David C.; 7 Nov 1914-8 Feb 1996
>Martha 5 Sept 1910-7 Dec 1985

Ollie A. 18 Jun 1908-11 Apr 1938
Rosa Reed w/o William C.; 2 Nov 1885-7 May 1978
Susie L. 19 Mar 1878-4 Jan 1964
Tillman N. h/o Ida H.; 4 Jan 1869-18 Nov 1952
William C. h/o Rosa Reed; 17 Nov 1884-20 Oct 1938

Summerall

Hubert Edgar 13 Feb 1919-20 Jul 1990

Talley

Ella Dean d/o J.A.; 6 Dec 1868-13 Jul 1935
Ella May d/o G.G.; d: 1885; 3m
Joseph Walter 11 Jul 1906-10 Dec 1948
Lelia A Grogan 27 Feb 1871-4 Jan 1943
J.T. h/o Martha E.D.; 1835-1909
Martha E.D. w/o J.T.; 1837-1911

Taylor

Carolyn Paden 1919-1982
Florence M. 26 Nov 1894-6 Jan 1976
Simeon Fred 14 Jun 1894-19 Aug 1959

Tedder

Amanda P. 23 Nov 1855-12 Jun 1943
Arminda d: 6 Feb 1888; 53y 9m
Elsie 1871-1916
Georgia 17 Jul 1889-21 Dec 1934
John W. D: 28 Jul 1832; 57y 10m
Lula 1869-1918
Nada 20 Jul 1892-20 May 1932
Pearl d/o Ransoms; d:1 May 1929;
Ransoms f/oPearl; d: 1 May 1929; 35y

Thomas

B. 25 Jun 1888-13 Aug 1965
Clinton Paul d: 18 Mar 1981
Elias B. 3 Oct 1914-15 Mar 1966
George Pierce 9 Sept 1854-22 Sept 1935
Louise Virginia 21 Oct 1860-4 Sept 1948
Mary O. 8 Dec 1892-20 Jul 1917
Packs 5 Mar 1911-21 Feb 1983

Thomason

Emma B. 20 Apr 1896-7 Aug 1964
Lucille M. w/o William G.; 12 Mar 1892-29 Mar 1968
Marion E. 5 Jun 1921-2 Mar 1960
Steve Michael 15 Jan 1954-2 Mar 1983

Warren H. 20 Feb 1896-7 Aug 1964
William G. h/o Lucille M.; 6 Sept 1894-8 Oct 1975
Thompson
    Ambry J. 26 Jul 1811-29 Mar 1905
    Mamie S. 5 Jun 1876-27 May 1968
    T.G. 5 May 1870-24 Jan 1930
Tinney
    John Elmer 9 Sept 1884-8 Mar 1914
    Lena L. 31 Aug 1882-12 Dec 1902
    Louie 4 May 1901-29 Jan 1902
    Maud Lillian 13 Nov 1880-30 Nov 1914
Tippens
    Samantha w/o R.S. Paden; 1834-1921
Tribble
    Jack Edwin 15 Mar 1927-31 Jul 1989
Tumlin
    George W. 1888-1965
    Leona w/o Ralph H. Kirk; 1881-1946
    Sarah k. 1883-1973
Turner
    Jessie J. 18 Jun 1889-2 Apr 1967
Vaughan
    Cliff P. 15 Sept 1890-25 Dec 1972
    Lorena G. 15 Sept 1888-1 Mar 1980
    Daisy E. 3 Jul 1910-2 Mar 1986
    Harsey T. h/o Lucile M.; 10 Apr 1917-5 Jun 1992
    Lucile M. w/o Harsey T.; 11 Apr 1920-22 Nov 1993
    Roy E. 1 Nov 1931-27 Nov 1954
    Willie E. 15 Aug 1906-19 Dec 1985
Vickery
    Chris William 25 Nov 1964-4 Sept 1991
    Floyd 2 Mar 1928-28 Jun 1983
    Lottie P. w/o Otis; 1907-1991
    William Alfred 7 Jun 1930-21 Apr 1993
Vinson
    Addie Carrie 6 Oct 1871-29 Jul 1931
    Elijiah 21 Oct 1828-2 May 1887
    K.T. 5 Sept 1865-1 Mar 1898
    Martha Alice 7 Aug 1870-28 Jun 1912
Voss
    Nancy A. 10 Aug 1845-29 Jul 1916

P.M. 2 Jan 1835-14 Oct 1903
Waldrop
    Chessie L. 25 Jan 1897-2 Mar 1970
    John H. 8 Jun 1871- 2 Mar 1970
Walker
    Pamela E. Scott 13 Aug 1955-20 Apr 1978
Wall
    John T. 10 Nov 1907-27 Aug 1955
Wallace
    Julie Ann 26 Jul 1872-24 Mar 1829
    Mary M. 26 Feb 1885-8 Jul 1886
Walraven
    Joe P. 24 Nov 1898-26 Mar 1957
    John 12 Dec 1872-1 Sept 1948
    Linnie 13 Dec 1870-1 Jun 1939
    Mae R. 23 Sept 1899-31 Jan 1977
Warner
    Harold 1920-1991
Waters
    A.M. 3 Feb 1906-23 May 1967
    Denise Flynn 16 Jun 1958-4 Feb 1990
Watkins
    Lyman W. 5 Apr 1892-4 Nov 1969
    Verna Hill 1899-1974
Weaver
    Floyd 2 Sept 1909-31 Oct 1954
    Mettie w/o H.I.; 5 Jun 1876-14 Jul 1901
Webb
    A. Thomas 3 Feb 1922-7 Nov 1946
    Bertha Annie w/o Claude; 13 Jul 1894-15 Apr 1980
    C.M. h/o Amanda Drake; d: 1928; 82y
    Casandra F. 27 Aug 1895-11 Apr 1983
    Claude h/o Bertha Annie; 16 Jun 1887-24 Apr 1958
    Clinton Tolliver h/o Edna L.; 7 Aug 1863-15 Mar 1915
    Edward T. 4 May 1885-2 Sept 1905
    Eonalula McNeely 11 Sept 1866-9 Jan 1949
    Hattie S. w/o Thomas E.; 1874-1965
    Jack 26 Jan 1889-6 Jun 1958
    Johne May d: 13 Jan 1936
    Ralph 1910-1993
    Roy 2 Dec 1892-18 Jun 1921

S. Gober 17 Jan 1886-8 Feb 1980

Thomas E. h/o Hattie S. ; 10 Oct 1873-29 Apr 1923

Weldon

Robert A. 26 Sept 1954-15 Sept 1990

Westbrook

Annie l. 26 Feb 1911-2 Jan 1990

Brenda Earl 21 Jul 1956-11 Nov 1988

Ella 24 Dec 1873-10 May 1924

G.R. 22 Nov 1959-22 Nov 1959

L.T. 10 Jan 1872-18 Oct 1948

Wett

Betty Gene 24 Jun 1924-20 Jan 1935

Whatley

FAughney S. 19 Mar 1868-18 Aug 1890

Margaret I. 25 Dec 1843-1 Aug 1898

Mary N. w/o Robert A.; 6 Mar 1874-9 Feb 1965

Robert A. h/o Mary N.; 7 Sept 1871-19 Dec 1952

Wilson M. 22 May 1835-21 May 1912

Wheeler

Buford 25 Dec 1905-9 Apr 1954

Eliza A. w/o William E.; 17 Sept 1874-12 Mar 1952

Levis 20 Apr 1917-7 Apr 1984

Lillie 20 Dec 1901-28 Jun 1970

Rovanna 8 Dec 1903-8 Apr 1965

William E. h/o Eliza A.; 8 Mar 1877-22 Jan 1957

Whiten

Carolyn Yvonne 15 Aug 1940-15 Jul 1941

Whitfield

Lucile A. 2 Jun 1910-19 May 1953

Whitley

Annie s/o Henry; 30 Apr 1890-26 Oct 1950

Ella d: 11 Nov 1860

Henry b/o Annie; 20 Sept 1886-29 Sept 1966

Ina V. 13 Oct 1881-16 Sept 1962

J.H. 21 Sept 1881-30 Jun 1902

Lula 8 Sept 1870-15 Jun 1898

Ola 4 Dec 1898-24 Jun 1944

Robert L. 27 Aug 1877-3 Feb 1958

Roy Dean 1925-1978

William 1 Sept 1832-7 Jan 1916

Wiley

    A.C. 5 Mar 1888-7 Jun 1953

    D.T. 1892-1973

    Guy R. 5 Dec 1913-2 Jun 1914

    Helen 14 Feb 1930-2 Dec 1930

    Herman R. D: 23 Nov 1958; 59y

    J. Huford 1910-1963

    Mae 13 Aug 1893-25 May 1915

    Marvin J. 27 Mar 1895-25 Sept 1956

    Mary A. Hughes 16 Mar 1859-18 May 1941

    Odessa 17 Dec 1884-21 Nov 1940

    Odessa Adams 26 Jan 1897-22 Sept 1986

    Olary Burdent 25 Oct 1886-2 Jan 1914

    Robert O. 25 Feb 1855-5 Oct 1927

    Rosa S. 12 Dec 1892-1 Sept 1958

    Sarah E. 24 Dec 1853-15 Aug 1922

    William C. 31 Jul 1923-5 Apr 1944

    William O. 17 Aug 1856-23 Dec 1929

Williams

    Dellar Harring w/o John B.; 6 Jul 1865-13 Mar 1907

    Joann W. 11 May 1836-12 Feb 1972

    John B. h/o Dellar Harring; 23 Apr 1861-18 Oct 1918

Wilson

    J.L. 25 Aug 1829-10 Dec 1893

    Susan S. 17 Nov 1867-15 Sept 1928

    Susan S. 9 Jun 1833-17 Jan 1904

Wingo

    Almond 5 Aug 1915-15 Aug 1967

    Claude Linton 16 Jul 1891-22 Jul 1986

    Lavada H. 5 Jun 1892-10 Mar 1986

Winkler

    Catherine Ellington 12 Feb 1903-19 Oct 1986

    John Elbert 20 Oct 1900-20 Jun 1958

    Julia A. w/o Thomas M.: 6 Feb 1883-16 Feb 1963

    Thomas M. h/o Julia A.; 20 Jan 1870-26 Nov 1952

Womad

    James Cole 20 Nov 1970-20 Nov 1970

Wood

    Chas D. 27 Jul 1882-9 Jun 1949

    H.P. h/o Julia Blair; 9 Jul 1860-25 Jun 1936

    Julia Blair w/o H.P.; 18 Jul 1976-9 Mar 1933

Louanna 11 May 1861-19 Aug 1920
Word
 Susan 1862-1922
Worsham
 George 28 Nov 1922-11 Jul 1977
Wright
 Alice R. 22 Nov 1862-24 Dec 1886
 Amanda E. 3 Jul 1861-31 Oct 1939
 Clyde Jamison 23 Jul 1892-15 Jul 1914
 Gladys D. d: 6 Jun 1911
 Henry E. 17 Jan 1896-13 Nov 1980
 J.I. h/o Nettie Reed; 2 Aug 1888-17 Dec 1971
 James B. 27 May 1858-19 May 1942
 James Hugh 1913-1914
 Julia Smith w/o Robert T.; 19 Jul 1888-22 Jul 1932
 Kate V. w/o Clarence; 1890-1975
 Laler Mae 18 Sept 1900-20 May 1924
 Mary J. Waller w/o Robert T.; 10 Jul 1861-8 Feb 1908
 Nettie Reed w/o J.I.; 26 Aug 1889-3 Jul 1976
 Olive 29 Aug 1885-24 Aug 1887
 Ralph A. 30 Sept 1906-20 Nov 1977
 Robert T. h/o Julia Smith & Mary J. Waller; 25 Mar 1856-
 23 Nov 1939
Yarbrough
 Henry h/o Oma Matline; 29 Sept 1866-7 May 1943
 L.H. 22 Jan 1931-19 Aug 1993
 Oma Matline w/o Henry; 22 Jul 1900-26 Jul 1977
Young
 Cliff H. Coleman 27 Jun 1907-3 Oct 1947
 Dillard T Winkler 25 Aug 1925-4 Jul 1952
 Flora E. Coleman 15 Oct 1910-31 May 1981
 Julia A. 6 Feb 1883-16 Feb 1963
 Michael G. 7 Sept 1958-11 Oct 1981
 Thomas M. 20 Jan 1870-26 Nov 1952
 William E. 25 Nov 1916-31 Jan 1976

Fulton County
Mt. Pisgah Cemetery

Abernathy
>Carris E. 15 Feb 1886-8 Dec 1947
>Fred L. 1906-1973
>Grady 1 Mar 1895-21 Dec 1964
>Mary Delilah 9 Oct 1873-6 Oct 1905
>Milton M. h/o L.; 1868-1939
>Roxie Ann 21 Jan 1857-8 Feb 1925
>Valentine Alax 28 Feb 1860-12 Sept 1939

Adams
>Guy S. 23 Sept 1887-2 Feb 1902
>Maud A. 8 Sept 1880-3 Sept 1883

Alexander
>S.A. 29 Mar 1862-6 Sept 1894

Allen
>Anthony W. 1 Dec 1956-17 Jun 1975
>Ronnie T. 30 May 1950-7 Mar 1988
>Tony G. 26 Mar 1954-22 Jan 1958

Allgood
>Franklin Z. h/o Sarah Annie; 15 Nov 1864-16 Aug 1923
>Sarah Annie w/o Franklin Z. 16 Mar 1869-4 Jul 1935

Anderson
>Charles Allen 1941-1977

Anglin
>Henry O. 28 Dec 1876-10 Sept 1950
>Ola Belle 1890-1917

Autrey
>Joe B. h/o Marsceanie; 1873-1951
>Marsceanie w/o Joe B.; 1875-1958

Autry
>Dewey Edward f/o Meridethy; 1946-1968
>Meridethy d/o Dewey Edward; 7 Oct 1967-7 Oct 1967

Ballard
>Marvin R. 15 Jul 1948-12 Aug 1968

Barnes
>J. Jane Brown 15 1947-4 Sept 1978

Barrett
>U. Lamar 17 Jun 1925-12 Nov 1962

Benson

    Claude W. 18 Jul 1888-15 Jun 1962

    Ida Lee 11 Dec 1875-15 Dec 1959

    James Edward b/o Jerry Euel; 16 Apr 1942-16 Apr 1942

    Jeffie M. h/o Naomi T.; 23 Aug 1878-15 May 1942

    Jerry Euel b/o James Edward; 16 Apr 1942-16 Apr 1942

    Naomi T. w/o Jeffie M.; 16 Jan 1886-20 Dec 1971

    Oscar T. 14 Oct 1842-6 Jun 1917

    Tempie J. 15 Nov 1847-10 Feb 1936

Blake

    Effat w/o Wade H.; 18 Mar 1887-28 Apr 1958

    Nonnie B. 21 Jan 1896-2 Jun 1925

    Wade H. h/o Effat ;18 Jan 1879-12 Feb 1955

Boyd

    Estelle Nov 1931-30 Mar 1933

Brown

    Charles L. 20 Apr 1951-15 Apr 1992

    F. Lucille 4 Feb 1928-18 Feb 1993

    Shirley A. 29 Oct 1959-1 Feb 1960

    Tammy M. 22 Mar 1967-22 Mar 1967

Brumbelow

    Eugene J. h/o Willene J.; 17 Jun 1922-23 Mar 1987

    Jimmy 27 Dec 1950-18 Jan 1980

    Tommy 7 Jun 1957-30 Jun 1957

    Willene J. w/o Eugene J.; 19 Jan 1924-29 Sept 1983

Burce

    Richard barry 13 Sept 1944-13 Sept 1944

Burgess

    Christopher 13 Mar 1955-2 Apr 1984

Burns

    Grayson h/o Nomie; 24 Jun 1910-27 Feb 1990

    Nomie w/o Grayson; 11 Dec 1914-3 Jan 1988

Byrd

    Albert T. 29 Jul 1894-14 Jun 1983

    Mattie J. 20 Apr 1901-27 Jan 1991

Campbell

    Helen Bourne w/o Henry Dean; 4 May 1931-27 Apr 1991

    Henry Dean 11 May 1980-21 Sept 1944

    Henry Dean h/o Helen Bourne; 28 May 1927-1 Sept 1980

    Hulon 24 Jul 1931-1 Nov 1990

    J.H.H. h/o Martha Jett; 13 Mar 1851-12 Jun 1921

John Robert d: 6 Jun 1958; 1y 2m
Martha Jett w/o J.H.H.; 21 Aug 1852-10 May 1909
Robert s/o J.H. & Martha Jett; 9 Sept 1885-20 Dec 1909
Sam J. s/o J.H. & Martha Jett; 5 Jan 1898-8 Feb 1918
Trenton d. 23 Nov 1949-31 Mar 1974

Carlan
Rosa J. w/o Thomas H.; 27 Mar 1901-7 Sept 1965
Thomas H. h/o Rosa J.; 30 May 1900-3 Feb 1974

Chamblee
Allies w/o Emmett L.; 7 May 1890-20 Mar 1963
Emmett L. h/o Allies; 20 Feb 1887-19 Oct 1962
Scott Curtis 21 Jan 1921-31 Jan 1989

Chandler
Annie May d/o W.H.; 27 Dec 1893-28 Dec 1894

Chastain
Norma Jea 19 Sept 1962-19 Sept 1962

Clark
Annie Lou w/o Macon A.; 8 Aug 1913-13 May 1953
Bessie w/o James; 1881-1951
James h/o Bessie; 1879-1958
Macon A. h/o Annie Lou; 18 Sept 1912-23 Jun 1939
Zora Estie 24 Nov 1909-8 May 1967

Clayton
John W. 27 May 1930-February 1997
Peggy Harriett 24 Jan 1955-2 May 1965
Thomas W. 16 Aug 1926-20 May 1974

Cleveland
Hallie M. w/o Garrett W.; 22 Feb 1908-15 Jun 1937

Cobb
Ada F. w/o Jim W.; 28 Sept 1885-8 Sept 1935
Annie w/o Homer L. Lackey; 31 Dec 1909-10 Apr 1965
Jeanette w/o W.Walter: 1915-1989
Jim W. h/o Ada F.; 2 Sept 1880-26 Aug 1950
John Robert s/o R.F. & Leaner; 20 May 1903-13 Nov 1918
Mary Jane w/o Thomas Shutle; d: 12 Mar 1914
Sim 22 Nov 1912-20 Jul 1972
W.Walter h/o Jeanette; 1904-1963

Coker
Grady S. 22 Nov 1912-20 Jul 1972

Compton
Nora lee 2 Jun 1925-9 Jun 1965

Conner

Janie T. 1875-1972

Offie E. 1866-1912

Cook

Andrew J. h/o Frances B.; 6 Oct 1900-18 Jun 1971

Frances B. w/o Andrew J.; 30 Jun 1902-29 Aug 1966

Cooper

Sarah E. 18 Jun 1856-12 Feb 1924

William A. 19 Sept 1845-24 Dec 1921

Cott

Agnes w/o William H.; 22 Jun 1902-3 Jan 1986

William H.: h/o Agnes 27 Mar 1904-5 Nov 1973

Cox

Ernest C. 13 Jan 1912-27 Feb 1961

Crocker

Bertie E. 6 Nov 1889-14 Aug 1975

Gaines V. 15 Apr 1881-8 Oct 1955

J.W. 27 Jul 1915-15 Mar 1987

James Leroy s/o J.W.; d: 24 Mar 1950

William Leon s/o J.W.; d: 5 Jan 1949

Dalton

Carrie N. 3 Mar 1882-6 Sept 1914

Herbert Clay 10 May 1917-3 Nov 1989

Martha Emma 26 Dec 1888-17 Jun 1978

Pearl E. 24 Nov 1892-24 Feb 1974

Robert G. 26 Sept 1882-23 Mar 1950

Robert Veston 14 Apr 1907-26 Oct 1908

Willie C. 8 May 1909-8 Jul 1909

Darnell

Mary w/o S.J.; 26 Mar 1855-21 Nov 1907

Davis

Lonie S. w/o Nelson M.; 25 Nov 1888-21 Jan 1966

Nelson M. h/o Lonie S.; 4 Feb 1884-13 Jun 1961

W.S. 1858-1941

Dean

Ivey M. 1902-1939

Johnny B. 1902-1980

Lillie 1897-1968

Dixon

Jeanette M. 4 Jul 1932-2 Oct 1993

Drake
    Elizabeth J. w/o James M.; 10 Apr 1833-22 Apr 1903
    James M. h/o Elizabeth J.; 3 Feb 1832-23 Nov 1908
    Robert L. h/o May N. Martin;10 May 1856-9 Apr 1915
Durham
    Roy 18 Jun 1900-23 Sept 1946
Edwards
    Bobby Grimes 15 Sept 1918-6 Nov 1987
Eison
    D.S. h/o Mollie & S.C.;1853-1938
    Jimie G 12 Jun 1867-17 Jan 1898
    Mary E. 21 Jan 1846-16 May 1923
    Mary I w/o W.S.; 1 Jan 1826-10 Jul 1918
    Mollie w/o D.S.; 13 May 1857-12 Jun 1889
    Nancy O. w/o Verbia V.; 1 Jan 1902-29 Oct 1957
    Odus s/o D.S. & Molly; 24 Dec 1886-8 Jan 1887
    S.C. w/o D.S.; 19 Jun 1874-13 Jan 1909
    Sarah E. 6 Sept 1861-28 Nov 1942
    Verbia V. h/o Nancy O.; 24 Feb 1889-1 May 1949
    W.S. h/o Mary I.; 2 Apr 1823-11 Dec 1908
    W.S. 19 Dec 1878-6 Nov 1962
Ferrell
    Bill 19 Mar 1909-30 Sept 1976
    Donnis Jewell 20 Dec 1929-20 Nov 1942
    Marian 18 Jun 1952-8 Oct 1957
    Reba Fay 14 May 1949-28 Nov 1989
Fields
    Edna M. 28 Jun 1842-11 Feb 1910
Fleeman
    Reece M. 19 Dec 1903-9 Nov 1985
Fousts
    Esther w/o Everett; 26 Jan 1902-25 Feb 1972
Fouts
    A. Pauline 5 Mar 1899-7 Oct 1945
    Bessie May 6 Sept 1926-6 Feb 1948
    Bill D. 15 Jan 1908-8 May 1986
    Clara E. w/o John H.; 29 Feb 1886-19 Dec 1950
    Dwight K. 23 Sept 1946-27 Feb 1960
    Edith E. 3 Aug 1920-9 May 1964
    Everett h/o Esther; 20 Dec 1899-1 Jul 1945
    Henry s/o John H. & Clara E.; d: 28 Dec 1921

Irene 19 Oct 1911-9 Aug 1932
James C. 5 Feb 1942-1 Mar 1967
Jerry William 9 Oct 1941-27 Nov 1993
John C. 29 Oct 1915-28 Mar 1995
John H. h/o Clara E.; 19 Feb 1883-25 Dec 1960
John J. s/o John H. & Clara E.; d: 18 Sept 1918
Luster 11 May 1907-1 Aug 1976
Mark Lindsey 6 Jan 1896-4 Apr 1959
Nellie E. 1901-1970
Paul W. 1893-1963
Syblee 27 Aug 1916-19 Nov 1993
Velva Cleo w/o William Edgar; 9 Nov 1907-24 Oct 1986
William Edgar h/o Velva Cleo; 14 Aug 1905-17 Jun 1985
Frazier
Carl C. 14 Feb 1906-11 Oct 1980
Martha W. 12 Dec 1894-12 Mar 1974
Ralph R. 15 Sept 1916-24 Nov 1926
Fuller
Georgia w/o T.R.; 22 Jun 1859-1 Sept 1919
Futrelle
James E. 4 Feb 1926-31 May 1987
Garren
Eliza Odell 23 Jan 1857-21 Oct 1894
John L. 16 Oct 1854-28 Sept 1924
Garrett
W. Luther 18 Nov 1908-19 Mar 1993
Garrot
Vernon Troy 1932-1934
Gero
Alice O. 19 Oct 1901-10 Nov 1922
Gibson
Ben h/o Nancy; 8 Aug 1885-26 Dec 1950
Julian 21 Aug 1916-24 Nov 1993
Nancy w/o Ben; 22 Sept 1878-9 May 1966
Gipson
Bobbie Anne w/o Hilliard G.; 13 Jan 1895-16 May 1990
Grover Cleveland 1897-1941
Hilliard G. h/o Bobbie Anne; 18 Aug 1892-1 Dec 1971
Gobb
Floyd 1863-1900

Goodson
	Hester w/o H.M.; 19 Oct 1884-10 Jul 1917
Gravitt
	Daniel A. h/o Ellen I.; 28 Apr 1884-20 Sept 1974
	Ellen I. w/o Daniel A.; 4 Feb 1888- 6 Jul 1977
Green
	Edsel L b/o Elsie & Estelle; 2 Mar 1930-19 Jun 1953
	Elsie s/o Edsel L. & Estelle; 22 Apr 1939-19 Jun 1953
	Elvis 27 Sept 1920-19 Oct 1960
	Estelle s/o Edsel L. & Elsie; 10 Feb 1936-19 Jun 1953
	Paul Lester 7 Feb 1896-17 Feb 1977
Hamil
	Arthur 27 Aug 1895-28 Aug 1973
	Donald Lamar 8 Oct 1950-28 Jun 1969

Hamilton
	Ricky L. 13 May 1961-14 Oct 1965
	Valeria 29 Nov 1925-7 Aug 1981
Hardman
	Hattie m/o Lester; 1847-1888
	Lester s/o Hattie; 1877-1886
Harmon
	Jewel G. 5 Jul 1928-10 Aug 1957
Harris
	E.L. w/o John C.; 4 Mar 1872-18 Oct 1906
	Ettie L. 2 Apr 1904-2 Oct 1904
	Eva A w/o John T.; 28 Aug 1896-5 Apr 1984
	George W. 6 Dec 1898-8 Dec 1898
	Hubert G. 1919-1961
	John C. h/o E.L.; 2 Sept 1868-22 Jan 1937
	John T. h/o Eva A.; 29 Jun 1892-30 Jul 1958
	Mary B. 8 Jan 1831-11 Jun 1898
	Robert S. 4 Sept 1854-9 Dec 1854
Harrison
	Audley T. h/o Betty J.; 30 May 1911-25 Mar 1971
	Betty J. w/o Audley T.; 30 Aug 1927-10 Feb 1977
Hawkins
	Betty d: 15 Apr 1937
	Clyde H. 10 Feb 1904-5 Mar 1971
	Etha L. 7 Feb 1904-11 May 1963
	James d: 15 Apr 1930

L.C. 1910-16 Sept 1966
Pamela Ann 4 Jun 1943-16 Jun 1943
Ruth d: 25 May 1923
Hembree
  Frona E. 6 May 1894-23 Jun 1975
Henderson
  Clarence H. f/o L.T.; 1902-1979
  L.T. s/o Clarence H.; 1933-1965
Hester
  Fate 19 Apr 1865-9 Sept 1950
  Lizer 10 Dec 1869-29 Nov 1931
Hindes
  Delynn Noell 14 Dec 1956-13 Jun 1987
Hughes
  Jesse Mae w/o J.T. Grimes; 28 Nov 1887-22 Feb 1920
Jackson
  Elizabeth 4 Oct 1858-2 Mar 1935
  Fannie R. w/o James Newton; 14 Feb 1869-10 Aug 1900
  James Newton h/o Fannie R.; 4 Sept 1859-17 Jun 1939
  Willie M. 26 Nov 1875-26 Mar 1876
Jenkins
  Alice J. w/o Gus; 1 Jan 1883-14 Apr 1934
  Arthur E. 1902-1941
  David E. 8 Dec 1910-5 Jun 1942
  Edward L. h/o Emma J.; 24 Aug 1876-28 Apr 1951
  Emma J. w/o Edward L.; 18 Sept 1889-9 Aug 1982
  Gus h/o Alice J.; 10 Apr 1879-6 Sept 1936
  James A. h/o Pauline; 21 Jun 1906-21 Jan 1977
  Mae G. 1910-1933
  Mary I. 18 Sept 1892-17 Feb 1968
  Melvin H. 1919-1970
  Pauline w/o James A.; 8 Sept 1914-29 Jan 1955
  Thomas C. 1908-1959
Jerkins
  Della w/o Walter S.; 22 Jan 1877-4 Feb 1939
  Gene 15 Dec 1980-15 Jun 1994
  Walter S. h/o Della; 16 Oct 1872-1 Feb 1959
Jett
  Adam h/o Sarah Ann; 7 Nov 1848-17 Feb 1926
  C. Harold h/o Julie L.; 17 Jan 1896-2 Feb 1970
  Ellen A. w/o John; 5 Apr 1868-29 May 1942

James 9 Sept 1846-28 Sept 1926
John h/o Ellen A.; 24 Jul 1854-24 Jul 1930
Joseph H. 29 May 1933-29 May 1933
Julie L. w/o C. Harold; 18 Oct 1910-17 Jun 1980
Laural 18 Feb 1865-3 Dec 1872
Mary 19 Aug 1845-19 Jun 1927
Menerril E. 9 Dec 1828-12 Jan 1905
Sarah Ann w/o Adam; 15 May 1853-13 May 1923
T.B. 24 Jun 1801-29 Oct 1826
Theo Philus 8 Dec 1893-9 Oct 1895
Theodosia d/o Adam & Sarah Ann; 1892-1895
Johnson
Aubry W. 22 Oct 1906-8 Jul 1966
Jackie Eugene 31 May 1936-16 Oct 1992
Jones
Earnest J. h/o Lula E. 14 Apr 1905-11 Mar 1967
Evans R. 12 Sept 1923-23 May 1984
Ira P. 19 Mar 1894-19 Aug 1959
J.T. 4 Jun 1825-21 May 1877
Josephine 1878-1940
Laura C. 16 Apr 1893-6 Jun 1972
Lula E. w/o Earnest J.; 21 Feb 1909-31 Dec 1991
Mary Jane w/o William H.; 22 Sept 1875-29 Nov 1958
Nancy J. w/o Barnett; 7 Sept 1849-May 1895
Sarah 15 Apr 1832-5 May 1923
William H. h/o Mary Jane; 27 May 1870-21 Jul 1917
Kelley
B.M. h/o Jimmie Ann; 15 Dec 1887-3 Mar 1940
Jimmie Ann w/o B.M.;21 Dec 1892-20 Mar 1970
Kimbrell
Alfred Sam d: 22 Feb 1960; 28y
Samuel d: 22 Feb 1960; 44y
King
Allie Mae w/o Clifford; 1909-1968
Charles Edward 24 Dec 1891-20 Jul 1964
Clifford h/o Allie Mae; 1906-1968
Frances 1880-1968
Lackey
Homer L. h/o Annie Cobb; 17 Sept 1900-6 Apr 1980
Lee
J.W. 2 Oct 1853-14 Feb 1901

Lingefott
    Raymond 7 Apr 1916-26 Apr 1994
Loner
    Alter E. 17 May 1895-27 May 1923
    Donald Ferry 5 Jan 1945-7 Apr 1945
    Eva M. 17 Jun 1910-7 Apr 1945
    Frances 30 Jun 1931-5 Apr 1947
    Franklin D. 3 Feb 1934-19 Jun 1935
    George P. 6 May 1919-6 May 1919
    Henry Franklin 23 Oct 1941-27 Jan 1987
    Henry H. h/o Rebecca P.; 13 Nov 1882-29 Apr 1950
    John L. h/o Ruth L. 9 Feb 1906-9 Feb 1983
    Mary Elizabeth w/o Perry Oliver; 19 May 1867-20 Jul 1944
    Perry Oliver h/o Mary Elizabeth; 16 Oct 1861-19 Oct 1930
    Rebecca P. w/o Henry H.; 5 Nov 1889-6 Jan 1984
    Ruth R. w/o John L.; 14 Jun 1907-6 Dec 1988
    Tressie Renee 5 Mar 1965-7 Mar 1965
    William H. 28 Apr 1923-30 Apr 1923
    Willie 30 Apr 1907-21 Feb 1987
Long
    Angelia Diane 1967-1967
    David L. 22 Aug 1884-8 Oct 1963
    Elizabeth M. 15 Sept 1892-1 Feb 1963
    Emory E. h/o Maude R.; 10 Jun 1887-24 Jun 1960
    Homer L. 7 Apr 1920-24 Sept 1983
    Jamie F. 7 Sept 1899-15 Aug 1977
    Johnny George 5 Nov 1948-24 Oct 1949
    Lee Ola 18 Oct 1887-17 Mar 1917
    Maude R. w/o Emory E.; 9 Aug 1884-19 Oct 1955
    Nancy C. w/o William F.; 25 Oct 1858-24 Feb 1912
    Sylvia Gene 1942-1943
    William F. h/o Nancy C.; 4 Jul 1852-1 Feb 1934
Lord
    Inas 22 Jun 1910-8 Oct 1983
Lowe
    D.B. 8 Dec 1861-31 Dec 1918
    Nancy E. 8 Jan 1859-22 Jul 1949
Lowry
    Adderson H. h/o Mary Alice; 8 Jun 1864-25 Jul 1925
    Buran E. 9 Jul 1897-10 May 1931
    Mary Alice w/o Adderson H.; 7 Aug 1872-27 Jan 1950

Robert H. 20 Feb 1844-5 Jun 1876

Loyd

J.D. 27 Oct 1908-27 Jun 1934

Manders

Robert Lewis h/o Vera Lucille; 22 May 1925-24 Jan 1985
Vera Lucille w/o Robert Lewis; 6 Sept 1924-10 Apr 1990

Martin

Georgia O. w/o John H.; 24 Sept 1892-9 Dec 1962
John H. h/o Georgia O.; 20 Aug 1892-4 Jun 1956
Martha A. 9 Aug 1851-27 Jan 1911
May N. w/o Robert L. Drake; 14 Jun 1875-17 Aug 1931
Rayman L. 31 Jan 1892-1 Apr 1918

Massey

Amanda Jane 6 Aug 1880-7 Jul 1943
Andrew C. h/o Lula M.; 31 Oct 1889-29 Oct 1945
Claude F. 1891-1966
Ethel 1903-1988
George T. 25 Apr 1911-1 Aug 1970
Hubert 1899-1984
L. Montez 27 May 1918-3 May 1979
Lula M. w/o Andrew C.; 2 Feb 1894-13 Oct 1927

McLendon

Alice M.w/o Arbyto; 7 Jan 1911-1 Apr 1991
Arbyto h/o Alice M.; 18 Oct 1898-15 Jun 1983

McPherson

Hozay H. 20 Mar 1901-20 Nov 1977

Medley

Fred Monroe 8 Jul 1920-6 Jun 1975

Mikel

Henry 4 Dec 1881-2 May 1883
Henry Briton 2 Jun 1835-8 Jan 1920
Jemima 16 Mar 1845-6 Feb 1901
Mattie J. 19 Dec 1868-10 Oct 1901
Samuel H. 3 Jun 1872-2 Jul 1973

Mitchell

Mary O. w/o Walter B.; 3 Nov 1872-30 Sept 1928
Walter B.; h/o Mary O.; 3 Jun 1878-9 Dec 1958

Moore

Nora Pearl 27 Nov 1909-4 Dec 1976
Rollin B. 25 Jun 1907-28 Mar 1971

Morgan
>Ada L. w/o James O.; 31 Dec 1890-24 Mar 1957
>Alice A. w/o C.B.; 16 Sept 1918-3 May 1950
>C.B. h/o Alice A.; 12 Sept 1912-15 May 1968
>Howard O. 2 Apr 1928-27 Oct 1944
>James O. h/o Ada L.; 26 May 1880-19 Apr 1954
>Mildred Jane 29 Jun 1940-5 Nov 1955

Morris
>Annie E. Campbell 17 Oct 1907-31 Jan 1990
>Drew B. Jul 1861-17 Mar 1909
>George C. 8 Mar 1886-2 Dec 1903
>Laura Viola 29 Dec 1883-22 Apr 1901
>Rosa Lereno 30 Jul 1917-4 Mar 1971

Naab
>Leo A. 1913-1980

Nalley
>Silas W. 1887-1946

Nelson
>Mary E. 15 Mar 1925-3 Apr 1991

Nesbit
>C.P. 1872-1932
>Caroline Lively 1843-1939
>Josephine F. 1867-1959
>Orin 17 Aug 1968-24 Mar 1893
>Robert C. 1863-1959
>S.G. d: Unknown; 50y
>William Otis 6 Jun 1877-24 Dec 1886

Norton
>Anderson h/o Lillie Mae; 3 Aug 1885-6 Nov 1925
>Henry E. 21 Sept 1925-2 Feb 1974
>Lillie Mae w/o Anderson; 20 Jul 1891-29 Aug 1949
>Marvin 12 Jul 1919-19 Oct 1982

Owens
>Lena 2 Jan 1831-3 Feb 1916
>Mattie w/o J.R.; 15 Jan 1867-30 Jul 1914

Pannell
>Carrie Bell 8 Jan 1906-31 Aug 1969
>Charlie G. h/o Cora Lee Fouts; 18 Mar 1895-23 Jan 1931
>Cora Lee Fouts w/o Charlie G.; 24 Aug 1896-31 Aug 1987
>Dewey W. 28 Apr 1902-14 Aug 1990
>Eliza Jane w/o William Thomas; 1878-1931

Henry Carriel 1900-1932
William Thomas h/o Eliza Jane; 1866-1961
Pittare
Ralph C. 9 Jun 1923-9 Mar 1974
Powell
Cora P. 26 Oct 1887-8 Nov 1954
Fannie May 18 Jul 1884-4 Aug 1886
J.W. h/o Mary F.; 19 Apr 1844-23 Jan 1922
John B. h/o Cora P.; 13 Oct 1886-9 Mar 1955
Mary F. w/o J.W.; 18 May 1849-13 Apr 1921
Rhodes 4 Sept 1910-11 Apr 1996
Prater
George Robert 31 Mar 1903-30 Jul 1955
Lelar Amalee 10 Jun 1901-7 Apr 1975
Leonard M. 1 Aug 1916-28 Dec 1974
William A. 1900-1972
Pritchett
Charles L. 5 Apr 1934-18 Mar 1961
Reeve
Cussie 13 Feb 1901-15 Jun 1902
Mary Ann w/o W.N.N.; 19 Nov 1978-3 Nov 1961
Sister 3 Oct 1914-3 Oct 1914
W.N.N. h/o Mary Ann; 17 May 1875-3 Feb 1940
Roberts
Valpha 24 Dec 1848-22 Sept 1919
Virgil Monroe 12 Aug 1888-1 Apr 1918
Rogers
Earl Mansfield 8 Nov 1915-10 Jun 1993
Edward Gene 7 Aug 1941-7 Apr 1988
Marie Vera 20 Apr 1918-23 Nov 1992
Roper
Charles A. 13 Jul 1921-11 May 1990
Russell
Della I w/o William N.; 28 Jan 1881-25 Nov 1963
William C. 1904-1988
William N. w/o Della I.; 6 Dec 1876-23 Jan 1948
Scott
A.J. 2 Apr 1865-21 Sept 1913
Alma 26 May 1889-17 Aug 1958
Ann s/o Dan; 1 Nov 1941-9 Dec 1941

Calvin f/o J. Michael & Calvin Michael Steven; 25 Jan 1933-2 Sept 1995
Calvin Michael Steven s/o Calvin; 3 Aug 1961-5 Feb 1983
Carrie N. d/o J.G.& M.;12 Mar 1900-7 Aug 1900
Carter Tate 27 Feb 1893-2 May 1960
Chandler 1884-1927
Claud Weldon 16 Oct 1959-16 Oct 1959
Cora Ethel w/o William Claude; 31 Aug 1886-30 Jan 1951
Dan b/o Ann; 1 Nov 1941-16 Dec 1941
Emma w/o James G.; 27 May 1871-28 Nov 1940
Eugene C. s/o J.G.&M.; 18 Jan 1889-8 Feb 1889
Evia m. 20 Mar 1928-19 Aug 1988
Frances Emiline w/o W.G.; 22 Jul 1851-20 Oct 1903
Gary Wayne 10 Jul 1946-1 Feb 1973
Glenn 18 Nov 1900-16 Oct 1974
Homer D. 1887-1912
J. Michael s/o Calvin 27 Nov 1953-2 Feb 1954
James Eugene 29 Dec 1952-1 Jan 1953
James G. h/o Emma; 1 Sept 1867-23 Aug 1934
James H. h/o Ruby; 15 Aug 1898-15 Apr 1939
John F. h/o Mary M.; 1851-1907
John T. s/o R.A.&M.; d:Unknown; 3y 4m
Johnnie Bell 4 May 1904-13 May 1991
Leara 29 Nov 1890-23 Oct 1918
Luna B. 12 Jul 1898-22 Mar 1984
Marion 10 Nov 1920-24 Jul 1936
Mary E. 24 Sept 1932-19 Feb 1978
Mary M. w/o John F.; 1853-1915
Mary S. w/o R.W.; 11 Nov 1854-27 Feb 1935
Mattie 22 May 1853-2 Jul 1918
Myrtie Kate 16 Mar 1904-17 Jan 1991
Obeen B. 19 Oct 1817-5 Jul 1876
Oscar Cobb 14 May 1894-4 Feb 1971
R.M. 1847-1901
Rachel Ann 15 Nov 1936-21 Sept 1937
Robert A. 4 Feb 1863-20 Sept 1921
Robert Lee 9 Sept 1908-10 Feb 1985
Rosa Louise 7 May 1933-20 Feb 1936
Rosette w/o William; d: 4 Jun 1893; 64y
Ruby B. d/o James G.& Emma; 22 Nov 1906-29 Jun 1914
Ruby H. w/o James H.; 20 Feb 1908-30 Oct 1966

Vertice L. d/o J.G.&M.; 12 Aug 1913-23 Jun 1916
W. Claud 17 Jun 1918-29 Aug 1977
W.G. h/o Frances Emiline; 19 Feb 1848-7 Feb 1906
William h/o Rosette; 18 Mar 1816-10 Mar 1892
William Claude h/o Cora E. 10 Mar 1887-30 Dec 1936
William Clayton 27 Jun 1924-9 Jul 1988
William H. 12 Jul 1894-23 Feb 1974
Seay
Callie V. 13 Oct 1868-16 Aug 1945
John A. 15 Sept 1861-14 Jul 1927
Samantha E. 5 Oct 1911-10 Apr 1929
Veston Dec 1909-Sept 1919
Segy
Lewis M. 18 Oct 1888-8 Nov 1912
Octavia 6 Jun 1857-9 Jun 1984
Shaw
R.B. 10 Mar 1841-4 Dec 1924
William 18 Jul 1893-16 Feb 1971
Shirley
Amanda Janie 8 Aug 1880-7 Jul 1943
Shutley
Robert Lee 5 Aug 1872-7 Dec 1935
Skinner
Beverly Marie 30 Nov 1951-9 Jan 1952
Ralph O. 1929-1986
Smith
Albert Walter 13 Mar 1875-12 Sept 1953
Angus William 23 Aug 1926-16 Jan 1980
Carrie V. w/o James P.; 1884-1986
Elizabeth d: 4 Feb 1892; 85y
George C. 1908-1936
Henry d:18 Apr 1892; 75y
Ida w/o Richard A.; 1879-1957
James Loyd 28 Mar 1951-17 Sept 1982
James P. h/o Carrie V.; 1882-1954
Richard A. h/o Ida; 1873-1943
Sarah F. 20 Oct 1841-4 Jul 1908
W.A. 3 Feb 1946-7 Mar 1914
Sparks
Austin Chance 15 Jun 1994-16 Jan 1996

Spruill
>Alice B. 22 Jan 1917-26 Dec 1972
>Charlie M. h/o Mary P.; 5 May 1885-12 Mar 1966
>Lucile W. w/o Howard; 22 Nov 1933-9 Jul 1996
>Mary P. w/o Charlie M.; 6 Jan 1890-25 Feb 1968
>William Roy 7 May 1909-13 Dec 1911

Standridge
>Andy R. h/o Emma; 5 Jun 1869-21 Jul 1945
>B. Brown 29 Mar 1909-9 Jan 1978
>Emma w/o Andy R.;13 Dec 1877-24 Oct 1918
>James P. h/o Nettie L.; 11 Feb 1900-15 Sept 1957
>Joe K. 10 Nov 1910-6 Nov 1987
>M. Ruth 26 Feb 1925- 26 Dec 1986
>Nettie L. w/o James P.; 15 Mar 1908-25 Nov 1958

Stephens
>Lou 1862-1923

Stephins
>Betty Lou 9 Apr 1900-27 Aug 1901
>W.P. 17 Aug 1865-4 Sept 1920

Stewart
>John L. 30 Aug 1910-23 Apr 1968

Strapler
>Grady Alfred 8 Mar 1942-8 Aug 1982

Strayhorn
>Bessie L. 19 Jun 1941-10 Jan 1994

Tai
>Juanita M. 16 Mar 1928-28 Aug 1991

Tatum
>Willie M. s/o G.W. & S.A.; 2 Mar 1871-9 Jun 1885

Tench
>Betty L. d: 24 Jan 1929
>Gregory L. 23 May 1961-10 Dec 1976

Thomason
>Addie S. 28 Mar 1871-25 Nov 1953
>Henry W. b/o John; 21 Sept 1903-21 Sept 1986
>James P. h/o A.S.; 22 Aug 1859-20 Feb 1923
>John Wesley h/o Mittie M.; 28 Oct 1897-26 Feb 1963
>Mittie M. w/o John Wesley; 10 Aug 1911-8 May 1971

Tilton
>Eller 1901-1970

Treadway
- Barbara 31 Aug 1933-21 Jan 1983
- David R. 1943-1977
- Fannie M. 30 Jul 1912-29 Mar 1980
- Hugh D. 19 Sept 1921-10 Sept 1958
- Mary Alice 1 Jul 1919-26 May 1977
- Nora S. 12 Mar 1889-9 Mar 1963

Tribble
- Elizabeth d:19 Oct 1897
- James R. 6 Feb 1815-4 Mar 1887
- Maggie E. 12 May 1888-22 Sept 1904

Tuggle
- Kenneth 18 Dec 1951-18 Dec 1951
- William Thomas 19 Sept 1953-19 Sept 1953

Turner
- Annie 28 May 1898-19 Sept 1972
- E. Elmina 27 Aug 1884-3 Jan 1953
- James A. 1886-1932
- James Anderson 14 Feb 1917-7 Jun 1959
- John B. 15 Apr 1888-18 Feb 1938
- W.J. 3 Feb 1840-14 Sept 1905
- William 20 Aug 1884-17 Mar 1919

Vaughan
- G.B. 16 Nov 1911-21 Jul 1970
- G.M. h/o N.E.; 4 Oct 1858-1 Aug 1933
- N.E. w/o G.M.;2 Mar 1857- 31 Oct 1933
- Eliza J. 10 Mar 1842-14 Jul 1928

Waites
- Warren Thomas 2 Feb 1931-3 Sept 1992

Waits
- Eula R. w/o R. Earl; 30 Sept 1903-22 Nov 1966
- R. Earl h/o Eula R.; 22 Jun 1900-11 Dec 1947

Warren
- Thomas B. 26 Dec 1907-31 Jul 1987

Waters
- Almesta 12 Nov 1911-11 May 1913
- Charles Claude 12 Sept 1914-17 Dec 1987
- Chasbert h/o Lula A.; 22 Sept 1892-1 Sept 1954
- Claudine d: 12 Sept 1914
- Edward E. 23 Nov 1919-6 Apr 1993
- Henry J. f/o J.C.; 12 Jul 1885-18 Feb 1955

J.C. s/o Henry J.; 17 Sept 1847-7 Dec 1910

Lula A. w/o Chasbert; 13 Apr 1888-3 Aug 1944

Luna May d/o Mary E.; 30 Apr 1888-31 Aug 1954

Mary d: 23 Nov 1913

Mary E. m/o Luna May; 30 Jun 1854-28 Oct 1918

Weathers

Dewey 1903-1970

Jerry Lyish 23 Oct 1949-1 Jan 1968

Webb

C.C. 20 Mar 1860-31 Mar 1916

Frank 25 Nov 1891-21 Jan 1909

Ruth O. d: 2 Aug 1995; 79y 10m

Webster

Beulah M. 1906-1965

Herbert H. 1900-1953

Westbrook

Cora Mae w/o Wiley W.; 10 May 1881-12 Jan 1944

Junnie E. w/o Holice McClain; 18 Feb 1905-23 Aug 1942

Wiley W. h/o Cora Mae; 1 Mar 1874-29 Dec 1964

Wilbanks

Franklin R. h/o Rosa Alta; 1888-1959

Richard Deariso 11 Oct 1922-13 Jan 1993

Rosa Alta 1927-1927

Rosa Alta w/o Franklin R.; 1895-1927

Ross Alvin 1927-1927

Wilkens

H.B. h/o Carrie H.; 22 Aug 1913-11 Aug 1968

Hattie W. w/o Lewis M.; 11 Jun 1890-15 Oct 1979

Lewis M. h/o Hattie W.; 11 Jun 1890-15 Oct 1979

Wilkins

Betty d/o Herman & Carrie H.; d: 12 May 1942

Carrie H. w/o Herman; 5 Jun 1915-12 May 1994

Herman s/o Herman & Carrie H.; 11 Sept 1934-14 Aug 1938

Will

J. 14 Aug 1897-15 May 1979

Williams

Naomi 8 Apr 1886-2 Oct 1924

Willingham

Alma Nesbit 1874-1944

Wilson

Alice Abbie 26 Apr 1967-28 May 1967

Irene J. w/o Woodrow Wilson; 28 Mar 1912-17 Oct 1993
Woodrow   h/o Irene J.; 8 Jan 1913-26 Aug 1950
Woodall
Belle 7 Feb 1884-8 Dec 1976
James P. h/o Martha; 4 Mar 1840-6 Jul 1915
Martha w/o James P.; 22 Feb 1845-18 Jan 1918
Wright
Carlton J. 1940-1988
Thelma Lowry 1902-1993
Yearwood
Hannah Elaine d: 3 May 1990
Young
Lucy Jones w/o William Tell; 17 Apr 1874-6 Feb 1919
Palmer Eugene 23 Jan 1900-27 Jan 1960
William Tell h/o Lucy Jones; 2 Mar 1874-3 Oct 1940

Fulton County
Maxwell Cemetery

Buice
Elisha b/o Fannie; 2 Sept 1845-9 Jan 1930
Fannie s/o Elisha; 7 Aug 1843-29 Dec 1928
Clayton
Diane Connie 13 Dec 1956-2 May 1965
Cobb
Annie Clyde 17 Aug 1902-3 Oct 1921
Carrie E. 2 Dec 1848-11 Jul 1904
Charlie 1898-1973
Clarence B. h/o Willie F.; 1 Feb 1892-6 Apr 1969
Cora C. s/o William E.; 24 Feb 1887-11 May 1957
H.T. 11 Jun 1890-30 Nov 1908
Little Ida d/o R. & E.; Apr 1870-Jul 1870
Lucile D. 1905-1970
Sarah J. w/o William E.; 19 Apr 1869-10 Aug 1913
William E. h/o Sarah J.; 20 Apr 1866-9 Feb 1944
William Otis 20 Nov 1895-16 Jul 1928
Willie F. 4 Aug 1900-6 Mar 1929

Dempsey
    Alta w/o James T.; 19 Dec 1875-21 Nov 1942
    Elizabeth C. w/o J. Miles; 1882-1974
    J. Miles h/o Elizabeth C.; 1882-1958
    James T. h/o Alta; 3 Sept 1862-13 Mar 1921
    Mattie I. d/o James T. & Alta; 24 Sept 1900-21 Dec 1900
Duff
    Edna Mae 1903-1968
    Harry G. 1890-1973
Erwin
    Frances Turner s/o Harold; 22 Mar 1921-1 May 1995
    Wm. Douglas 17 Jul 1910-22 Nov 1993
Fogelson
    Jack 24 Jul 1903-23 Jun 1983
Freeman
    Calvin McDuffie 18 Jan 1918-11 Mar 1979
Hembree
    Sophia A. 23 Jan 1876-9 Oct 1949
    G.J. d/o Robert & Samantha A.; 20 Mar 1878-10 Jul 1884
    H.W. d/o Robert & Samantha A.; 28 Oct 1884-9 Jul 1886
    J.L. d/o Robert & Samantha A.; 30 May 1880-15 Jul 1886
    Robert A. h/o Samantha A. Maxwell; 30 Dec 1842-28 Oct 1914
    William Sept 1898-20 Aug 1899
    Willis Edgar h/o Mattie Meline Tinney; 15 Sept 1872-17 Feb
    1938
Holbrook
    Ralph E. 10 Jan 1904-12 Jul 1944
Holland
    Hoyt M. 19 Oct 1883-10 Nov 1957
Hook
    Minnie G. 5 Jun 1873-7 Dec 1907
Hutchinson
    Blanche 22 May 1910-27 Feb 1995
    Winston L. 16 Mar 1909-29 May 1986
Jenkins
    Bernetta K. 17 Oct 1879-1938
Johnson
    Beatrice J. w/o Loyd T.; 30 Jun 1905-9 Jun 1985
    Fannie Turner w/o John David; 12 Aug 1883-26 Feb 1964
    John David h/o Fannie Turner; 19 Jul 1883-19 May 1952
    Loyd T. h/o Beatrice J.; 11 Oct 1906-26 Jul 1994

Jones

 Brenda Sue 1946-1948

 Henrietta 1869-1934

 James Alvis 1863-1938

 James Carroll 25 Sept 1927-6 Sept 1994

 John H. 1905-1957

 Ruth D. 1910-1989

Maffett

 Clyde W. h/o Eulah I.; 22 Aug 1892-24 Sept 1957

 Eulah I. w/o Clyde W.; 1 Jul 1895-19 Feb 1987

Maxwell

 Aby Tinney w/o James T.; 22 Dec 1873-8 Feb 1951

 Arthur b/o Conway; 17 May 1862-14 May 1936

 Audrey L. 22 Jul 1913-27 Mar 1970

 Carl Allen 6 Sept 1888-25 Jan 1960

 Carrie May d/o William Benson& Mary Ann; 7 Nov 1896-28 Oct 1907

 Charles Henry s/o William Benson& Mary Ann; 23 Apr 1912-22 Sept 1927

 Conway b/o Arthur; 15 May 1865-5 Dec 1907

 Emily Florence w/o A.C.; 27 Jul 1858-9 Jul 1911

 James T. h/o Aby Tinney; 9 Jan 1875-3 Sept 1959

 Jessie Norris w/o Wade Hampton; 29 Nov 1878-28 Mar 1951

 John d: 1975

 John E. 4 Jun 1848-1 Mar 1914

 John W. 21 Nov 1898-18 Sept 1977

 Lillian Holbrook 1 May 1904-12 Mar 1998

 Mary Ann w/o William Benson; 6 May 1850-15 Sept 1930

 Myrtle V. 11 Sept 1890-6 Jul 1979

 Pearl 7 Dec 1895-12 Feb 1938

 Samantha A. w/o Robert A.; 9 May 1845-30 Nov 1908

 Sarerta 5 Sept 1813-15 Oct 1875

 Wade Hampton h/o Jessie Norris; 17 Feb 1872-24 Sept 1941

 William Benson h/o Mary Ann; 29 May 1842-23 Feb 1931

McConnell

 Barry Maxwell s/o B.&M.; 30 Nov 1957-12 Dec 1974

McGinnis

 Charles Lee 9 Apr 1930-20 Mar 1978

McKinney

 Harold D. h/o M.; 18 May 1910-26 May 1996

Morris
>Carrie Mildred 15 Apr 1914-5 Aug 1914
>J.L. h/o Odessa H.;10 Sept 1878-18 Mar 1904
>James Hembree 7 Jun 1921-25 Feb 1929
>Odessa H. w/o J.L.; 10 May 1880-1 Sept 1969

Moulder
>Jep d: 1911
>Mattie d: 1930
>Ted d: 1953

Phillips
>Catherine L. 15 Oct 1925-1 Mar 1928
>Nora P. 25 Jan 1896-9 Sept 1958
>Will E. 2 Feb 1894-5 Apr 1979

Roberts
>Jessie Morris 1 Jun 1922-3 Oct 1996

Samples
>Danny Elmer 28 Nov 1949-17 Sept 1987
>Mary J. w/o Elmer; 9 Apr 1916-6 May 1994

Shirley
>Chase Tyler d: 30 Jan 1988

Teasley
>Isham h/o Mary; 12 Jul 1807-23 Nov 1888

Thomas
>Otella Martha 1 Sept 1890-14 Sept 1942

Tinney
>Mattie Meline w/o Willis Edgar; 7 Jan 1869-3 Apr 1950

Trammell
>Maude E. w/o Montiner R.; 6 Jul 1880-11 Dec 1918
>Montiner h/o Maude E.; 24 Oct 1880-19 Oct 1966

Turner
>Bessie E. w/o Byron L.; 28 Feb 1921-10 Aug 1981
>Bessie M. w/o Guy L.; 12 Jun 1900-13 Dec 1977
>Caroline E. w/o Mark H.; 10 May 1844-5 Dec 1890
>Conley W. 14 Jul 1888-9 Jan 1929
>Elizabeth June 1843-Jan 1881
>George G. s/o John H & Martha E.; 18 Jan 1879-6 Aug 1879
>George T. h/o Lela S.; 27 May 1885-12 Mar 1964
>Guy L. h/o Bessie M.; 23 May 1894-20 Feb 1970
>Harold S. 30 Jan 1925-26 Jan 1995
>Jane R. 1 Mar 1858-11 Mar 1943
>John H. h/o Martha E.; d: 1 Aug 1911; 72y 11m

Lela S. w/o George T.; 11 Oct 1885-8 Feb 1966
Lisa Marie 28 Jun 1963-3 Apr 1967
Martha E. w/o John H.; 27 Dec 1838-9 Feb 1905
Mathew L. h/o Nancy C.; 27 Jun 1813-9 Jan 1886
Minnie B. 30 Apr 1882-16 May 1941
Nancy C. w/o Mathew L.; 3 Feb 1813-25 Jul 1889
Pierce 16 Oct 1892-10 Feb 1946
Scott C. h/o Jane R.; 1 Nov 1856-23 Mar 1911
William 1917-1920
William H. s/o John H & Martha E.; 6 Jun 1878-Sept 1878
Vaughan
Louise M. 18 Jul 1906-30 Jul 1968

Fulton County
Mt. Oliver Cemetery

Allen
Alice M. w/o Paul w.; 12 Feb 1882-31 Oct 1972
Anglin
Archie 15 May 1929-15 Aug 1929
Henry h/o Nancy A.; 11 Mar 1854-28 Feb 1936
Ida T. 8 Aug 1893-15 Apr 1922
Mandye 14 Oct 1889-13 Jan 1976
Nancy A. w/o Henry; d:10 Jan1923
T. Early 6 Aug 1885-26 Nov 1961
Bailey
Cecil M. w/o Harry L.; 4 Jun 1904-8 Dec 1988
Harry L. w/o Cecil M.; 4 Feb 1903-17 Jul 1992
James P. h/o Meek; 27 May 1873-5 Jul 1944
Joseph s/o Harry L. & Cecil M.; d: 4 Mar 1930
Meek w/o James P.; 1 Sept 1876-6 Oct 1956
Bates
James Homer h/o Nancy L.; 11 Apr 1896-2 Sept 1971
Nancy L. w/o James Homer; 4 Oct 1895-7 Jul 1986
Booker
B. Frank h/o Nettie L.; 24 Feb 1901-23 Aug 1964
Dalier O. w/o John W.; 29 Jun 1882-31 May 1936
Hubert E. 27 Jun 1909-24 Aug 1918
Infant d/o B. Frank & Nettie L.; d: Sept 1924

Jennie w/o Robert; 1876-1965

John W. h/o Dalier O.; 31 Jul 1875-3 Feb 1946

Nettie L. w/o B. Frank; 16 Jul 1905-24 Mar 1977

Robert h/o Jennie; 1882-1952

Bowen

William Floyd d: 1 Dec 1940

Bradley

Robert 1903-1922

Brown

Clinton Bascomb 18 Jan 1904-28 Jul 1975

M.O. d: 7 Jun 1949; 74y

Buice

Agnes 22 Oct 1882-21 Feb 1967

Butterworth

William Thomas 25 Sept 1895-23 Sept 1956

Willie V. 25 Jun 1902-14 Feb 1994

Carter

William Lewis h/o Florence Chester; 4 Jan 1898-19 Mar 1962

Carver

Betty Oliver 23 Feb 1930-31 Aug 1966

Chester

Emoline Ryder w/o Jesse Soloman; 26 Oct 1862-1 Nov 1952

Florence w/o William L. Carter; 9 May 1901-29 Jul 1986

Jesse Solomon h/o Emoline Ryder; 9 May 1862-26 Nov 1959

Mary w/o Idas A. Kent; 29 Oct 1883-16 Oct 1923

Coker

C. Wyndell h/o Averil B.; 25 Sept 1936-7 Feb 1986

Homer G. h/o Maggie B.; 18 Apr 1892-18 Jan 1950

Maggie B. w/o Homer G.; 2 Feb 1900-5 Aug 1975

Conner

Delphia Jackson w/o John Harvey; 20 Sept 1900-28 Nov 1968

James Ray s/o John H. & Delphia J.; 25 Oct 1927-25 Oct 1927

John Harvey h/o Delphia Jackson; 28 Dec 1895-27 Nov 1969

Marian Elizabeth d/o John H.& Delphia J.; 25 Oct 1927-
25 Oct 1927

Wayman Norman s/o John H. & Delphia J.; d: 30 Jun 1935

Daniel

James Claude 1895-1984

Davis

Paul 1918-1925

Dinsmore
 Tracy Thomas 6 Dec 1961-14 May 1992
Duncan
 Infant d/o R.O.; d: 19 Jul 1923
 Infant d/o R.O.; d: 2 May 1922
Dunson
 Flora S. w/o Lewis L.; 1902-1957
 Lewis L.; h/o Flora S. 1882-1953
Elkins
 Mary Frances w/o James Worth; 29 Aug 1925-7 Apr 1990
Fillingim
 Ronald Dewey 24 Mar 1945-1 Oct 1973
Fitch
 James Don d: 9 Jul 1945
Fowler
 Ernest N. h/o Gussie Green; 15 Jan 1904-27 May 1968
 Gussie Green w/o Ernest N.; 11 Jul 1906-29 Apr 1974
 Robert s/o R. & G.; 16 Feb 1926-Oct 1926
Guy
 J.S. b/o Laura; 27 Mar 1865-12 Jul 1917
 Laura s/o J.S.; 14 Jun 1887-22 Mar 1927
Hodson
 Daniel Hubert 2 Mar 1924-15 Nov 1984
Hopkins
 Harvey h/o Pearl A. ; 8 Apr 1901-17 May 1966
 Pearl A. w/o Harvey; 9 Feb 1898-24 Jan 1961
Hulsey
 J. Roland b/o Ralph E.; 14 Jun 1917-20 Feb 1957
Jackson
 Howard b/o Lula Coker; 27 Dec 1895-16 May 1916
 Lula Coker s/o Howard; 2 Jul 1879-10 Apr 1916
Johnson
 Anna w/o W.B.; 1880-1972
 Arthur J. h/o Dovie; 29 Oct 1880-17 Jan 1964
 Dorothy d/o Arthur & Dovie; 2 Sept 1927-2 Sept 1927
 Dovie w/o Arthur J.; 30 Dec 1882-8 Dec 1960
 Luvina w/o W.B.; 1880-1927
 W.B. h/o Anna & Luvina; 1879-1963
Kent
 Floyd 1919-1998
 Idas A. h/o Mary Chester; 26 Oct 1880-18 Jul 1949

Leroy h/o Nora Inez; 28 Jun 1912-30 May 1984
Mable C. w/o Troy H.; 5 Sept 1908-29 Apr 1985
Nora Inez w/o Leroy; 16 Mar 1917-12 Sept 1983
T. Nelson s/o Troy H & Mable C.; 27 Apr 1934-20 Jun 1934
Troy H. h/o Mable C.; 4 Oct 1910-30 Sept 1986
Willie B. 4 Mar 1928-25 Jun 1928
Zonie A. 1892-1969
Lackey
Clyde Clemmons 18 Aug 1904-23 Jun 1949
Harley Buren 18 Sept 1911-22 Dec 1964
Twin d/o D.C.; d: 4 Jul 1917
Lawson
Clara M. w/o Homer N.; 5 Jun 1895-19 Mar 1965
Cora 4 Sept 1870-29 Apr 1962
Doyle E. 27 Sept 1914-30 Oct 1983
Edward N. 31 Jan 1924-16 May 1953
Homer N. h/o Clara M.; 4 Sept 1889-9 Mar 1978
Leavell
Carlton Wesley 27 Nov 1940-22 Jan 1941
Lingerfelt
Nettie 1900-1975
Perry 1890-1964
Vera Lucile 1935-1952
Maffett
Brownlow h/o Susan; 1859-1940
Susan w/o Brownlow; 1862-1951
Maloney
Addie Louise w/o Charles F.; 14 Jun 1915-10 May 1946
Charles F. h/o Addie Louise; 8 Oct 1930-8 May 1951
Cora B. w/o Forrest C.; 15 Sept 1897-17 Jan 1967
Forrest C. h/o Cora B.; 3 Mar 1897-27 Aug 1969
Fronie J. w/o Henry D.; 24 Feb 1893-29 Mar 1977
Henry D. h/o Fronie J.; 2 Feb 1893-8 Mar 1974
Henry Jack 27 Aug 1917-9 Jun 1919
Howard F. 26 Aug 1919-18 Jan 1920
Marcus
Kenny A. 20 Dec 1884-2 Feb 1929
Massey
Estell B. m/o James A.; 8 Nov 1906-27 Oct 1973
James A. s/o Estell B.; 23 Apr 1939-30 Dec 1940

Maxwell
    A.C. h/o E.F.; 4 Feb 1840-7 Apr 1904
Meeks
    Betty Lou 1931-1996
Mitchell
    Ethel C. w/o James H.; 1885-1948
    James H. h/o Ethel C.; 1878-1967
    Rossie L. w/o Thomas Glenn; 28 Jun 1912-19 Jan 1982
    Thomas Glenn h/o Rossie L.; 22 Oct 1908-24 Feb 1982
    William Doyal h/o Ruth B.; 1915-1960
Morris
    Cara Chester 3 Jan 1896-29 Nov 1963
Moulder
    Thomas J. h/o Betty J.; 6 Oct 1929-20 May 1991
Oliver
    Annie Pearl w/o Fermon D.; 31 Jul 1899-26 Mar 1991
    Barbara Ann d/o J& R; 10 Jun 1940-7 Feb 1960
    E. Orana w/o William M.; 30 May 1866-29 Jul 1938
    Fermon D. h/o Annie Pearl; 5 Sept 1896-6 Dec 1951
    James Arthur h/o Ruby W.; 27 Sept 1892-9 Jan 1959
    Johnny Lamar s/o J&R; 21 Sept 1951-1 Feb 1979
    Ruby W. w/o James Arthur.; 4 Sept 1902- 22 Feb 1985
    William M. h/o E. Orana; 20 May 1870-11 Jan 1944
Pack
    George W. 1883-1960
Patterson
    Hubert H. h/o Pearle E.; 22 Aug 1916-2 Sept 1990
    Pearle E. w/o Hubert H.; 24 Mar 1918-8 Nov 1951
Pearl
    M. 1889-1984
Pink
    J. 1881-1951
Rakestraw
    Neal Barry s/o W.R.; 14 Feb 1951-26 Feb 1951
Ransom
    Cocia w/o W.A.; 8 Aug 1859-22 Oct 1927
    W.A. h/o Cocia; 8 Jan 1866-16 Jun 1929
Richards
    M.J. h/o Roberta A.; 28 Jul 1918-4 Feb 1985
    Roberta A. w/o M.J.; 3 Jan 1918-19 Aug 1975

Rucker

Jessie 14 Feb 1901-18 Sept 1971

Samples

F. Mittie w/o L. Olen; 9 Oct 1868-29 Aug 1942

L. Olen h/o F. Mattie; 14 Dec 1856-13 May 1941

Sanders

Bertie E. Chester 22 Oct 1906-10 Apr 1997

Scoggins

Charles P. 1957-1957

James C. 1959-1959

Joseph William h/o Verdie D. Nix; 30 May 1899-21 Jan 1989

Robert W. 22 Dec 1922-18 Jan 1984

Verdie D. Nix w/o Joseph William; 12 Mar 1905-16 Apr 1985

Smith

Clyde Joe h/o Fannie P.; 12 Nov 1893-30 Oct 1967

Fannie P. w/o Clyde Joe; 4 Sept 1895-26 Oct 1985

Herbert Troy h/o M.L.; 30 Nov 1921-14 Mar 1987

J. Edwin h/o Myrtle I.; 16 Apr 1920-18 Apr 1997

Malaney A. 11 Apr 1894-1 Sept 1983

Myrtle I. w/o Edwin J.; 3 Mar 1920-4 Feb 1987

Stephens

Arthur h/o Edith; 29 Apr 1905-12 Apr 1989

C.O. h/o F.E.; 13 Aug 1867-4 Oct 1942

David P. 30 Sept 1878-4 Oct 1942

Edith w/o Arthur; 9 Dec 1907-11 Sept 1993

F.E. h/o C.O.; 20 Aug 1868-14 Mar 1948

Flossie Marie 8 Sept 1905-24 Jan 1924

Henry Grady h/o Nola L.; 24 Feb 1899-5 Dec 1984

James Clyde h/o Rossie; 7 Nov 1907-3 Jan 1991

Jessie M. 27 May 1881-24 May 1959

Jewell B. w/o Paralee B.; 16 Mar 1909-14 Dec 1980

Louise d/o A; 31 Oct 1925-31 Oct 1925

Manda d/o A.; 13 Mar 1929

Nola L. w/o Henry Grady; 15 Mar 1900-12 Apr 1995

Paralee B. h/o Jewell B.; 9 Oct 1909-12 Oct 1990

Rossie w/o James Clyde; 14 Nov 1913-26 Feb 1998

Stewart

Jackie Lamar 23 Mar 1936-2 Sept 1956

Ruth Agnes 26 Jun 1922-15 Nov 1926

Vaughan E. 2 Jul 1898-21 Oct 1943

Thompson
> Cora A. w/o Lewis; 21 Jun 1896-29 Jan 1958
> Lewis h/o Cora A.; 27 Sept 1897-21 Apr 1945

Voyles
> Lester G. h/o Vellar B.; 1899-1989
> Norman E. 1926-1979
> Vellar B. w/o Lester G.; 1906-1973

Whitfield
> C.C. h/o Mattie; 3 Nov 1871-7 Sept 1933
> Carl h/o Cleo; 26 Mar 1904-5 Jul 1956
> Clarence G. h/o Peggy; d: 18 Oct 1937
> Cleo w/o Carl; 24 Mar 1909-29 Jun 1991
> Clyde s/o C.C.& Mattie; 13 Dec 1910-25 Nov 1943
> Mattie w/o C.C.; 10 Jul 1880-21 May 1939
> Peggy D. w/o Clarence G.; d: 8 Apr 1946

Williams
> Hugh Taylor 15 Oct 1937-24 Nov 1937
> Oma 30 Nov 1890-25 Jun 1979
> Taylor h/o Sibyl; 20 Jan 1909-28 Sept 1986

Woodson
> Scarlet Elaine 29 Oct 1962-24 Nov 1962

Fulton County
Pleasant Hill Historical Cemetery

Bailey
> Lois K. 1913-1961

Barnes
> Dorcus 5 Aug 1876-19 Nov 1939

Bell
> Rosa d: 3 Nov 1962

Blackwell
> Lawton s/o Lawton G.&Virginia P.; 3 Oct 1927-9 Jul 1948
> Lawton G. h/o Virginia P.f/oLawton; 31 Dec 1900-28 Jun 1970
> Virginia P. w/o Lawton G.m/oLawton; 10 Feb 1906-
> 24 Feb 1983

Brown
> Annie Kirk d:22 Aug 1960

Burse
>Herman Emanuel h/o Maude Strickland; 13 Oct 1910-
>3 Feb 1996
>Maude Strickland w/o Herman Emanuel; 3 Mar 1903-
>7 Dec 1995

Champion
>Jessie Cook 19 Oct 1892-5 Oct 1938

Clayton
>Sarah Grogan 30 Aug 1900-14 Dec 1944

Cook
>Frank J. h/o Marie M.; 5 Jun 1897-31 Mar 1959
>Marie M. w/o Frank J.; 9 Sept 1900-18 Jan 1932
>Parthenia d: 8 Dec 1924; 74y

Cooley
>John J. h/o Mahalie; 10 Feb 1886-14 Nov 1957
>Mahalie w/o John J.; 26 Dec 1893-26 Aug 1979

Curtis
>Ernest 12 Jun 1948-15 Jan 1988

Delaney
>Samuel h/o Lottie S.; 16 Apr 1910-10 Sept 1962

Dupree
>Francis Sarah 7 Aug 1911-11 Mar 1971

Garrett
>John Aaron 21 May 1917-15 May 1919

Griggs
>Johnnie Mae 12 Jun 1906-12 Mar 1960

Grogan
>A.J. 14 Jul 1873-28 Jun 1954
>Lillie Cook 13 Dec 1883-11 Apr 1932
>Samuel 2 Jul 1910-24 Sept 1954
>Willie 2 May 1900-8 May 1944

Hammond
>Robert Lee 25 Dec 1945-8 Apr 1993

Hargrove
>Nora Strickland 23 Jun 1905-14 Apr 1991

Hembree
>Queen d: 15 Oct 1935; 52y
>Will 18 May 1902- 6 Sept 1923

Hill
>Evie 12 May 1894-9 Jan 1986
>Janie Mae 5 Apr 1904-23 Mar 1931

Willie S. 27 Jun 1902-4 Jul 1922
Kilcore
    Willie E. D: 2 Feb 1987
King
    James W. 2 Sept 1922-18 May 1982
Knuckles
    Gartrell F. 20 Jul 1909-19 Jul 1974
    Samuel D. 15 May 1916-5 Jan 1994
Martin
    Minnie R. w/o Harmon; Feb 1899-Mar 1953
    Samuel R. 1942-1973
    Viola B. w/o Sam; 30 May 1895-18 May 1965
Moore
    Homer 8 Mar 1901-7 Jan 1964
Morland
    Lizzie 1881-1941
Newell
    Harvey 28 Nov 1880-17 Apr 1945
    Mollie d:7 Aug 1957
Rainwater
    Wesley 1897-1927
Ransby
    Bertha M. Heath 19 Aug 1923-8 Apr 1993
Strickland
    Elizabeth 22 Nov 1920-1 Feb 1987
Taylor
    Price W. 27 Apr 1922-28 Mar 1992
Webb
    Morgan Faye 28 Sept 1995-20 Jan 1996
Wells
    Mary Lee w/o Otis; 5 Feb 1914-8 Apr 1984
    Otis h/o Mary Lee; 1 Jun 1914-28 Oct 1981
Williams
    Bertha Lee 28 Nov 1918-7 Apr 1981
    Elizabeth d; 10 Aug 1981
    Jessie Juanita 5 Apr 1932-20 Nov 1976

Abernathy
    Kate Adams 21 Aug 1895-4 Aug 1986
Adams
    Chessie M. 1 Dec 1902-1 Jan 1933
    Emma C. w/o Shockley C.; 17 Nov 1864-1 Jan 1933
    Gobel Sanford 21 May 1899-20 Dec 1979
    John H. 31 Aug 1888-22 Jul 1951
    Shockley C. h/o Emma C.; 24 Apr 1846-1 Dec 1942
Alexander
    Frankie F. w/o J. Henry; 16 Sept 1885-25 Sept 1956
    J. Henry h/o Frankie F.; 20 Jun 1885-27 Aug 1966
    Myrtle C. 4 Oct 1908-26 Aug 1997
Armistead
    Ann 3 Aug 1946-27 Jan 1982
Ayers
    Emma E. 1869-1956
    Neva D. 1905-1972
Bagwell
    Carl h/o Jeffie A.;24 Dec 1885-24 Dec 1935
    Hewlett 2 Jun 1910-12 Jun 1980
    Jeffie A. w/o Carl; 23 Jan 1889-5 Apr 1957
Bailey
    Alice S. 1872-1949
    Frances M. 1860-1944
    Lizzie R. w/o J. Henry; 1893-1963
Ballew
    Charles 1890-1941
Barett
    Dewey C. h/o Sarah J.; 23 Apr 1900-9 Apr 1961
    Sarah J. w/o Dewey; 26 Jun 1899-26 Apr 1990
Barnett
    Claude N. 2 Oct 1990-18 Nov 1992
    Myrtie Inez 2 Apr 1908-15 Oct 1958
    Willard N. 18 Mar 1940-19 Jan 1987
Barrett
    Clarence A. 23 Apr 1912-13 Dec 1968

Howard T. 4 Aug 1914-30 Jan 1973

Bennett

Ray Carrole 1946-1946

Bird

Charles L. 29 Oct 1915-17 Sept 1974

James R. 18 May 1911-8 Aug 1975

Marvin R. 28 Apr 1913-27 Mar 1993

Thomas 31 Oct 1907-1 Aug 1989

Bowen

Mattie J. w/o N.S.; 12 Jan 1871-19 Jun 1907

Rachel 9 Apr 1827-27 Jun 1906

Sarah A. w/o Joel L.; 4 Jul 1848-2 Jul 1918

Brackett

Elizabeth w/o J.A.; 17 Nov 1867-9 Dec 1966

J.A. h/o Elizabeth; 8 Aug 1860-17 Feb 1927

James B. 23 Oct 1912-27 Aug 1973

Brady

Loyal B. 30 Oct 1909-15 Dec 1988

Ollie M. 29 May 1916-9 May 1963

Brannon

Fannie I. w/o James; 1886-1958

James h/o Fannie I.; 1882-1967

Ruth A. 1929-1965

Brewton

Bennie D. 31 Dec 1955-6 Jan 1976

Brock

Frankie L. 3 Mar 1954-9 Nov 1995

Broodwell

Fannie Belle w/o Thad Pickett; 28 Nov 1885-31 Aug 1978

Thad Pickett h/o Fannie Belle; 19 Oct 1888-4 Dec 1965

Brooke

George Carter 1891-1951

J.P. h/o Maude; 1860-1932

Maude w/o J.P.; 1866-1935

Maude Myrtle 1904-1993

Mildred Packard 1893-1987

Brooks

Charles S. 10 Feb 1906-29 May 1992

Burdette

Nallie M. Smith w/o Robert C.; 17 Jun 1922-2 Mar 1985

Robert C. h/o Nallie M. Smith; 23 Jul 1916-29 Oct 1986

Burge
Cecil W. 13 Oct 1907-20 May 1967
Dixie V. w/o Guy J.; 12 Mar 1901-10 Jan 1966
Guy J. h/o Dixie V.; 13 Jan 1899-8 Feb 1970
Mary Ann 19 May 1934-1 Sept 1968
Steven A. 25 Sept 1955-27 May 1956
Burnette
Annie w/o G.B.; 1868-1932
G.B. h/o Annie; Feb 1860-Feb 1919
Herbert Leo 28 Sept 1916-16 Nov 1986
Wynell 11 Apr 1925-31 Jan 1950
Burton
Martha Clark d: 19 Dec 1893
Busch
Harlod 17 Feb 1904-14 Jan 1948
Cable
Thelma B. 27 Apr 1922-13 Feb 1970
Cantril
Ernest E. 4 Jul 1947-6 Jul 1972
Castleberry
Emory 4 Dec 1888-9 Dec 1972
Rosia L. w/o James E.; 12 Oct 1880-12 Feb 1961
John K. h/o Nettie C.; 12 May 1885-16 Jun 1944
Billy h/o Katherine; 21 Mar 1925-5 Sept 1976
Emory Howard s/o Emory; 26 Sept 1918-10 Apr 1928
Harry Lamar 11 Oct 1958-12 Nov 1977
Henderson 25 Feb 1011-1 Oct 1968
Jack T. s/o John K. & Nettie C.; 16 Aug 1921-22 Aug 1923
James E. h/o R.L.; 27 Jul 1878-12 Jul 1944
Katherine w/o Billy; 5 Aug 1924-26 Jun 1994
Louie J. h/o Sarah C.; 4 Aug 1906-20 Dec 1955
Martha Frances d/o John K. & Nettie C.; 3 Nov 1919-27 Jun 1920
Nettie C. w/o John K.; 16 Feb 1894-25 Dec 1970
Robert F. 28 Apr 1985-23 Mar 1986
Rossie S. 8 Jun 1896-2 Jul 1963
Roy E. 27 Apr 1915-13 Jan 1994
Sarah C. w/o Louie J.; 2 Jun 1915-6 Jun 1993
Cates
Hattie P. w/o Hubert B.; 25 Dec 1915-11 Aug 1989
Hubert B. h/o Hattie P.; 2 Apr 1919-25 Sept 1983

Chathim
    Margaret H. w/o Virgil; 8 Aug 1898-29 Mar 1986
    Virgil h/o Margaret H.; 19 Sept 1889-10 Jul 1954
Chester
    Infant 4 Dec 1921-4 Dec 1921
Christian
    Minnie 1878-1965
    Pearl 1882-1957
Christopher
    Pat W. 30 Mar 1936-30 Oct 1975
Coalson
    Clyde L. 1 Apr 101-9 Feb 1980
    Emmett W. 10 Jul 1897-1 Feb 1980
    John L. 14 Dec 1920-29 Mar 1964
Collins
    Ata Howell 1874-1957
Cooper
    Charles M. D: 16 Dec 1938
    Mamie 1868-1921
    Will M. 17 Mar 1863-25 Dec 1892
Coswick
    Delsie 1908-1975
    Fred E. 1875-1944
    John h/o Margaret; 24 Sept 1839-27 Mar 1922
    Margaret w/o John; 3 Mar 1838-27 Oct 1910
    Walter J. 1909-1976
Cowart
    Belle F. w/o Ernest L.; 15 Aug 1902-8 Mar 1968
    Ernest L. h/o Belle F.; 23 Mar 1902-15 Nov 1966
Cox
    Ebbert D. 5 Aug 1894-28 Apr 1969
    Maude S. 1 Jul 1890-3 Dec 1972
Crawford
    Berner J. 1892-1965
    John C. 1887-1952
Crisler
    Maude Apr 1876-Nov 1966
Davidson
    Louis S. h/o D.; 13 Sept 1913-24 Feb 1967

Dempsey

George Thomas h/o Luna Treadwell; 21 Jul 1881-25 Dec 1957

Luna Treadwell w/o George Thomas; 16 Nov 1880-16 Mar 1937

Mozella T. w/o Robert G.; 6 May 1909-28 Jun 1991

Robert Calvin 27 Feb 1927-7 Dec 1991

Robert Grady 8 Jan 1905-17 Jun 1970

Roy h/o Jewell; 10 Sept 1908-2 Oct 1970

Dennis

Pauline E. 1869-1957

Pauline H. 19 Nov 1848-31 Mar 1933

Dildy

Frances w/o L.W.; d: 6 Dec 1872

J.S. h/o Nancy; 1870-1919

Joe 1904-1918

Marie 1917-1917

Nancy w/o J.S.; 1883-1977

Dinsmore

Horace L. h/o Louise A.; 2 Sept 1910-14 Jun 1972

Louise A. w/o Horace L.; 10 Nov 1915-24 Jun 1954

Martha Nell 18 Sept 1932-30 Nov 1951

Willis Jackie 30 Sept 1935-31 Jul 1991

Dodd

Amy Tucker w/o Ira Homer; 2 Sept 1895-10 Mar 1981

Carlos s/o C.A.; d: 10 May 1929

Ira Homer h/o Amy Tucker; 28 Sept 1893-28 Oct 1976

James M. 16 Apr 1828-14 Aug 1895

Leon A. h/o Viola Odessa; 12 Jun 1897-22 Oct 1965

Sallie 1830-1916

Viola Odessa w/o Leon A.; 8 Aug 1895-12 Feb 1977

Dodds

Alice Noel 29 Oct 1849-26 Dec 1915

J.M. 16 Apr 1828-14 Oct 1895

Melvin W. 19 Aug 1857-29 Oct 1929

S.A. Jun 1878-28 Feb 1892

Eison

Carrye E. w/o Vester E.; 1887-1989

Vester E. h/o Carrye E.; 1883-1982

Findley

Mary Frances 24 Dec 1914-24 Dec 1914

Sarah Ann d/o J.R.; d: 30 Aug 1918
Floyd
 Coy E. 7 Oct 1894-25 Mar 1965
 May Teasley 11 Jan 1871-5 Aug 1923
 Oscar P. 22 Feb 1896-29 Jan 1979
Flynn
 William h/o Doris; 5 Aug 1930-12 Jan 1992
Foster
 Betty Louise 28 Dec 1935-9 Oct 1983
Francis
 Isaac T. h/o Mary A.; 1860-1945
 Mary A. w/o Isaac T.; 1861-1941
 Mattie O. 5 May 1893-8 Aug 1973
 W.A. 20 Aug 1887-8 Oct 1933
Gardner
 Dora L. w/o Sherman L.; 1893-1977
 Sherman L. h/o Dora L.; 1879-1948
Gilbert
 Billy Joe 1952-1958
 James W. 6 Jun 1921-12 Sept 1985
 Jason Bryan 31 May 1979-2 Sept 1982
 Ollie M. 17 Nov 1925-17 Nov 1993
Gilstrap
 Benjamin D. 9 Sept 1828-1 May 1911
 Mary Ann 9 Oct 1880-16 Jul 1918
Green
 B. Cantrill h/o Naomi F.; 12 Jun 1891-10 May 1981
 Bessie 24 Jul 1886-1 Nov 1963
 Claude T. 29 Mar 1919-18 May 1944
 Erwin 27 May 1925-4 Jan 1926
 J.G. 28 May 1879-18 Oct 1963
 Naomi F. w/o B. Cantrell; 11 Nov 1898-11 Jul 1978
Griffeth
 Edith W. 24 Apr 1927-4 Jun 1990
Grizzle
 Siddelle Cox 20 Feb 1916-1 Mar 1956
Haggod
 Herbert C. s/o Herbert C.; 8 Jun 1945-14 Jun 1945
 Herbert C. f/o Herbert C.; 30 Jun 1913-1 Mar 1959
Hall
 Frank F. h/o Nadean M.; 1912-1959

Holbrook
>Byron Edward 2 May 1919-19 Mar 1964
>Clara C. w/o William E.; 9 Aug 1875-18 Jan 1961
>Judson S. 1893-1963
>Leon 17 Mar 1910-26 Dec 1983
>Rudine Chandler 19 Feb 1933- 9 Feb 1942
>William E. h/o Clara C.; 28 Nov 1871-1 Jun 1950

Holden
>W.M. h/o Annie; 22 Dec 1908-19 Dec 1986

Hood
>J.H. 10 May 1847-21 Oct 1922
>L.E. 1 Dec 1847-25 Feb 1894

Hook
>George O. h/o Nora E.; 3 Nov 1871-21 Dec 1950
>Nora E. w/o Nora E.; 20 Dec 1876-26 Jan 1968

Huddleston
>Adline ; w/o John;d: 19 Aug 1908; 75y
>J.W. 11 May 1858-25 Nov 1935
>Mary Maygood w/o J.W.; 3 Sept 1858-16 Dec 1917

James
>Alfred Cleveland 1888-1969
>Bessie Mae 1909-1910
>Lily Ruth 1910-1911
>Lucy B. 1879-1966
>Nettie C. 1890-1929
>Rueben 1866-1939
>S.J. 26 Jun 1884-20 Jun 1932

Jenkins
>Carl 4 Aug 1909-4 Oct 1972
>Carl G. h/o Cleo B.; 1898-1976
>Carl Green 20 Aug 1925-20 Jan 1943
>Cleo B. w/o Carl G.; 1907-1957
>Fred H. 28 Jul 1887-8 Jun 1965
>Jessie E. h/o Mary J.; 1857-1923
>Mamie P. 3 Apr 1894-22 May 1978
>Mary Belle 11 Aug 1914-23 Oct 1992
>Mary J. w/o Jessie E.; 1853-1950

Jones
>Alma o. 8 Jan 1875-10 Oct 1901
>Carra Estes 1889-1941
>Crawford 22 Nov 1845-23 Dec 1906

Janice Hazel d/o G.& S.R.; 7 Apr 1954-23 Jan 1966
Mattie Webb 7 Dec 1860-29 Sept 1928
May J. 15 Jun 1889-6 Oct 1961
William C. 3 Aug 1919-5 Aug 1919
William G. 9 Jun 1877-27 May 1942
Kay
Effie Harben w/o Walter R.; 11 Oct 1890-26 Apr 1980
Walter R. h/o Effie Harben; 7 Oct 1888-25 Apr 1978
Landrum
Flonnie A. w/o S.Calvin; 16 Sept 1912-17 Mar 1980
S. Calvin h/o Flonnie A.; 7 Apr 1914-8 Feb 1996
Lane
Charlie L. 6 Aug 1874-24 Nov 1916
Lawson
N. Bobbie h/o Aubrey; 18 Aug 1932-21 Dec 1993
Nellie E. w/o David L.; 27 Jun 1912-18 Oct 1954
Lee
Fannie w/o Floyd S.; 19 Jan 1899-27 Dec 1984
Floyd S. h/o Fannie; 9 Apr 1892-1 Oct 1974
Margaret Leona w/o William; 29 Jan 1877-20 Dec 1937

Letterman
Rita R. D: 30 Aug 1946
Light
H. Stephens 13 May 1955-26 Aug 1957
Little
Bobbye Howell 1881-1858
Lowery
Homer B. h/o Stella S.; 16 Nov 1888-4 Nov 1953
Stella S. w/o Homer B.; 18 Nov 1892-21 Apr 1945
Maddox
Blanche Rucker 27 Apr 1890-25 Feb 1980
C. Emmerson 12 Apr 1883-15 Jun 1946
C.C. 13 Aug 1858-6 Jan 1920
Cicero Holt w/o Meda Fowler; 19 Aug 1895-11 Jun 1958
Elizabeth Burnette 15 May 1923-4 Dec 1985
Emerson Rucker d: 8 Aug 1916
Eulalia 11 Sept 1860-1 May 1923
George Emerson 13 Nov 1919-23 Sept 1987
Joe Rucker 23 Aug 1929-29 Nov 1950

Meda Fowler w/o Cicero Holt; 6 Dec 1898-6 Oct 1983

Marshall

Flonnie W. w/o Henry Ford; 14 Jan 1923-22 Jan 1994

Henry Ford h/o Flonnie W.; 24 May 1920-24 Mar 1996

Martin

Hugh Dorsey 23 Mar 1916-14 Feb 1925

John N. 13 Mar 1883-21 Sept 1969

Ruth Shirley w/o W.D.; 17 Jul 1892-14 Dec 1947

W.D. h/o Ruth Shirley; 1880-20 Jan 1925

W/D. 28 Jan 1913-12 Nov 1951

Mask

Angie w/o Robert Edgar; 12 Dec 1922-28 Jan 1992

Robert Edgar h/o Angie; 5 Jan 1923-21 Oct 1985

McDaniel

Joseph L. h/o Mary J.; 1872-1950

Mary J. w/o Joseph L.; 1882-1982

Miers

Edith Jenkins 22 Jan 1912-10 Jun 1981

Moore

Almeda 15 Sept 1861-8 May 1920

Bill E. h/o Mollie Susan; 18 Mar 1919-25 Jul 1978

Bright G. h/o Margaret E.; 9 Dec 1852-21 Sept 1933

Carl Raphael s/o Bill E. & Mollie S.; 12 Jun 1922-23 Jan 1923

Grady 3 Jun 1894-1 Oct 1965

Hollis G. h/o Mary C.; 10 Oct 1917-2 Oct 1954

Margaret E. w/o Bright G.; 4 Jul 1857-10 Feb 1933

Mollie Susan w/o Bill E.; 13 Jun 1903-14 Feb 1924

Nancy 1 Sept 1862-9 May 1924

Robert C. 9 Mar 1889-29 Aug 1911

William Durell 28 Feb 1943-26 Apr 1996

Morris

Alice O. 1888-1976

Charlie A. 1863-1930

Cynthia Louise 14 Apr 1952-15 Apr 1994

James M. 1891-1969

Randall H. 1913-1968

Moss

H. Carroll 1911-1955

Mullins

M.F. Paul 8 Dec 1915-24 Jan 1975

Murphey
>G. Fred 31 Aug 1906-23 Sept 1975
>Hazel E. 15 Sept 1909-13 Dec 1995

Neal
>David G. 11 Nov 1934-5 Mar 1996

Neeley
>Robert David 31 Mar 1904-24 Jun 1963

Nesbit
>Willie Carl 1889-1959

Nichols
>George C. h/o Myrtle C.; 1893-1959
>Myrtle C. w/o George C.; 1901-1978

Nix
>Fred Charles 29 Dec 1897-2 Apr 1965
>Luther S. 12 Aug 1908-20 Jan 1945
>Nelson J. h/o Susan B.; 16 Dec 1859-26 Nov 1939
>Susan B. w/o Nelson J.; 1 Oct 1871-30 May 1966

Norman
>C. Pierce h/o Nancy S.; 10 Oct 1880-1 Feb 1968
>Clifford P. 10 Feb 1923-6 Jan 1924
>Nancy S. w/o C. Pierce; 20 Jul 1881-20 Jun 1968
>P. Elizabeth 4 Jan 1908-22 Feb 1984

Paris
>Carrie S. w/o Charles N.; 27 Aug 1865-11 Nov 1943
>Charles N. h/o Carrie S.; 10 Nov 1864-28 Mar 1953

Phillips
>Adena P. w/o Walter W.; 12 Apr 1889-2 Aug 1963
>Catherine Waters 7 Jun 1914-19 Nov 1994
>Raymond Edwards 15 Jan 1912-15 Sept 1997
>Walter W. h/o Adena P.; 29 Jan 1883-18 Oct 1963

Polts
>Gail l. 1 Dec 1949-17 Dec 1980

Powell
>Octavia H. 5 Jan 1909-19 May 1942

Purcell
>Theora 4 Jun 1907-28 Jul 1950

Rainwater
>Charles E. 15 Jan 1923-29 Dec 1982
>Jimmy 5 Jan 1946-29 Aug 1960
>Lonnie d:12 Jul 1921
>Nannie B. 26 Aug 1886-14 Aug 1903

Ramsey

    Estelle M. w/o John L.; 25 Apr 1894-23 Mar 1982

    John L. h/o Estelle M.; 13 Jun 1899-8 Aug 1991

Randall

    Frederick T. h/o Mary T.; 1904-1976

Rayner

    Glen E. 7 Nov 1936-7 Nov 1936

    Glen Richard 13 May 1957-20 Jun 1957

    Kate Roe 19 Aug 1910-22 Aug 1980

    Noah 18 Apr 1901-5 Dec 1986

    Paul L. 1 Jul 1903-17 Jan 1990

    Robert Perry 1934-1996

Roe

    Albert E. h/o Jeppie G.; 15 Dec 1883-10 Mar 1963

    Flossie Popper 1891-1980

    Jeppie G. w/o Albert E.; 7 Jun 1888-7 Jan 1976

    Julius Curt 1886-1965

    Lillian W. w/o Lewis H.; 14 Jun 1917-21 Nov 1997

    Noima Jean 1933-1934

Rucker

    Florence Teasley w/o George D.; 1867-1933

    George D. h/o Florence Teasley; 1867-1922

    Von Teasley s/o George D & Florence T.; 1892-1898

Rudassil

    Don B. 4 May 1950-29 Sept 1987

    Katherine Smith w/o W.L.; 9 Aug 1913-20 Sept 1982

    W.L. h/o Katherine Smith; 11 Nov 1909-7 Jan 1994

Ruth

    E. Turner Hagood Barett 30 Nov 1924-4 Mar 1995

Sanders

    John Alfred 22 Jun 1937-27 Dec 1993

Scoggins

    Cleo w/o George; 5 Jul 1902-3 Dec 1983

    George h/o Cleo; 30 Aug 1897-29 Oct 1984

Shaw

    C. Warren h/o Mary Dildy; 9 Sept 1912-16 Oct 1977

    John R. h/o Nettie O.; 1881-1960

    John Robert 21 Jun 1911-30 May 1977

    Mary Dildy w/o C. Warren; 14 Apr 1915-17 Apr 1944

    Nettie O. w/o John R.; 1885-1937

    W.I. 1866-1964

Sheffield
> Thomas W. h/o M.; 16 Jul 1927-22 Feb 1984

Shelton
> Felix J. h/o Lessie L.; 8 Jan 1904-8 Feb 1973
> Lessie L. w/o Felix J.; 30 Sept 1907-29 Jun 1980

Shirley
> B.N. h/o Jennie Webb; 6 Oct 1847-23 Dec 1928
> Carlos V. h/o Lucille P.; 2 Oct 1889-21 Jul 1973
> Jennie Webb w/o B.N.; 2 Feb 1857-26 Nov 1940
> Lucille P. w/o Carlos V.; 23 Jun 1900-1 Sept 1986

Sims
> Amanda L. w/o J.R.; 20 Feb 1900-5 Aug 1990
> Faye Ann Shaw 27 Sept 1928-13 Apr 1996
> J.R. h/o Amanda L.; 19 Jan 1895-10 Oct 1973

Sloan
> Marylou w/o R.L.; 1873-1921
> R.L. h/o Marylou; 1870-1924

Smith
> Dolores M. 31 Mar 1896-14 Apr 1947
> Edna M. w/o J. Clifford; 17 Oct 1891-29 Jun 1930
> Emerson 11 Jan 1920-4 Mar 1939
> Ernest L. 28 Sept 1885-29 Aug 1931
> J. Clifford h/o Edna M.; 1 Jun 1886-26 Nov 1938
> Lola W. w/o Roy; 27 Apr 1885-3 Oct 1972
> Maggie Williams 30 Oct 1894-19 Sept 1989
> Philip L. 26 Aug 1929-17 Oct 1970
> Phillip Ermon 7 Feb 1891-19 Jul 1967
> Roy h/o Lola W.; 8 Mar 1889-8 Apr 1971
> Rufus 4 Mar 1906-10 Sept 1987
> Zollie B. 6 Oct 1884-3 Mar 1965

Sosebee
> Jack T. h/o K.S.; 28 Mar 1962-17 Feb 1985

Spence
> Cecil Franklin 21 Jan 1953-18 Dec 1973
> E. Dewitt 12 Feb 1910-23 Oct 1898
> Mary A. 7 Aug 1888-26 Apr 1987
> Stacy 15 Oct 1954-16 Oct 1964
> Tracy 1 Jan 1966-3 Jan 1966

Stephens
> Fannie P. 15 Nov 1918-13 Dec 1968
> Luna L. 12 Oct 1892-21 Jul 1956

Robert V. 15 Nov 1880-26 Nov 1970
Strickland
David M. h/o Ollie L.; 1884-1943
Ollie L. w/o David M.; 1892-1982
Florence A. w/o Mat A.; 26 Oct 1872-8 Apr 1934
Mat A. h/o Florence A.; 26 Oct 1868-12 Aug 1946
Stozier
Henry M. h/o Ola Teasley; 1861-1942
Henry Milton 16 Jan 1906-6 Apr 1919
Joel h/o Lillian; d:22 Aug 1960
Ola Teasley w/o Henry M.; 1873-1953
William A. h/o Winnie H.; 13 Jan 1897-28 Apr 1989
William A. 13 Apr 1925-24 Apr 1994
Winnie H. w/o William A.; 2 Jan 1900-11 Jun 1985
Sutton
Arthur C. h/o Ollie May; 5 Apr 1891-17 May 1949
John h/o Addie; 8 Aug 1866-6 Oct 1953
Ollie May w/o Arthur C.; 1893-1953
Swafford
Elena 1880-1921
Tatum
John B. h/o Hattie; 29 Jul 1912-7 Sept 1962
Terrel
Len E. 2 Aug 1907-22 Jul 1997
Thomas
Florence 27 Jun 1914-15 Aug 1981
Polly 15 Sept 1943-3 Mar 1944
Thompson
Agnes 1878-1951
Fannie Anderson w/o Isaac Newton; 12 Dec 1881-30 Jun 1966
Isaac Newton h/o Fannie Anderson; 26 May 1875-1 Jun 1963
Tollison
Clifford G. h/o T.P.; 22 Jul 1900-23 Nov 1971
James H. 28 Sept 1895-16 Apr 1973
Myrtle S. 1 Jun 1895-1 Dec 1983
Trammell
James Robert h/o Mary Dennis; 3 Nov 1867-9 Sept 1937
Mary Dennis w/o James Robert; 18 Jul 1877-17 Sept 1916
Tribble
Eva G. 30 Sept 1894-13 Jun 1978
Herman L. 27 Jun 1918-4 Mar 1942

Homer 16 Jul 1891-25 Jul 1953

Turner

Fern C. 5 Dec 1922-10 Oct 1963

Harrison H. h/o Maudie Mae; 28 Feb 1890-9 Oct 1953

Hazel L. 10 Jan 1929-2 Dec 1991

John W. 3 Apr 1893-2 Jun 1983

Lizzie R. 21 Apr 1899-6 Jun 1984

Maudie Mae w/o Harrison H.; 18 Nov 1896-10 Apr 1964

Ronnie 23 Oct 1947-26 Mar 1969

Upshaw

Arah Ann 9 Jul 1901-20 Jul 1901

Dora Teasley 30 Sept 1859-22 Mar 1929

Florence Alma w/o George; 23 May 1890-28 Aug 1917

William T. 28 Feb 1863-31 May 1912

Wade

James B. h/o Ruby V.; 14 Sept 1914-28 Jan 1986

James E. h/o Essie H.; 24 May 1892-30 Oct 1965

Ruby V. w/o James B.; 23 Oct 1917-9 Jun 1983

Walker

Fred D. 17 Oct 1901-8 May 1902

Ina Mae 18 Jan 1895-12 Oct 1960

John W. 9 Mar 1885-8 Nov 1961

Julia A. 24 May 1858-9 Feb 1914

Laura E. w/o R. Mack; 27 Mar 1865-25 Oct 1948

R. Mack h/o Laura E.; 7 Apr 1859-20 Jan 1910

Robert M. h/o E.B.; 22 Jul 1927-29 Dec 1993

Teddy Roosevelt 17 Oct 1901-4 Dec 1984

W.A. 1848-1920

Waters

Agnes G. w/o J. Arvil; 16 Aug 1908-3 Oct 1983

Cleo Shirley w/o Ralph A.; 4 Nov 1886-2 Dec 1957

David P. 5 Apr 1852-3 Jan 1918

Dora B. 27 Jan 1858-8 Jan 1923

E. Marion 17 Feb 1884-20 Jan 1963

Edwin G. h/o Betty M. Waters; 1 Aug 1930-15 May 1996

Glenon R. 7 Aug 1934-10 Jun 1981

Henry G. 11 Apr 1881-17 Jun 1922

J. Arvil h/o Agnes G.; 28 Nov 1908-29 Jun 1965

Josephine C. w/o William M.; 1860-1932

Ralph Alston h/o Cleo Shirley; 21 Aug 1883-8 Nov 1954

William M. h/o Josephine C.; 1857-1928

Watkins
Eppie M. w/o R. Dozier; 10 Sept 1872-2 Mar 1955
Louis Carl 16 Apr 1914-2 Mar 1983
R. Dozier h/o Eppie M.; 1 Oct 1864-29 Jul 1926
Ruby 28 Jun 1908-28 Jun 1908
Ruth 27 Jan 1906-22 Jun 1907
Velma 15 Jul 1909-26 May 1910
Weatherford
Nora Lou 11 Oct 1910-8 Mar 1936
Webb
C. Byron 30 Jul 1896-30 Aug 1916
Charles M. 26 Apr 1866-22 Jul 1897
Curtis h/o Reath N.; 1890-1973
Hubert 16 Feb 1923-23 Feb 1978
Joseph J. h/o Mollie C.; 14 Oct 1858-1 Feb 1938
Mary Hawkins 1870-1943
Mollie C. w/o Joseph J.; 6 Jan 1865-27 Nov 1911
Odessa L. 4 Jan 1895-12 Jul 1974
Quilton 6 Sept 1929-19 Oct 1997
R.O. 27 Jan 1892-29 Oct 1952
Reath N. w/o Curtis; 1893-1973
Robert J. h/o Samantha; 24 Feb 1856-24 Jun 1938
Samantha w/o Robert J.; 30 Aug 1859-12 Nov 1934
Virginia K. w/o H.S.; 4 May 1924-21 Oct 1984
William 22 Jan 1861-13 Jul 1896
Westbrook
Amanda Bailey w/o Marion Francis; 11 Apr 1900-20 Jul 1985
John Ed. h/o Patricia A. Threatt; 10 Mar 1943-22 Aug 1958
Marion Francis h/o Amanda Bailey; 15 May 1898-14 Sept 1995
Maude M. w/o Thomas; 3 Mar 1889-5 Jul 1972
Patricia A. Threatt w/o John Ed.; 26 Sept 1945-27 Feb 1982
Thomas h/o Maude M. 7 Jan 1888-2 Jun 1955
Westbrooks
Berlene d/o F.; 9 Nov 1925-6 Jul 1926
Whiting
Ada w/o Thomas G.; 11 Nov 1881-21 Jun 1961
Thomas G. h/o Ada; 5 Dec 1876-22 Aug 1961
Whitt
Ethell D. 28 Jun 1918-27 Feb 1972
Williams
Cory B. w/o G. Arthur; 2 Mar 1902-7 Apr 1987

D.G. Puckett 27 Sept 1923-29 Dec 1974
G. Arthur 23 Oct 1901-17 Oct 1978
Mildred P. 14 Dec 1919-6 Dec 1939
Minnie A. 11 May 1870-8 Jan 1944
W.D. March 1918-Dec 1951
W.N. 23 Apr 1877-28 Jun 1959
Wood
Cicero F. 8 Jun 1866-26 Apr 1942
Colline P. 24 Dec 1902-24 Jul 1973
General W. h/o Irene; 19 May 1904-17 Aug 1958
Harold D. 12 Dec 1920-17 Jan 1955
Irene w/o General; 8 Jan 1906-3 Jul 1966
Isham Young h/o Mary Purn; 22 Feb 1876-14 Jan 1964
J. Will 27 Nov 1884-8 Aug 1976
Mamie Hagood 28 Apr 1898-6 Sept 1970
Mary Purn w/o Isham Young; 24 May 1877-29 Mar 1955
O.W. 12 Jul 1898-17 Oct 1955
Ruby B. 9 Jun 1904-7 Aug 1987
Sally Day 7 Oct 1869-28 Jul 1945
William Grady h/o Mamie Hagood; 30 Jun 1896-21 Apr 1950
York
Jo Ann 9 Aug 1947-1 Jul 1989

Fulton County
Providence Baptist Cemetery

Andrews
Jasper H. 1875-1941
Arbouth
J. 1889-1937
Baldwin
Chester 28 Oct 1938-26 Jun 1980
Jessie F. 24 Jun 1916-24 Jun 1975
Sebern Thesta 14 Oct 1928-5 Jan 1967
Barnett
Minnie L. w/o W. Cicero; 14 Nov 1878-17 Apr 1957
W. Cicero h/o Minnie L.; 16 Jul 1873-20 Jul 1957
Barrett
Albert J. 29 Apr 1899-29 Mar 1976

Claude 7 Apr 1921-7 Dec 1978
Daisy Mae Dodd 15 Apr 1899-20 Aug 1983
Bates
George Lee h/o Ida Mable; 27 Dec 1877-14 Nov 1937
Ida Mable w/o George Lee; 14 Feb 1879-7 Apr 1946
Bearden
Sarah Elizabeth 25 Mar 1872-8 Apr 1943
Berry
Roxie d: 1921
Bibikan
Seteven D. 11 Jun 1955-1 Nov 1978
Branyon
Frances Sutton 19 Mar 1919-1 Nov 1978
Bridwell
Jesse J. D: 17 Aug 1901; 8y
Broadwell
Hamelton 14 Apr 1859-10 Sept 1862
Lavina 5 Nov 1837-25 Jul 1867
Sarah J. 22 Mar 1865-17 Jul 1867
Sophrona 8 Dec 1936-8 Oct 1881
W.H. 14 Dec 1860-21 Mar 1878
Brown
Barbara A. 1956-1965
Catherine 1875-1917
Donia 13 Mar 1893-27 Oct 1895
Jannie 10 Nov 1878-28 Jul 1895
John Henry 4 Oct 1907-23 Apr 1992
Lizzie B. w/o William J.; 1873-1916
M.A. 1850-1921
Mary J. 1855-1927
William J. h/o Lizzie B.; 1877-1963
Buice
Robert L. 29 Dec 1918-29 Jan 1961
Castleberry
Alice T. w/o Thomas O.; 1887-1972
Thomas O. h/o Alice T.; 5 Mar 1888-20 May 1968
Chamblee
Sallie G. 21 Jun 1841-7 Dec 1908
Chatam
Beul h/o Gertrude; 18 Jul 1913-9 Aug 1981
Gertrude w/o Beul; 8 Apr 1911-29 Nov 1986

Willie B. 30 Jul 1935-24 Oct 1983

Cogburn

Bob Earle 26 Oct 1889-31 May 1891

Eveline w/o J. Floyd; 10 Feb 1824-17 Sept 1912

J. Floyd h/o Eveline; 28 Dec 1820-18 May 1897

Lillie Agnes d/o J.&M.; 18 Feb 1875-30 Jul 1892

Collett

Melissa 18 Dec 1961-18 Dec 1961

Theresa Sue 26 Aug 1960-14 Jan 1961

Cook

Claud C. 13 May 1906-13 Apr 1966

Edward C. 1831-1918

General R.L. 14 Jan 1867-29 Mar 1936

Jimmie 5 Jun 1939-6 Jun 1939

John h/o Rebecca A.; 17 Dec 1823-9 Jan 1888

Lou w/o John H.; 1836-1860

Mamie 30 Mar 1892-9 May 1892

Mattie 24 Dec 1885-11 Jan 1945

Mattie Lou 7 Jul 1910-8 Mar 1984

Rebecca A. w/o John; 10 Oct 1838-4 May 1911

Cowart

Annie O. w/o John W.; 28 Dec 1865-12 Nov 1951

Charlie P. 3 Apr 1897-30 Nov 1958

Fannie N. w/o J.H.; 30 Jan 1867-6 Jun 1941

Geneva 25 Nov 1901-16 Nov 1970

Infant s/o C.M.; 17 Nov 1920-17 Nov 1920

J.H. s/o Fannie N.; 21 Dec 1861-1 Apr 1928

John W. h/o Annie O.; 20 Jan 1859-23 Apr 1926

Mary Pauline d/o L.B.; 6 Apr 1909-14 Jun 1910

Maurine 18 Apr 1909-25 Apr 1989

Cox

Alice 28 Oct 1880-16 Mar 1915

DeVore

A.W. h/o L.C.; 4 Oct 1839-6 Aug 1897

D. Williams 27 Oct 1846-5 Feb 1925

Daisy G. w/o Roy E.; 4 Sept 1896-7 Jun 1980

David h/o Lucinda B.; 27 Feb 1802-16 Apr 1887

George G. 22 Mar 1870-2 May 1870

J. Elzorah 30 Sept 1846-7 Aug 1891

L.C. w/o A.W.; 14 Aug 1837-6 Jan 1921

Lawrence Hunter 1920-1990

Lillie Mae 30 May 1886-11 Jul 1886
Lucinda B. 6 Jul 1811-3 Oct 1898
Mary E. 6 Jun 1850-4 Jan 1918
Mary Lou 2 Dec 1847-2 Dec 1899
Missouria w/o B.R.; 11 Apr 1852-16 May 1886
Roy E. h/o Daisy G.; 16 Sept 1897-17 Oct 1988

Dilbeck

Mae Walker 9 Nov 1899-9 Nov 1961
Merrill Walker 17 May 1937-15 Jun 1988
Susan Ashley 29 Oct 1970-1 Nov 1970

Dinkins

Joseph d:30 May 1854; 19y; "The Lone Boy"

Dinsmore

Agens L. w/o Archie C.; 17 Oct 1884-9 Sept 1925
Archie C. h/o Agens L.; 20 Apr 1885-29 Nov 1961
Aubrey 31 Jan 1913-23 May 1957
Carl C. 1 Nov 1927-10 Jun 1956
Glenn 29 Nov 1892-19 Apr 1959
Ida 1 Nov 1900-4 Jul 1979
Ina May d/o William M.& Lessie I.; 4 Aug 1908-14 Nov 1910
J. Apr 1929-Nov 1982
Keith R. 1906-1969
Lessie 7 Nov 1904-18 Apr 1905
Lessie I. w/o William M.; 5 Apr 1890-7 Dec 1965
Martha E. 9 Apr 1876-23 Dec 1960
Mary N. 5 Oct 1862-17 Jun 1898
Maude O. 8 Jul 1905-6 Oct 1987
S.N. 18 Oct 1858-27 Jan 1941
W.I. s/o William M.&Lessie I.; 10 Feb 1915-30 Jun 1916
Walter 4 Jan 1907-25 Mar 1971
William M. h/o Lessie I.; 12 Jun 1885-5 Apr 1958

Dodd

Annie Babikan 27 Aug 1929-13 Nov 1935
Odius 21 Jun 1885-12 Apr 1974

Earley

Elizabeth 3 Jul 1822-16 Dec 1895
John Green w/o Viola Graham; 23 Oct 1873-5 Apr 1972
Viola Graham w/o John Green; 10 Dec 1880-5 Jul 1947

Estes

Carlos Y. 1920-1922
Charlie P. 1899-1968

Hudson M. 1972-1959
Mollie M. 1879-1954

Etris
Amanda Stover w/o William S.; 1875-1956
Gus L. 26 Jul 1909-26 Oct 1936
J. Frank h/o Sallie W.; 2 Dec 1873-31 Jan 1953
James Nolan 14 Aug 1911-14 Jun 1968
Rolph 21 Oct 1900-26 Jul 1925
Sallie W. w/o J. Frank; 23 Sept 1873-11 Jun 1943
William S. h/o Amanda Stover; 1875-1965

Farnes
August W. 8 Dec 1895-27 Oct 1920

Ferguson
Avie C. 20 Apr 1884-28 Sept 1900
John W. 17 Jul 1885-23 Aug 1958

Fowler
Frances 1828-1854
George T. 1825-1889
Jessie O. 17 Sept 1901-27 Sept 1976
Telitha C. 1835-1892

Gillespie
C.C. h/o Nancy C.; 23 Jul 1819-9 Mar 1882
Nancy C. w/o C.C.; 24 Nov 1818-5 Jan 1909

Goodwin
Warren Lee 1873-1934

Graham
Willie M. s/o J.& M.; 26 Jul 1864-18 Jul 1970

Grant
Anthoney Norman 26 Dec 1964-24 Jan 1965
Maude W. w/o William Augustus; 28 May 1886-20 Jul 1978
Stephanie Renee 6 Aug 1963-4 Mar 1987
W.A. s/o William A.& Maude W.; 15 Feb 1910-7 Jul 1923
William Augustus h/o Maude W.; 1881-1947

Gravis
Harold h/o Irene; 30 Aug 1909-8 Feb 1965

Green
Marvin 29 Dec 1922-21 Jun 1987

Griffin
Dora B. w/o Jesse W.; 1895-1954
Jesse W. h/o Dora B.; 1894-1984

Gunter
Camilia d:1942
Charles 1924-1950
Charles 1878-1950
Douie Self 29 Jul 1891-28 Feb 1948
Ed 1926-1973
Martha Louise 1927-1932
Nettie L. 1881-1964
Pearl Wood 1891-1928
Samuel M. 18 Jun 1884-4 Aug 1952
Sarah 7 Apr 1919-1 Sept 1946
Tony Lamar 25 Jan 1959-8 Feb 1959
Hardeman
B.M. 26 Jul 1824-4 Mar 1904
Lou Ella w/o J.; 16 Jul 1875-6 Jul 1916
Serepty 28 Jul 1856-14 Feb 1918
T.D. 16 Sept 1845-9 Sept 1915
Hatcher
Lillie L. 16 May 1912-2 Mar 1984
Holcomb
Clyde M. h/o Mary Lee; 18 Dec 1903-5 Dec 1969
Mary Lee w/o Clyde M.; 15 Oct 1907-30 Nov 1967
Holcombe
Fannie D. w/o John W.; 6 Jul 1881-1 Dec 1968
John W. h/o Fannie D.; 25 Aug 1873-12 Dec 1945
Holden
Buney V. w/o W.D.; 8 Sept 1856-14 Sept 1916
Buren Ivan s/o G.&C.; 15 Oct 1915-21 Mar 1916
Luther R. s/o J.J.&M.O.; 28 Apr 1902-15 Aug 1902
W.D. h/o Buney V.; 15 Mar 1859-8 Feb 1930
Jackson
David M. 3 Mar 1893-21 Jan 1964
Jones
Daisy 1896-1912
John D. 1 Jun 1952-23 Jan 1972
Leonard 1899-1913
Kennignton
Samantha 1858-1934
William W. 1847-1924
Landrum
Grace Mandy 21 Sept 1907-17 Dec 1991

Lane
    W.D. 1850-1914
Lee
    Fairy 1916-1916
Legg
    C.T. h/o Nora Lee; 30 May 1891-25 Mar 1971
    Nora Lee w/o C.T.; 3 Feb 1898-5 Jul 1949
Makin
    Andrew J. s/o J.J. &V.M.; June 1865-Jun 1867
    Sarah E. w/o J.W.; Nov 1868-23 Jun 1964
Mansell
    Gincy w/o J.W.; 1844-1922
    Hannah w/o Robert; 1815-1903
    J.W. h/o Gincy; 1844-1913
    Robert h/o Hannah; 1820-1862
Manus
    John B. 27 Apr 1911-30 Oct 1978
Marshall
    B.H. 25 Jul 1860-24 Dec 1918
    Ezzard T. h/o Wanda J.; 1906-1950
    Wanda J. w/o Ezzard T.; 1912-1986
Mashburn
    Edmond W. 1913-1996
    Fred M. 14 Nov 1923-2 Feb 1925
    Julia 28 May 1924-18 Apr 1996
    Willie D. 8 Dec 1918-28 Oct 1979
McClesky
    L.E. 28 Aug 1882-4 Jan 1961
    Ida 8 Sept 1883-27 Feb 1929
McCollum
    Easter H. 1796-1857
    Infant s/o W.F.; 30 Mar 1898-30 Mar 1898
    John B. h/o Sophronia C.; 2 Sept 1822-14 Dec 1891
    Sophronia C. w/o John B.; 22 Jul 1826-16 Jun 1910
    William 1789-1876
Moore
    E.B. h/o Mary J,; 26 Apr 1834-13 Feb 1899
    Loyd W. 1897-1921
    Mary J. w/o E.B.; 22 Feb 1838-20 Feb 1903
Nix
    C. Oscar h/o Lilian M.; 1902-1978

Charles 1836-1927
Charles Samuel s/o C. Oscar & Lilian M.; 1928-1933
John R. 1871-1939
Lilian M. w/o C. Oscar; 1902-1966
Roxie A. 1861-1905
Susan G. 1840-1907
Wade H. 1866-1894
Norton
M.E. 1841-1877 "Mother & Baby"
Perry
Franky w/o William H.; 8 May 1812-26 Nov 1868
William H. h/o Franky; 18 Aug 1804-3 Oct 1878
Phillips
Harriet E.w/o H.P.; 8 Dec 1880-16 Nov 1901
Phalonia P. w/o John W.; 2 Jul 1856-11 Sept 1939
Thomas J. 18 Jan 1881-15 Feb 1952
Willie 3 Sept 1878-28 Dec 1908
John W. h/o Phalonia P.; 31 May 1849-11 Jan 1912
Pool
Luther S. 1896-1956
Sarah A. 1871-1917
William L. 1867-1954
Poole
Truman Rex 9 Dec 1925-30 Nov 1956
Pruitt
Beatrice 1927-1984
James Woodrow 13 Mar 1914-8 Oct 1984
Railey
Vickie J. 1955-1993
Rapp
William M. 1921-1984
Redd
John L. h/o Martha G.; 1 Jan 1847-22 Ju 1910
Lee Tucker 1902-1990
Martha G. w/o John L.; 26 Nov 1847-13 Nov 1925
Rilliat 1894-1988
William P. 1891-1958
Reece
A.L. s/o E.A.&M.F.; 10 Aug 1880-5 Jun 1893
D.W. s/o E.A.&M.F.; 29 Jul 1880-13 Oct 1881
E.A. w/o M.F.; 18 Jul 1844-6 Feb 1904

E.M. s/o E.A.&M.F.; 18 Jun 1886-18 Jun 1887
Eli 22 Apr 1847-11 Apr 1921
Emma C. w/o Eli; 25 Dec 1854-22 Nov 1902
J.L. s/o E.A.&M.F. 26 Jul 1876-5 Jul 1887
Rusk
William Henry h/o Clarenda Upshaw; 24 May 1872-
10 Apr 1929
Samples
Jennifer Lynn 1 Dec 1976-1 Dec 1976
Shelton
Curtis C. h/o Ruby Lee; 2 Oct 1913-9 Apr 1994
Ruby Lee w/o Curtis C.; 1 Jul 1904-3 Apr 1979
Shuler
John D. 1891-1980
Nellie 1891-1932
Smith
Fannie P. 1883-1911
Hartwell 1906-1926
Lonzo 1898-1921
Nancy P. 1879-1931
Spence
Aytch B. 24 Aug 1892-13 Mar 1962
Hattie C. 7 Aug 1907-12 Jul 1983
Jeff 13 Mar 1911-17 Oct 1969
William Cody 30 Oct 1908-7 Jan 1971
Stover
Buchie 1886-1975
George W. 1871-1937
Thompson
Albert W. 26 Sept 1866-4 Feb 1895
Esther 20 May 1895-5 Feb 1896
Martha A. w/o William J.; 1 May 1850-12 Apr 1936
William J. h/o Martha A.; 16 Aug 1843-28 Aug 1914
William Mark 13 Mar 1961-6 Jun 1997
Tippens
Daryl Richard 13 Feb 1961-6 Jun 1997
Richard T. 2 May 1927-14 Jan 1980
Treadwell
Eli H. h/o Mary G.; 1845-1903
Mary G. w/o Eli H.; 1853-1898

Tucker
>Beulah 1906-1997
>Delia 1870-1939
>Dialphia Jane 16 Apr 1853-16 Jul 1940
>J.W. h/o Octava E.; 1867-1939
>Julia C. w/o W. Rollin; 1885-1957
>Octava E. w/o J.W.; 1869-1920
>W.Rollin h/o Julia C.; 1878-1963
>Willis Cass 15 May 1849-30 Jun 1925

Upshaw
>Charlie 9 Nov 1867-12 Nov 1891
>Clarenda w/o William H, Rusk; 19 Feb 1875-27 Aug 1926
>J.M. h/o S.C.; 24 May 1844-20 Nov 1920
>S.C. w/o J.M.; 25 May 1844-30 Sept 1907

Vaughn
>Eliza 1866-1898

Walker
>A.A. 22 Jul 1851-28 Feb 1921
>J.C. 20 Mar 1889-29 Jul 1918 "Killed In France"
>J.W. 4 Jul 1848-20 Mar 1915
>Jane 10 May 1873-9 Oct 1935
>Joseph Alvin 18 Aug 1919-6 Nov 1984
>Sallie C. 7 Mar 1877-5 Mar 1959
>V. Ernest 5 Nov 1893-20 Jan 1969

Warren
>Andrew J. 11 Jan 1916-20 Sept 1969

Westbrook
>C. Paul 21 Feb 1953-7 Apr 1985
>Ellen Irene w/o William Glenn; 18 Aug 1901-15 Feb 1996
>Gertrude W. 6 Apr 1932-1 Jan 1966
>William Glenn h/o Ellen Irene; 9 May 1897-6 Oct 1964

Wheeler
>Mary Arminda w/o J.J.; 27 Nov 1833-1 Oct 1891

White
>J.T. 10 Aug 1825-Aug 1862

Winkler
>Flonnie E. w/o Wilbur C.; 17 Aug 1893-22 May 1927
>Wilbur C. h/o Flonnie E.; 25 Nov 1887-27 Oct 1966

Wood
>Alline L. w/o Joseph D.; 6 Apr 1872-10 Feb 1940
>Boyd F. 6 Jun 1886-29 Sept 1941

E. Glenn 11 Jul 1902-20 Dec 1969
Fannie 2 Apr 1847-26 Dec 1899
Frances w/o John J.; 1837-1884
General Lee 6 Jan 1881-29 Mar 1902
George 26 Jul 1906-16 Jun 1969
Howard F. 29 Apr 1858-14 Aug 1914
Ida w/ Paul; 30 Sept 1874-18 Feb 1956
James Doyle 30 Aug 1921-15 Jul 1996
John J. 1826-1916
John M. 23 Jan 1905-22 Apr 1958
Joseph D. h/o Alline L.; 13 Feb 1865-9 May 1943
Lola 31 Oct 1883-31 Oct 1951
Luster s/o L.J.& Rachel; d:6. 12d
M.W. d: 1 Oct 1892; 69y 5m
Mark Palmer 26 Dec 1921-15 Dec 1942
Mary Matilda 19 Nov 1840-29 Aug 1911
Mattie 1887-1969
Mattie Lee d/o L.&M.; 8 Mar 1899-8 Nov 1899
Mollie Belle 2 Jun 1909-23 Jul 1923
Paul h/o Ida; 10 Dec 1872-6 Jun 1964
Savilla 12 Jul 1885-25 Feb 1936
Willie Mae 28 Sept 1909-10 Feb 1984

Fulton County
Union Hill Baptist Cemetery

Bagwell
Ben R. h/o Ruth; 25 Mar 1871-5 May 1950
Delds s/o J.F. & I.L. 26 Nov 1906-15 Mar 1908
Ida L. w/o James F.; 21 Jan 1878-14 Jan 1919
James F. h/o Ida L.; 19 Aug 1875-26 Oct 1950
J.E. 8 Aug 1841-29 Dec 1929
Lou 23 Jul 1839-19 Dec 1909
M.W. 2 Feb 1869-14 Jul 1905
Robert Glenn 14 Aug 1921-21 Jun 1979
Ruth w/o Ben R.; 27 Feb 1874-17 Aug 1952
Stephen Lee 1834-1876
Bailey
A.L. 8 Jan 1854-23 Oct 1912

Baker
  L. Idean Strickland 23 Oct 1909-21 Jul 1961
Biddy
  Carol Elaine d: 6 Aug 1968
Booker
  Jane Swafford 27 Jul 1853-29 Jun 1929
  Jason R. 22 Aug 1845-24 Jan 1893
Burnett
  M.C. 1897-1966
  Ruby 1918-1983
Chelders
  Jackson d:19 Oct 1903; 35y
Chester
  Alta Jane 1903-1936
Cobb
  Douglas L. 30 Oct 1937-27 Jun 1984
Davidson
  Fannie D. w/o H.H.; 4 May 1852-14 Mar 1916
Durham
  Naomi w/o Paul D.; 19 Aug 1899-18 Mar 1989
  Paul D. h/o Naomi; 15 Jul 1898-5 Jul 1959
Estes
  Lala Strickland 28 Feb 1889-1 Sept 1967
Flynn
  Hattie H. w/o Joe Thomas; 1895-1973
  Joe Thomas h/o Hattie H.; 1905-1963
Gazaway
  George W. h/o Mary M.; 1861-1935
  Mary M. w/o George W.; 1861-1950
Gilstrap
  Bascomb 24 Dec 1896-23 Dec 1917
Gosden
  Charlorre H. 1 Apr 1921-21 Apr 1994
Hawkins
  Alfred J. 1 Mar 1863-8 Feb 1901
Heard
  Calvin J. h/o Frances L.;18 Jun 1838-30 Nov 1892
  Charles Ceveland 13 Feb 1890-18 Mar 1962
  Frances L. w/o Calvin J.; 10 May 1841-1 Oct 1895
Hudson
  Jonny 7 May 1896-9 Jun 1896

J.M. 23 May 1861-9 Jun 1984

Hunter

Nancy 18 Nov 1820-13 Jun 1878

Jhonas 10 Jun 1810-18 May 1872

Hyde

D.T. h/o Martha; 8 Jun 1835-1 Dec 1914

Martha w/o D.T.; 6 Oct 1848-21 Aug 1927

Jackson

Eugene 1941-1966

Keesee

Joseph Richard h/o Lillie May Heard;30 Jun 1880-2 Jun 1942

Lillie May Heard w/o Joseph Richard; 10 May 1886-
24 Sept 1944

Kilgore

Calvin D. 5 Feb 1924-3 Mar 1995

James E. 23 Jan 1916-7 Jul 1967

J.E. h/o Mamie; 12 Sept 1882-16 May 1957

J.T. 27 May 1853-6 Aug 1933

Mamie w/o J.E.; 16 Nov 1885-22 Sept 1950

Mary I. 1877-1972

Kuykendall

William Oscar 1915-1972

Lee

R.F. 5 Jun 1828-10 May 1896

Little

George h/o Georgia; 1931-1963

Georgia w/o George; 1929-1990

Jess 1931-1960

Martin

B.A. 12 Jun 1857-26 Mar 1928

George W. 19 Dec 1853-19 May 1903

J.H. h/o Martha A.; 14 Oct 1852-25 Dec 1909

John G. h/o Lucy C.; 15 Mar 1825-19 Jun 1899

Lucy C. w/o John C.; 2 Mar 1882-2 Aug 1903

Martha A. w/o J.H.; 15 Jan 1858-19 Oct 1913

Robert Lee h/o Effie E. Shirley; 11 Oct 1868-9 Oct 1939

Welton 1921-1980

William 1825-1897

Mathis

Athelda Caroline; w/o Clyde Franklin; 28 Jun 1890-28 Aug 1957

Clyde Franklin h/o Athelda Caroline; 6 Jun 1895-9 Jul 1944

Jessie Mae 26 Feb 1922-15 Sept 1923
Lee Baxter 10 Mar 1924-28 May 1924
Leona Elizabeth 10 Mar 1924-27 Apr 1924
Meeks
James C. 1907-1970
Merritt
Danny Otis 1957-1984
S. Ethel 1889-1968
Toy H. 1887-1973
Morris
Essie M. w/o T.J.; 23 Apr 1918-21 Jan 1988
T.J. h/o Essie M.; 20 Jan 1915-19 Aug 1956
Moss
Ben F. 4 Dec 1903-9 Nov 1946
Ida Shirley w/o Patrick David; 29 Jul 1866-25 Apr 1940
Patrick David h/o Ida Shirley; 26 Mar 1862-22 Jun 1931
Nalley
D.M. 1884-1962
Earley R. h/o Ethel B.; 1881-1931
Ethel B. w/o Earley R.; 1884-1981
Glenn H, s/o Earley R. & Ethel B.; 24 Jul 1914-29 Jun 1916
Parker
Ira 4 Apr 1898-29 Jul 1935
Robert P. 30 Sept 1902-22 Nov 1955
Potts
John W. 1890-1953
Ramsey
Shirley 9 Dec 1881-13 Jan 1953
Samples
Clarence A. 1893-1929
Daniel P. 1897-1949
G. Cleveland 23 Apr 1886-21 Jun 1940
Mattie Estell 9 Sept 1884-16 Dec 1960
Noah B. 1858-1921
Norama M. 1862-1937
Victor M. 1899-1946
Shirley
Dara J. 12 Aug 1870-1 Dec 1951
Edward R. 1909-1979
Effie E. w/o Robert Lee Martin; 15 Jan 1871-6 Aug 1964
Fannie 1907-1960

Horace s/o J.R.&J.B.; 7 Oct 1910-3 Feb 1911
Infant d/o J.R.&J.B.; 28 Aug 1906-29 Sept 1906
James P. 30 Jun 1868-15 Mar 1938
James W. 5 Sept 1868-6 Jul 1967
Jennie Belle w/o John Robert; 21 Mar 1878-17 May 1957
John F. h/o Mary G.; 3 Mar 1841-27 Sept 1906
John Robert h/o Jennie Belle;20 Jun 1873-22 Nov 1949
Lillie Mae w/o Wilburn C.; 1 Oct 1896-23 Oct 1949
Mamie Lee 16 Mar 1903-6 Jun 1986
Mary 1851-1925
Mary G. w/o John F.; 12 Feb 1846-10 Jan 1915
Mary H. 16 Mar 1913-15 Jul 1991
Sarah Magdalene w/o Tribble; 27 Oct 1872-21 Aug 1950
Shirley Ola Lucile d/o J.R.; 11 Feb 1897-20 Nov 1918
Tribble h/o Sarah Magdalene; 23 Sept 1860-30 Mar 1929
Wilburn C. h/o Lillie Mae; 23 Aug 1893-28 Nov 1978

Smith

Alpha h/o Mary; 21 Jun 1817-20 Apr 1905
Mary w/o Alpha; 30 Apr 1823-12 Mar 1896

Stone

Eva 1884-1972
Susan Effie w/o Thomas l.; 20 Oct 1883-10 Apr 1938
Thomas L. h/o Susan Effie; 29 Mar 1879-2 Mar 1958

Strickland

Anna Cox 10 Apr 1891-10 May 1976
Arlinta w/o Luke; 1888-1930
Carl 25 Dec 1907-13 Mar 1958
Effie w/o Mathew; 20 Aug 1884-10 Sept 1952
Harold 18 Mar 1914-23 Nov 1939
I.J. h/o Nancy; 16 Dec 1843-15 Dec 1916
Luke h/o Arlinta; 1887-1938
Mathew h/o Effie; 29 Feb 1881-29 Aug 1952
Nancy w/o I.J.; 5 Jun 1847-25 Dec 1909
R.A. 27 Nov 1881-25 May 1910

Sweatman

Sarah Martin 2 Sept 1898-4 Aug 1914

Thompson

C.J. 23 Oct 1832-10 May 1914
James W. 30 Oct 1858-10 Feb 1890

Tribble

J.W. d: 1851; 68y 1m 7d

Villyard

Grover 19 Apr 1929-27 Jun 1995

Wade

Collins R. 15 Jun 1935-3 Apr 1994

David R. 9 Nov 1957-19 Jan 1958

Warren

Louise R. 23 May 1929- 4 Jun 1969

Webb

Joel 28 May 1837-1 Feb 1900

Robert J. 3 Oct 1881-1 Feb 1903

Susan A. 9 Jan 1868-6 Nov 1910

Fulton County
Hopewell Baptist Church Cemetery

Aaron

Eula Hughes 28 Oct 1903-29 Jun 1990

Rochester 1896-1966

Armstrong

Mary J. w/o Thomas V.; 22 May 1883-4 Jun 1965

Thomas J. h/o Mary J.; 1 Jul 1881-15 Aug 1960

Thomas V. 1912-1973

Ballew

Elizabeth 14 Apr 1879-9 Jan 1936

R.M. h/o S.C.; 22 Dec 1844-1 Nov 1915

S.C. w/o R.M.; 13 Mar 1847-27 Apr 1919

Thomas Gordon 1872-1898

Bates

Ada L. 11 Apr 1881-31 Dec 1971

Annie Mae 1918-1991

Daisy Holden 1875-1962

Francis 24 Jul 1811-11 Dec 1888

George 10 Jul 1883- 17 Mar 1993

James h/o Ruth 1899-1975

James W. 13 Nov 1929-25 Feb 1930

J.K. (Mrs) w/o J.K.; 16 Jun 1851-18 Jun 1893

J.K. h/o Mrs; 16 Nov 1846-7 May 1920

John 22 Mar 1847-28 Dec 1923
Lillie M. 21 Feb 1905-1 Jun 1991
Mattie 13 May 1870-13 Aug 1949
Minnie G. 1907-1953
Ruth w/o James; 1901-1983
Sarah 30 Mar 1815-11 Dec 1910
Walter D. 1904-1977
Bell
Lula A. w/o John A.; 13 Jun 1902-3 Sept 1972
Jennings Gerald h/o Betty Westbrook; 28 Dec 1931-4 Mar 1991
John A. h/o Lula A.; 5 Oct 1892-11 Mar 1973
Blalock
Barbara S. w/o James E.; 3 Oct 1938-27 Dec 1938
Eugene h/o Maeoma 23 Jun 1912-13 Jun 1970
Howell Dean s/o Barbara S. & James E.; d: 28 Jul 1945
James E. h/o Barbara S.; 14 Jan 1940-12 Mar 1940
Maeoma w/o Eugene; 1 Jan 1917-3 May 1994
Brice
James E. 11 May 1920-13 Jul 1970
Bruice
Charles A. 1924-1924
Homer A. 1892-1980
Laura H. 1895-1980
Buice
Daisy h/o James R.; 4 Jun 1891-1 Jan 1937
J. Henry 12 Nov 1896-3 Oct 1942
James R. h/o Daisy; 12 Jun 1886-14 Jul 1958
Lillie Mae Fitch 27 Mar 1871-16 May 1967
Burgess
Clara Minnie w/o William Henry; 17 Jan 1874-24 Nov 1936
Toledo Parks h/o Estelle Wright; 13 Nov 1906-3 Jun 1987
William Henry h/o Clara Minnie; 13 Jan 1870-4 Dec 1956
Chadwick
Cecil 23 Aug 1893-3 May 1966
Infant s/o B.&D.; d:7 Apr 1961
Laura D. 8 Oct 1897-20 Oct 1986
Chatham
Columbus J. 11 Sept 1880-11 Jul 1920
Elizabeth w/o George W.; 12 Apr 1850-14 Mar 1930
George W. h/o Elizabeth; 12 Jan 1846-9 Mar 1930

Clayton

    Saacl 6 Dec 1829-6 Apr 1915

    Syrena 28 May 1827-4 Feb 1910

Cochran

    James Sexdon 23 Feb 1878-27 Aug 1940

    John 1 Dec 1855-17 Nov 1919

    Oscar D. h/o Zemma; 6 Sept 1883-1 Feb 1936

    Quincy h/o Dovie; 22 Oct 1905-16 Dec 1997

    Sarah 14 Sept 1882-8 Jan 1915

    Savannah 27 Apr 1861-27 Mar 1952

    T.B. 9 Sept 1817-27 Nov 1868

    W.J. s/o Oscar D. & Zemma; 30 Jun 1904-29 May 1905

    Zemma w/o Oscar D.; 2 Apr 1885-24 May 1975

Collett

    Charles J. 1 Jun 1939-9 Jun 1956

    Jimmy M. 25 Mar 1947-24 Jun 1965

    Willie A. 10 Apr 1915-31 Jan 1977

Corbee

    James Richard 15 Apr 1935-5 Oct 1935

Couly

    Buddy 25 Mar 1925-18 Mar 1926

    Jessie 24 Oct 1903-20 Apr 1966

    William 17 Jul 1891-16 May 1946

Covey

    Buddy 1925-1928

    William R. 1897-1946

Davis

    Robert Perry 24 Aug 1962-25 Aug 1962

    Roger Joseph 12 Aug 1940-25 Aug 1964

Day

    Benny Charles 4 Jun 1959-26 Mar 1960

    Emerson Newport h/o Margrett Jewell; 17 Feb 1913-21 Jan 1977

    J.C. h/o Mary; 15 Oct 1845-24 Feb 1926

    Margrett Jewell w/o Emerson Newport; 22 Nov 1911-10 Nov 1995

    Mary w/o J.C.; 18 Jan 1848-20 Oct 1925

    Ruby Jean 11 May 1910-31 Jan 1986

    W. Lucene 8 Oct 1910-25 Apr 1962

Deverell

    L.R. w/o W.S.; 26 Mar 1848-21 Nov 1897

Dimsdale
>A.P. 25 May 1873-22 Mar 1905
>Lee h/o Malinda; 8 Jul 1858-2 Dec 1951
>Malinda w/o Lee; 2 Jan 1855-9 Nov 1908
>Minnie E. w/o Robert L.; 14 Jun 1894-1 Feb 1986
>Robert L. h/o Minnie E.; 11 Jan 1890-14 May 1962
>W.I. 2 Jan 1875-20 Jan 1947

Dinsmore
>Anner M. Noris w/o Cicero L.; 1865-5 May 1935
>Cicero L. h/o Anner N. Noris; 20 Mar 1859-15 Jan 1936

Dooley
>Alma Wright Blackwell 1876-1969

Edward
>Iva 1922-1924

Estes
>Blanche W. 1920-1978
>Clyde h/o Onnie H.; 25 Dec 1904-21 Sept 1971
>Onnie H. w/o Clyde; 22 Dec 1907-16 Jun 1985

Fitch
>Estelle H. w/o James R.; 1857-1933
>James F. 12 May 1905-4 Nov 1971
>James R. h/o Estelle H.; 1856-1921
>Van 27 Jan 1882-26 May 1937

Gaddis
>John B. 1 Dec 1888-26 Jul 1983
>Margaret 13 Apr 1890-3 Dec 1971

Garrett
>E. 23 Jul 1867-29 Sept 1938
>Laura J. 30 Nov 1871-16 Nov 1956
>Wm. A. 15 Sept 1890-22 Nov 1907

Gravitt
>Carl C. h/o Nanniet; 1913-1956
>Nanniet w/o Carl C. 1917-1942

Green
>Mary Avis w/o Walton R.; 28 Jan 1905-16 Dec 1995
>Walton R. h/o Mary Avis; 8 Aug 1896-2 Aug 1985

Hamrick
>Carlton J. h/o Janice M.; 1 Oct 1929-10 Nov 1973
>Janice M. w/o Carlton J.; 9 Apr 1929-16 Nov 1994
>Parlee 1864-1918

Harbin
    Tammy Richards 25 Jul 1970-27 Jun 1989
Hardman
    T. Ernest 25 Oct 1906-8 Nov 1989
Heard
    Zoma 15 Aug 1874-19 Feb 1958
Henderson
    John 1886-1937
    Thomas K. 1885-1904
Holbrook
    G.C. h/o Ollie B.; 27 Feb 1892-7 Oct 1957
    Mary Redd 1873-1902
    Ollie w/o G.C.; 12 May 1892-4 Sept 1985
Holcombe
    Arthur M. h/o Lilie M. 1883-1962
    Lillie M. w/o Arthur M.; 1886-1967
    Martha 1889-1889
Hughes
    Essie Mae 17 Jul 1909-30 Aug 1978
    Wm.B. 10 Aug 1864-25 Jan 1977
Ivan
    Joel d:25 Jul 1972
Johnson
    Christopher J. 15 Feb 1987-15 Feb 1987
Keyes
    N. Thanetta w/o Donald H.; 16 May 1920-20 Oct 1986
Land
    Alice 6 Feb 1884-30 Aug 1961
    Bud h/o Mamie; 1887-1952
    Jesse Lee 22 Jun 1909-21 Dec 1901
    Levi M. 31 Oct 1875-9 Oct 1949
    Mamie w/o Bud; 1887-1981
    M.J. 17 Feb 1807-3 Jul 1818
    S. 20 Jul 1851-15 Apr 1926
Ledford
    Elizabeth w/o Hiram J.; 29 Feb 1887-5 Jan 1956
    Ernest L. h/o Lillie Mae 17 Jan 1907-24 Feb 1972
    H. David 30 Oct 1940-7 Feb 1959
    Hiram J. h/o Elizabeth; 2 May 1885-30 Apr 1968
    Jewell Reeves 6 May 1918-29 May 1989
    Lillie Mae w/o Ernest L.; 12 Mar 1908-28 Sept 1981

Little
>Paul 9 Jun 1934-3 Aug 1970
>Wayne 24 Feb 1958-5 Jun 1965

Maddox
>Wynette Parks 1921-1967

Mashack
>Noah 14 Jan 1877-16 May 1958

McClain
>Bessie w/o Dozier; 1900-1989
>Dozier h/o Bessie; 1889-1941
>J.D. 19 Jan 1925-21 Oct 1990
>Winton D. 1920-1962

McCleskey
>Dollie w/o Tom; 1886-1965
>Dovie Florine 7 Jan 1919-28 Jan 1919
>Estelle W. w/o Leo; 11 Feb 1905-7 Feb 1985
>Leo h/o Estelle W.; 19 Feb 1903-9 Oct 1977
>Telma Lee 8 Dec 1917-21 Jan 1918
>Tom h/o Dollie; 1879-1945
>Virginia w/o W.G.; 5 Oct 1868-5 Sept 1958
>W.G. h/o Virginia; 24 Dec 1873-7 Apr 1947

McCluskey
>Eura w/o Guss; 1892-1920
>Guss h/o Eura; 1889-1925

Northcutt
>Charles h/o Geneva M. 28 Apr 1928-3 Dec 1985
>John Emmett s/o Charles; 21 Sept 1963-12 May 1991

Pearson
>A.L. h/o L.E.; d:4 Oct 1917; 63y
>Clarence D. 26 Jun 1914-10 Nov 1974
>Infant d/o C.D.& Mary; d: 11 Apr 1938
>L.E. w/o A.L.; w/o A.L.; 31 Oct 1857-17 Jun 1920
>Liler 20 Mar 1895-18 Mar 1900
>Melvin 1944-1991
>Virgil s/o A.L.& L.E. 15 Mar 1884-13 Feb 1903

Pendley
>Brad Ford 10 Sept 1921-18 Jun 1995
>C. Corbet 11 Mar 1899-8 Sept 1985
>Dorres Willene 18 Jun 1932-24 Aug 1932
>Marie C. 28 Jan 1924-25 Jul 1993

Phillips
> Alma 8 Aug 1881-16 May 1960
> H.E. 18 Dec 1879-8 Jun 1929
> Janis H. h/o Mary E.; 1849-1928
> J. Felton w/o R. Forrest; 20 Mar 1888-11 Jan 1963
> Martha J. 1853-1966
> Mary E. w/o Janis H.; 1868-1950
> R. Forrest h/o J. Felton; 4 Jan 1886-7 Oct 1951

Rayford
> Mark 19 Mar 1926-24 Mar 1980

Redd
> Luther Cecil 11 Aug 1908-12 Mar 1910

Rogers
> R.C. (Mrs) w/o R.C.; 24 Aug 1815-21 Jan 1897

Rucker
> Horace W. h/o Deryle L. 25 Oct 1921-6 Nov 1998

Rydasill
> Elizabeth w/o Wm. 2 Oct 1891-4 Sept 1919

Sewell
> Penny JeDean 8 Feb 1969-28 Jan 1981

Smith
> Estelle P. w/o Wm. Gordon; 6 Sept 1905-24 Sept 1986
> George D. 30 May 1864-9 Mar 1910
> Launia 18 Jun 1869-21 May 1939
> Wm. Gordon h/o Estelle P.; 7 Jul 1899-14 Jul 1986

Thompson
> Annie L. w/o James H.; 31 Dec 1888-22 Jul 1952
> James H. h/o Annie L.; 23 Jul 1888-27 Jan 1981

Tucker
> Howell M. s/o A.H.&M.L.; 8 Mar 1903-26 Nov 1906

Vaughan
> Emmett C. 1917-1990
> Harry Mar 1949-Mar 1968

Waldrop
> George W. h/o Pauline A.; 16 Aug 1911-1 Jul 1992
> Pauline A. w/o George W.; 22 Dec 1912-24 Apr 1967

Walker
> Janelle G. w/o J.W.; 29 Apr 1915-7 May 1952
> J.W. h/o Janelle G.; 21 Jun 1915-7 Aug 1984

Watson
> Alma Lee w/o Julius Arell; 31 Mar 1879-29 Nov 1927

Julius Arell h/o Alma Lee; 8 Nov 1875-20 Jul 1934
West
    Joyce L. 18 Aug 1943-8 Aug 1988
Westbrook
    Cora D. w/o John B.; 6 May 1884-27 Jun 1980
    James W. 9 Oct 1879-25 Feb 1923
    John B.h/o Cora D.; 15 Apr 1882-27 Jan 1971
    Luther L.h/o Ruby M.; 14 Mar 1903-12 Feb 1966
    Opal 27 Oct 1913-23 Aug 1932
    Ophelia 23 Apr 1878-18 Jul 1955
    Ruby M. w/o Luther L.; 17 Oct 1902-10 Apr 1983
    Thomas M. 1871-1950
White
    Era P. 17 Jun 1898-9 Jun 1996
    Eura P. w/o James S.; 1875-1959
    James S. h/o Eura P.; 1868-1914
    J.C. s/o James S. & Eura P.; 20 Apr 1910-1910
    J. Vesta 17 Jan 1919-27 Mar 1972
    Maggie A. 26 Aug 1929-18 Apr 1971
    R.E. 19 Jun 1895-13 Jul 1973
    T.M. 17 May 1820-8 Jun 1919
Wilke
    Doyle 1908-1980
Wilson
    Celia Frances w/o Elijah; 1 Sept 1860-16 Jan 1898
    Elijah h/o Celia Frances; 21 Dec 1858-31 Jan 1937
    Emerson 1 Aug 1925-10 Jan 1996
    Infant s/o John & Mamie B.; d: 25 Jan 1917
    John h/o Mamie; 26 Nov 1892-18 Jul 1958
    Laura J. s/o Savannah; 31 Jul 1883-29 Jul 1968
    Mamie w/o John; 26 Mar 1896-8 Aug 1991
    Savannah s/o Laura J.; 29 Feb 1888-16 Aug 1951
Wood
    B.B. h/o Celia; 8 Feb 1876-8 Sept 1961
    Celia w/o B.B.; 22 Aug 1876-20 Nov 1944
    Clarence 1922-1935
    George F. 1917-1979
    Howard 11 Nov 1927-22 Apr 1964
    Linda 1900-1976
    Lizzie w/o G.W; 4 Sept 1875-3 Jul 1934
    G.W. h/o Lizzie; 4 May 1865-14 May 1923

Harry 1932-1935
Ila 1894-1986
Twigs W. h/o Vennie; 1885-1906
Vennie w/o Twigs W.; 1888-1944
W.B. 1890-1957
Wilborn 1917-1938
Wright
Charles E. 19 Aug 1886-21 May 1959
Charles E. h/o Elizabeth; 5 Mar 1850-5 Feb 1927
Elizabeth w/o Charles E.; 12 Jan 1892-7 May 1903
Ellene w/o John Elton; 4 Oct 1908-7 Apr 1984
Henry F. 13 Jul 1919-12 Feb 1983
Henry Fleming h/o Odessa Whitaker; 18 Aug 1890-17 Feb 1935
I.O. h/o Jewell B.; 1904-1993
Jewell B. w/o I.O.; 1909-1985
John Elton h/o Ellene; 16 Apr 1897-9 Jul 1976
Larry Charles 29 Sept 1943-10 Oct 1965
Lena Mae 23 May 1892-17 Mar 1965
Lucy Margaret 18 Nov 1850-16 Jul 1913
Minnie Lee 20 Jul 1899-28 Mar 1912
Nettie J. w/o William T.; 6 Dec 1888-10 Mar 1967
Odessa Whitaker w/o Henry Fleming; 26 Oct 1888-27 Nov 1986
Robert Charles 14 Sept 1913-11 Oct 1986
Thomas Ellis 13 Aug 1849-4 Jan 1935
Thomas Whitaker h/o Ruby Sewell; 30 Aug 1916-24 Aug 1981
Virgil T. 12 Jun 1911-23 Sept 1995
William T. h/o Nettie J.; 27 Feb 1888-1 Aug 1952
William Tarpley 1881-1926
Wm. Ivie s/o William T.&Nettie J.; 17 May 1919-6 Jan 1926

Fulton County
Greenlawn Cemetary

Abbattista
Joseph Michael 1915-1986
Abbott
Irene H. w/o Lawton B.; 1909-1989

Lawton B. h/o Irene H.; 1902-1984

Adams
Earl J. h/o Naomia 1910-1987
Elizabeth Ann 1968-1993
Emere w/o John T.; 1912-1999

Akselsen
Peter K. 1903-1990

Albuquerque
Mildred Tierney 1898-1984

Allen
Clarence E. 20 Mar 1930-21 Nov 1995
Dewey M 7 Nov 1941-1 Dec 1998
Jerry Brian 1971-1996
L. David 1956-1983
Roger J. h/o Etta K.; 12 Apr 1915-23 Apr 1994
Rosa R. w/o Thurmane E.; 1926-1982
Thurmane E. h/o Rosa R.; 1920-1984

Allshouse
Herbert G. h/o Catherine B. 1917-1996

Altobelli
Donato J. h/o Constance A.; 1934-1998

Alynn
Mary 6 Jan 1908-17 Jun 1981

Amato
Janet A. w/o Samuel V.; 1933-1984

Amos
Marion J. h/o Mildred S.; 1912-1980
Mildred S. w/o Marion J.; 1911-1996

Anderson
Atward h/o Wynette B.; 1922-1986
Carolyn E. w/o Dean; 1916-1980
Clarence Chester h/o Essie M.; 1900-1989
Dean h/o Carolyn E.; 1912-1988
Essie M. w/o Clarence Chester; 1903-1979
J. Garland h/o Laura M.; 1929-1991
J. Shelby h/o Mabell B.; 1915-1972
Julia Mae w/o Gordon K.; 1932-1972
Laura M. w/o J. Garland; 1935-1989
Mabell B. w/o J. Shelby; 1917-1972
Sheldon C. h/o Bonnie S.; 1914-1996

Andrews
   Walter S. h/o Montez C.; 1914-1977
Anger
   Edward W. h/o Harriette W.; 1912-1997
   Harriette W. w/o Edward W.; 1915-1990
Anglin
   Leaunia w/o Henry J.; 1927-1986
   Lewis M. h/o Catherine U.; 1924-1993
   Sarah H. w/o Toy C.; 1897-1983
   Toy C. h/o Sarah H.; 1896-1984
Anthony
   Sandra Carolyn Wing 17 Jan 1939-14 Aug 1983
Armstrong
   Donald E. 1928-1998
   Hugh D. h/o Ozelle 1917-1993
   Jeanne B. 1924-1993
   Ozelle w/o Hugh D.; 1923-1982
Arnold
   Gaynell 27 Dec 1921-11 Jun 1986
   Herbert 9 Jan 1921-20 Jan 1992
Asherbranner
   Buford L. h/o Lodius Corine; 22 Jun 1917-27 Jul 1988
   Lodius Corine w/o Buford L.; 25 Apr 1914-12 Feb 1993
Austin
   Andy 27 Sept 1979-19 Jul 1998
   G. Turner h/o M. Joyce; 1931-1990
Bacon
   David 22 Sept 1943- 28 Jan 1998
Bailey
   Genr R. h/o Sylvia 1945-1995
   Howard E. h/o Mattie A.; 1895-1983
   Mattie A. w/o Howard E.; 1906-1999
Baker
   George C. 1936-1994
   William Warren 23 Aug 1919-20 Jul 1993
Ball
   Howard Kelly h/o Mildred Barrows; 24 Jan 1929-25 Dec 1994
Bardin
   Charles A. 1940-1985
Barkshadt
   William E. 17 Nov 1969-23 May 1991

Barlett
   Richard   3 Sept 1946-13 Jun 1993
Barnett
   Henry I. 1911-1983
   Randy F. 15 Jan 1959-6 Aug 1992
   William A. 1929-1991
Barron
   Christy Michelle 20 Jan 1969-16 Jun 1979
   Riley R. 27 Jun 1924-23 Nov 1987
   Ruth Elaine Maxwell 14 May 1937-10 Jun 1995
Bartley
   Ruth E. 1921-1995
Barwick
   Eugene 1913-1993
Bates
   Charlie h/o Ellie M.; 1904-1978
   Effie S. w/o William N.; 1904-1996
   Ellie M. w/o Charlie; 1907-1975
   William N. h/o Effie S.; 1900-1974
Batter
   William 1905-1993
Baum
   Arthur 1903-1985
Bauman
   Michael G. 1971-1995
Bean
   Christopher L. 9 Aug 1969-13 Aug 1988
Beckham
   Mattie 18 Mar 1910-4 Mar 1983
Bell
   Lola B. w/o Robert T.; 1908-1983
   Robert T. h/o Lola B.; 1904-1992
Belling
   Maye P. 1906-1985
Bence
   Richard L. 1920-1996
Bennett
   Hershel C. h/o Evelyn G.; 1926-1992
   Myrtle P. 1922-1976
   William R. h/o Margaret; 1923-1974

Benning
    Karen Lou   1971-1998
Bentley
    Curtis Howard 28 Nov 1945-2 Nov 1989
Berry
    Henry C. h/o Nellie M.; 1919-1980
Bess
    Thomas Carl 1961-1989
Birchall
    Walter E. 1906-1980
Bird
    Beverly Anne 16 Dec 1955-10 Feb 1980
Birdsong
    Grace A. w/o Guy; 1905-1988
    Guy h/o Grace A.; 1906-1984
Bishop
    Carolyn R. w/o Gerald A. 1934-1995
    Ivalyne 1907-1991
Black
    Margaret 20 Dec 1924-3 Jun 1982
    Richard   1923-1985
Blake
    Martha F. w/o W. Forrest; 1933-1996
    W. Forrest h/o Martha F.; 1927-1982
Blalock
    Jerry B. h/o Linda J.; 1945-1989
Blankenship
    E. Erle 10 Sept 1916- 4 Mar 4, 1986
Blarr
    Flora E. w/o Jesse E.; 1912-1981
    Jesse E. h/o Flora E.; 1907-1980
Blassingame
    Walter 1927-1991
Blockowitz
    John M. 1 Mar 1943-11 Mar 1987
Bobo
    Frank Clifton 5 Jun 1941-23 Sept 1987
    James Lawrence h/o Geraldine A.; 1927-1991
    Sarah M. 16 Dec 1976-23 Dec 1976
    Tom Watson h/o Frances D.; 21 Jun 1921-18 Aug 1987

Bohannon
    David S. 21 Sept 1931-9 Nov 1993
    Henry h/o Jannie M.; 1914-1992
Booker
    Ruth w/o William Marshall Davis; 1916-1995
Bottoms
    Charles Franklin 29 Dec 1913-14 Feb 1978
Boudreau
    Betty I. 2 Sept 1920-9 Aug 1998
Boven
    Andrea C. 1946-1988
Boyd
    Carl H. 1903-1992
    Jessie T. 1908-1998
    Robert H. h/o Marion M.; 1915-1995
    Robert S. h/o Sarah F.; 1925-1990
Boylan
    Claudia w/o Warren J.;   1914-1997
    Warren J. h/o Claudia; 1913-1991
Bradbury
    Kay Earley 1925-1993
    Virgina P. 1948-1998
Bradford
    Cooledge W.   h/o Jeanette A.;   27 Dec 1923- 3 Oct 1984
Bradley
    Arthur 26, Dec 1935-16 Jan 1995
    Elizabeth W. w/o James H.; 1926-1974
    James H. h/o Elizabeth W.; 1922-1976
Branden
    H.N. Obino 1992-1992
Brandenburg
    Harry H. 1906-1980
Brannon
    Carrie E. w/o James E.; 1920-1993
    James Wesley 1917-1991
Brantley
    Charles A. 1924-1974
    Mildred L. 1915-1996
Braswell
    Bernice R. w/o Loy S.; 1909-1996
    James H. h/o Dorothy G.; 1926-1995

Loy S. h/o Bernice R.; 1903-1970
Brazzeal
    Samuel L. h/o Daisy W.; 1929-1995
Brewer
    Ella Louise w/o G.W.; 14 Jan 1915-17 Aug 1990
    G.W. h/o Ella Louise; 27 Nov 1912-4 Aug 1990
Briggs
    Aileen B. 17 Oct 1938-13 Dec 1995
    Marion 23 Mar 1923-26 Mar 1992
Brinster
    Ferdinand P. h/o Rose Mary; 1897-1984
    Rose Mary w/o Ferdinand P.; 1897-1987
Brock
    Earl A. h/o Willene H.; 1921-1981
Brook
    Jennifer 10 Dec 1965-23 Aug 1996
Brooks
    Charles Cecil 1 Oct 1959-10 Oct 1993
    Harley B. h/o Alma; 1905-1976
Brown
    James J.P. h/o Sallie E.; 1916-1979
    Shelia C. 1925-1993
Browne
    Frances M. 1907-1995
Browning
    Philip Macy 1930-1987
Brumbelow
    Charles W. h/o Maude L.; 1931-1989
    Effie D. w/o Oliver L.; 1898-1989
    Effie O. w/o W.T.; 1916-1991
    Glen h/o Ruby K.; 1913-1991
    Herbert B. 6 Dec 1929-21 Jul 1936
    Iona R. w/o Vurner J.; 1898-1987
    Joe C. h/o Zadie L.; 1900-1982
    J.Will h/o Ora M.; 1891-1954
    Margaret E. w/o Reps H.; 1895- 1989
    Maude L. w/o Charles W.; 1932-1989
    Oliver L. h/o Effie D.; 1898-1985
    Ora M. w/o J. Will 1895-1987
    Reps H. h/o Margaret E. 1895-1971
    Roger E. 13 Feb 1924-9 Jul 1997

Ruby K. w/o Glen; 1913-1991
Vurner J. h/o Iona R.; 1897-1972
William E. 27 Aug 1920-8 Jul 1944
W.T. h/o Effie O.; 1913- 1996
Zadie L. w/o Joe C.; 1908-1978
Brunson
Harold D. 1 Jun 1933-20 Apr 1992
James E. 21 Feb 1947-13 Jun 1993
Brusco
Charles A. 1913-1998
Bryant
Don R. 1934-1987
Linton L. h/o Erma R.; 1925-1981
Buckman
Frank 1929-1991
Bullard
Mary A. w/o Clarke T.; 1929-1989
Burdick
Jessie W. 1889-1972
Burley
Leila G. 1923-1979
Burnett
Kellie Barron 26 Jun 1962-25 Mar 1998
Raymond E. h/o Clemmie E.; 1938-1989
Burnette
C.C. h/o Mary M.; 1917-1992
Burrell
Richard Lee 15 Jun 1948-16 Sept 1995
Bush
Asa W. h/o Helen S.; 1916-1993
Helen S. w/o Asa W.; 1921-1996
Bustamante
German E. 8 Mar 1944-13 Jul 1997
Butler
Dorothy A. w/o Thomas D.; 1931-1997
Thomas D. h/o Dorothy A.; 1929-1989
Buzzard
James L. 14 Dec 1919-7 Feb 1998
Byers
Richard Carroll 17 Jun 1955-17 Jun 1990

Cagle
George L. 1899-1982
Hoyt N. h/o Mary Lou; 1915-1992
Lillian 1918-1994
Caldwell
Richard L. 1907-1984
Callaghan
J.P. 3 Sept 1918-5 Oct 1992
Callahan
Betty D. 1928-1990
Callaway
Evelyn W. w/o Leo O.; 1910-1995
Leo O. h/o Evelyn W.; 1913-1994
Campbell
Mary E. 1929-1980
Cannon
J.C. h/o Silvia M.; 1905-1998
Silvia M. w/o J.C.; 1903-1989
Carmon
J.C. h/o Lara Rose; 1914-1992
Carnes
Ethel H. w/o Jacob M.; 1899-1983
Jacob M. h/o Ethel H.; 1898-1973
Carper
Howard B. 1925-1975
Carruth
Hugh L. 1929-1981
Cash
Sam J. h/o Pearl B.; 1912-1976
Casselman
RoseMary L. 1949-1997
Cassidy
Charles E. 9 Jun 1932-3 May 1983
Cassis
Michael A. 1936-1993
Castile
Vivian W. 1923-1987
Castleberry
Fred R. h/o Gladys B.; 1912-1980
Gladys B. w/o Fred R.; 1914-1996

Cat

Z. Hong 1950-1995

Ceccherini

Rodolpho 31 Aug 1952-31 Mar 1993

Cerroni

Catherine L. 1949-1988

Foster J. 1925-1993

Cha

Jessica 6 Oct 1992-14 Jan 1994

Chadwick

Leland L. h/o Hazel J.; 1921-1986

Hazel J. w/o Leland L.; 1923-1997

Chambers

B. Gertrude w/o Leonard B.; 1906-1989

Leonard B. h/o B. Gertrude; 1901-1973

Chamblee

Charity C. w/o E.C.; 1913-1988

E.C. h/o Charity C.; 1914-1996

Chandler

Juan T. h/o Anne H.; 17 Feb 1921-14 Oct 1996

Chapman

Vincent A. h/o Freda F.; 1912-1990

Chase

Rita Eunice 1924-1991

Cheshire

F. Hout h/o Janet S.; 1921-1984

Ruth 1918-1996

Chester

James E. 1946-1977

Larry W. 1939-1987

Christian

Kenneth A. 1932-1998

Christopher

Homer J. w/o Ruby V.; 1897-1986

Ruby V. w/o Homer J.; 1899-1999

Church

Angela M. 1965-1987

Ciannetti

Norma J. 1926-1994

Ciccosello

Jean 2 Sept 1924-6 Jul 1996

Ciprari
  John Louis 20 May 1928-13 Feb 1998
Clark
  Benjamin David 9 Aug 1981-10 Apr 1999
  Geraldine E. w/o Alva O.; 1920-1988
Clayton
  Frank C. h/o Patricia Foley; 20 Jul 1924-24 Dec 1988
Clemenger
  Clinton A. 1905-1993
Clute
  Tracy B. 1924-1998
Cobb
  Claude C. h/o Evelyn 1904-1987
  Frances P. 1923-1988
  Hollis L. 1922-1988
Cochran
  Hubert C. h/o Angie L.; 1904-1996
  J. Junior 16 Aug 1912-21 Jan 1982
  Junior 1912-1982
  Mary R. w/o Joe C.; 1931-1986
  Ronald L. h/o Barbara R.; 1942-1993
  Vivian E. 1915-1998
Cole
  Barbara M. w/o Weldon V.; 1930-1995
Coleman
  Bryson Y. h/o Nona B.; 1899-1987
  Carolyn D. w/o Ralph R.; 1925-1985
  Herbert Woodrow 29 Mar 1917-12 Dec 1987
  Joseph W. 1925-1991
  Nona B. w/o Bryson Y.; 1901-1983
  Oretha L. 18 Nov 1937-24 Dec 1995
  Phillip M. 18 Jan 1965-7 Mar 1993
  Robert Lewis h/o Norma Jean; 29 Jun 1936-5 Apr 1995
Colliff
  Benjamin 1909-1955
Collins
  Darius Nathan 17 Jun 1997-20 Dec 1997
  Gale A. 1937-1994
  James J. 1936- 1992
Combs
  Lynda 28 Oct 1942-12 Jan 1994

Comer
George W. 1933-1991
Comerford
Debra K. Duncan 1950-1994
Conaway
Nina E. 1906-1995
Conner
John Marcin h/o Eva Lou 22 Dec 1918-2 Nov 1996
Conrad
Edith K. w/o Richard H.; 1905-1973
Richard H. h/o Edith K.; 1905-1983
Conti
Vincent S. h/o Rose H.; 1911-1997
Conway
Elizabeth Lily 1939-1992
Cook
Anne J. w/o James C.; 1909-1976
Chester C. h/o Mana L.; 1903-1987
James C. h/o Anne J.; 1907-1982
Jammie W. w/o Thomas E.; 1924-1993
Mana L.; w/o Chester C.; 1906-1990
Thomas E. h/o Jammie W.; 1924-1981
Wm. C. h/o Bertha E.; 1902-1971
Coombs
Frances Robert 1907-1977
Cooper
Carrie L. 6 Jun 1926-5 Aug 1983
Corbett
Frederick M. 1916-1984
Corey
Archie H. 1908-1995
Costley
Emmett T. h/o Jean M.; 1934-1995
Coursey
Adelia R. 1916-1999
Cowart
W.T. h/o Ruth F.; 1912-1977
Cox
Artie B. 1902-1989
Huiel h/o Bertha L.; 4 Feb 1926- 13 Jul 1993
J. Denver 1898-1971

Craddock
Lowell K. 2 Oct 1949-25 May 1997
Crain
Larry J. h/o Nickiel; 1950-1992
Crawford
Elizabeth A. w/o Ralph A.; 1914-1989
Ralph A. h/o Elizabeth A.; 1908-1985
Crisler
Donald Keith 1 Nov 1964-5 Nov 1988
Cronic
James C. 26 Feb 1937-15 Jun 1967
Crosby
Kathryn Michaela 1 Apr 1994-30 Jun 1994
Crow
Clifford E. h/o Margaret N.; 1914-1980
Margaret N. w/o Clifford e.; 1914-1999
Cuff
Howard R. 13 Sept 1924-4 Oct 1992
Cullen
Ester P. 1908-1993
Frank B. 1906-1992
Cunningham
Vantrice B. 1943-1993
Cushard
Thomas 18 Sept 1924-29 Dec 1994
Cusson
Beatrice L. 1916-1998
Dale
Cornelia B. w/o Francis Lillard; 8 Apr 1914-27 Jul 1997
Francis Lillard h/o Cornelia B.; 17 May 1912-14 Jul 1997
Darnell
W. Fred h/o Barbara S.; 1913-1993
Davis
James H. 1916-1981
Perry L. 1906-1988
William Marshall h/o Ruth Booker; 1912-1979
Winnie W. 1911-1994
Day
Wm. Louis 1933-1997
Dean
Joel S.L. h/o Willie Nell; 1916- 1992

Willie Nell w/o Joel S.L.; 1919-1977
Deardorff
    Janet w/o Scotty; 1912-1985
Deboor
    Walter E. h/o Emmie L.; 1919-1998
Dempsey
    Frances Pauline 5 Apr 1900-18 Oct 1981
    Paul C. 1943-1992
Deprimo
    Kevin 1968-1987
Devore
    Shirley 1916-1996
    Wendele O. 1911-1993
Dickens
    Darryl K. 1939-1972
Dickerson
    C.S. h/o Martha 1928-1988
Dickson
    Charles L. 1893-1981
Diego
    Gregorio h/o Luisa; 1930-1996
Dilbeck
    Dean M. w/o Jack L.; 1938-1989
Dildy
    Lucille W. w/o Joel ; 1908-1983
    James Larry 3 Dec 1938-22 Mar 1988
    Joel h/o Lucille W.; 1906-1975
Dill
    Christian E. h/o Louise H.; 1910-1980
Dimitrios
    Kohilis 1923-1986
Dinsmore
    A. Ford h/o Ida T.; 1906-1987
    Luther V. h/o Zona P.; 1905-1988
Disbrow
    Morgan S. 1925-1982
Disney
    Mamie D. w/o Richard S.; 1915-1985
Dixon
    Virlyn L. h/o Jacqueline Elliott; 21 Apr 1927-19 Apr 1997

Dobbs
   Asberry N. h/o Betty L.; 1929-1993
Dockery
   Lillie C. w/o Robert J.; 1917-1991
   Robert J. h/o Lillie C.; 1911-1993
Donegan
   Betty w/o Robert F.; 1926-1969
   Herman W. h/o Lorena H.; 31 May 1892-4 Mar 1963
   Lorena H. w/o Herman W.; 10 Apr 1899-29 Sept 1980
Dooley
   Ethel Blondine 29 Jun 1912-16 Feb 1996
Dormann
   Erwin F. 1904-1997
Dotson
   Beulah B. w/o Eugene H.; 10 Aug 1915-11 Nov 1998
   Eugene H. h/o Beulah B.; 10 May 1911-21 Mar 1995
Douglas
   Granger h/o Hazel; 1923-1988
Dow
   Robert Bruce h/o Joyce Powers; 22 Jun 1920-25 Jun 1995
   Violet, 194-1987
Drew
   Charles L. 4 May 1889-17 May 1982
   Katherine P. 8 Jun 1915-13 Apr 1981
Dudlees
   Linda Lee 1946-1992
Dudley
   James Glenn h/o Laura Lewis; 1911-1996
   Jeanne 8 Oct 1925-25 Jul 1996
Dulton
   Travis O. 1926-1984
Dumont
   M.E. June w/o William A.; 16 Mar 1919-15 May 1997
   William A. h/o M.E. June; 5 Jul 1919-12 Aug 1991
Duncan
   Rex W.; 1951-1997
Dunn
   Dan C. 2 Jul 1956-19 Feb 1993
Dusseau
   Roy J. h/o Vera M.; 1910-1980
   Vera M. w/o Roy J.; 1913-1998

Dutton
  Emmett Irvin h/o Mary Swann; 1908-1986
Earley
  Bertha C. w/o B.L.; 1895-1974
  B.L. h/o Bertha C.; 1897-1981
Edelman
  Joseph h/o Jeanne F. 1916-1989
Edwards
  David L. 1953-1996
Eggersman
  Arthur F. h/o Margaret F.; 1915-1980
  Margaret F. w/o Arthur F.; 1920-1996
Eichner
  Ronald h/o Patricia 1939-1990
Eifert
  Donald M. 1929-1989
Eller
  Gus W. h/o Syble R.; 1914-1983
  Syble R. w/o Gus W.; 1918-1997
Ellington
  Ruby Claudine 7 Nov 1925-12 Oct 1994
Elliot
  Alice J. w/o J. Carroll 15 Jun 1907-11 Aug 1979
  J. Carroll h/o Alice J.; 21 Feb 1905-27 May 1983
Elliott
  Lois T. 1900-1984
  Van B. 1940-1988
  William C. h/o Jewell P. 1927-1990
Engel
  Herbert Joseph 1905-1987
English
  J.D. h/o Addie Aileen; 20 Jul 1920-25 Apr 1994
Ervin
  Amelia 11 Sept 1910-23 Mar 1993
  Mary Louise 1917-1989
Evans
  Barbara H. w/o Jack R.; 1935-1987
  Jack R. h/o Barbara H.; 1933-1996
Everhart
  Betty J. 1928-1992

Everton
  Virginia L. 1916-1997
Eves
  Arnold W. h/o Jeannette W.; 1915-1994
  Jeannette W. w/o Arnold W.; 1920-1992
Falcitelli
  Joe 9 Sept 1938-19 Oct 1991
Farley
  Hester M. 1919-1993
  Raymond W. 1918-1991
Farmer
  Rupert S. 1923-1988
Farrell
  James R. 7 Mar 1953-29 Nov 1993
  Ronald J. h/o Betty V.; 1912-1998
Favero
  Elizabeth T. 22 Sept 1951-11 May 1996
  Franco 14 Feb 1945-11 May 1996
  Laura Elizabeth 13 Feb 1982-11 May 1996
Feigel
  Charles Louis 1918-1976
Feind
  Emroy E. h/o Geraldine W.; 1899-1996
  Geraldine W. w/o Emroy E.; 1902-1981
Fell
  Nelda W. w/o Roland E.; 1924-1995
  Roland E. h/o Nelda W.; 1919-1994
Fenley
  Harper 1907-1994
Ferrari
  Catherine M. 12 Jul 1919-20 May 1997
Ferrell
  Margie w/o Wm. Charles; 1934-1998
  Wm. Charles h/o Margie; 1930-1989
Flatley
  Maureen S. 22 Nov 1959-10 Jan 1993
Floyd
  Kendell Douglas 13 May 1935-17 Sept 1998
Foley
  Lauren Alexandria 22 Aug 1982-24 Dec 1993
  Patricia w/o Frank C. Clayton; 3 May 1928-7 Sept 1991

Ford
Craig A. 1900-1989
Earnest J. 26 Jul 1970-3 Nov 1990
Joseph 24 Jun 1924-3 Oct 1994
Forehand
John L. h/o Lee; 1925-1981
Forrester
Samuel C. h/o Mildred R.; 1917-1991
Foster
Roy E. h/o Frances C.; 1923-1986
Wilberg 1914-1998
Wm. C. 12 Jul 1961-20 Sept 1992
Fournier
Calvin E. 1952-1992
Foust
Floyd J. 1932-1987
Fox
Elizabeth Jane 1963-1980
Mary Jean 1929-1997
Frances
Jean 1914-1993
Franklin
Louise W. w/o Nat; 1903-1986
Nat h/o Louise W.; 1905-1989
Fraser
Lucille R. w/o Jesse R.; 1915-1992
Fredine
Rita 1925-1993
Fredericks
Pearl E. 1906-1994
Fredrickson
Lindsey Elizabeth 3 Mar 1985-6 Feb 1986
Fright
John 16 Jan 1910-3 May 1980
Frisby
Ruby Jewell 3 Jul 1920-27 Oct 1995
Frizzell
John Scott 13 May 1936-18 Jul 1994
Frost
Herbert h/o Agnes H.; 1921-1992

Fry
    Clair V. 1901-1995
    Maudi L. 1905-1992
Fulton
    Bonnie w/o Jack; 1927-1992
    Jack h/o Bonnie; 1921-1994
    Scott Richard 11 Sept 1965-1 Feb 1994
Furr
    Alene W. 1918-1986
    W. Craig 1913-1992
Gallagher
    Heba A. 22 Jan 1928-7 Oct 1998
    Michael E. 1938-1998
Galosky
    Catherine 1909-1997
Gargal
    Fred H. h/o Ozella H.; 1908-1994
    Ozella H. w/o Fred H.; 1924-1996
Garrett
    Bobbie A. h/o Jeanette B.; 1945-1998
    Charlie h/o Ruby; 1917-1999
    Ruby w/o Charlie; 1914-1997
Garrison
    David Cole 10 Sept 1985-5 May 1993
Gaymon
    Allen 8 Jun 1954-3 Jan 1993
    Harold T. h/o Hilda S.; 1920-1989
    Hilda S. w/o Harold T.; 1917-1995
Gaynair
    Carmen 1906-1996
Gayton
    Artie L. w/o Ernest A.; 1907-1992
    Earnest A. h/o Artie L.; 1903-1979
Geeslin
    Marvin E. 1957-1988
Gentry
    Geo. Obie h/o Nellie C.; 1907-1979
    Nellie C. w/o Geo Obie; 1908-1987
Gerheim
    John W. h/o Alyce S.; 1912-1993

Gerwig
  Arthur Robert 15 Dec 1943-21 Jun 1995
Giardot
  Norman F. h/o Ruth M.; 1915-1998
  Ruth M. w/o Norman F.; 1921-1995
Gilliam
  Jolantha 12 Dec 1946-14 May 1987
Gilmore
  Marsha Cox w/o Roger C.; 2 Oct 1945-28 Jun 1994
Glascock
  Maxine R. 1933-1986
Gleason
  Helen Hall w/o Neil Arden; 16 Apr 1920-21 Oct 1998
Glesias
  James T. 1924-1991
Glickman
  Sheree L. 1955-1995
Glover
  Augustus Hoyt 1914-1976
  Doris 1 Apr 1929-5 Jul 1992
  William 7 Apr 1969-15 Nov 1985
Goldstein
  Barbara w/o Joseph F.; 4 Dec 1927-16 Jul 1997
  Joseph F. h/o Barbara; 20 Jun 1925-18 Jan 1997
Gomes
  Antoinette V. 10 Jun 1928-18 Jun 1997
Gonzales
  F. Eugene 27 Mar 1923-10 Sept 1994
Good
  Dorthyann w/o Raymond L.; 1923-1982
Goodrich
  Don G. h/o Peggy T.; 1925-1990
Gordon
  Cena Y. w/o Michael; 1945-1992
  Grace O. 11 Jun 1911-22 Dec 1995
  Mattie Davis 1 Oct 1912-29 Apr 1992
Goss
  Hiram D. 1929-1984
Graham
  C. Edward 18 Dec 1945-8 Oct 1994
  L. Pauline 4 Jul 1918-19 Oct 1996

Grant
 John B. 12 May 1979-20 May 1979
 Vollie F. w/o Harold D.; 1914-1997
Gravitt
 A. Hubert h/o Alice C.; 1904-1984
 Alfred H. w/o Nettie R.; 1929-1989
 Alice C. w/o A. Hubert 1905- 1992
Green
 Gary Lynn 1961-1987
 James R. h/o Sandra S.; 1932-1996
 Richard Louis 13 Jan 1944-6 Mar 1992
 Sandra S. w/o James R.; 1933-1972
Greenwalt
 Helen S. 1942-1994
Greves
 Alfred C. 1906-1986
Grice
 Pamela L. 1958-1989
Grillo
 Mary J. 24 Apr 1913-3 Feb 1995
Grimes
 Helen L. w/o Luther; 1917-1997
 Luther h/o Helen L.; 1912-1986
Grippo
 William F. 1909-1987
Grizzle
 Hollis Theford 24 Jan 1923-23 Aug 1997
Grobe
 Richard A. 1944-1987
Gunter
 E. Hugh 1914-1969
 Elton H. 1914-1995
Gyure
 Barbara Jea 20 Aug 1927-23 Dec 1990
Hackett
 Walter T. h/o Margaret M.; 1907-1996
Hager
 Frank L. 17 Oct 1925-13 Feb 1992
Hagood
 Grady L. h/o Cora C.; 1935-1997

Hale

Clifford G. h/o Cecile A.; 31 May 1945-20 Apr 1993

Nelson A. h/o Fay I.; 1923-1982

Hall

Charles Roberts 12 Jan 1929-1 Aug 1983

Halverson

Jacob Cecil 5 Mar 1988-22 Sept 1990

Hamm

James Christopher 12 Feb 1989-13 Feb 1989

Hancock

L.C. h/o Virginia; 1924-1989

Haney

James Olan 25 Jul 1925-19 Jul 1989

Hanley

Repa 5 Jul 1916-2 Oct 1984

William 31 May 1938-22 Apr 1989

Hansard

James J. 1920-1998

Hanson

Elizabeth G. w/o Harold T.; 1914-1993

Harold T. h/o Elizabeth G.; 1911-1994

Hardin

Thelma W. w/o Everett ; 1923-1984

Harley

James R. 17 Sept 1913-15 Dec 1995

Harmon

Howard B. 1952-1989

Harrell

Jack L. 1914-1985

Harrington

Alexander B. h/o Frances R.; 1910-1993

Harris

Allen G. h/o Lillian H.; 1901-1976

Kathleen 9 Jul 1926-18 Mar 1985

Lillian H. w/o Allen G.; 1903-1988

Harrison

Linda S. 4 May 1954-24 Jun 1998

Vera 1901-1993

Hartter

David E. 2 Nov 1961-30 Jan 1990

Harvey
    Margaret R. 1924-1996
Hatcher
    Henry G. h/o Willie B.; 1914-1994
Hawkins
    Corrine w/o Ernest F.; 1901-1988
    Emery E. h/o Nannie L.; 1901-1983
    Ernest F. h/o Corrine; 1900-1982
    Frank L 12 Apr 1934-11 Sept 1997
    J. Harold h/o Leila S.; 1921-1990
    Margaret w/o Ivey O.; 1937-1990
    Nannie L. w/o Emery E.; 1905-1983
Hawrey
    Margery E. w/o Robert S.; 1917-1994
    Robert S. h/o Margery E.; 1917-1995
Hayes
    Brenda M. 1946-1993
    Robert M. h/o Helen C.; 1929-1992
Heath
    Louise Dec 1928-May 1997
    Sydnor Laffitte 1906-1996
Hecht
    Loretta B. 1932-1997
Heinold
    Frieda w/o Paul; 1896-1986
    Herbert 1937-1988
Henderson
    Fannie J. w/o Henry I.; 1895-1988
    Henry I. h/o Fannie J.; 1890-1974
    Louise T. 1925-1992
Hendrix
    Rachel J. 26 Apr 1956-28 Apr 1983
Hensley
    B. Gene 4 Sept 1928-6 Dec 1987
Herpin
    Joseph E. h/o Lola R.; 1906-1989
    Lola R. w/o Joseph E.; 1910-1986
Herren
    Willie J. h/o Mary F.; 1916-1994
Hester
    Michael E. 22 Apr 1954-14 Feb 1991

Hickey
    Henry Hillman 22 Nov 1923-14 Sept 1981
Hicks
    Clyde Wesley 1911-1973
    Ralph W. h/o Betty W.; 16 May 1930-11 Mar 1997
Highnight
    Richard F. 1919-1978
Hill
    Alice I. 1931-1995
    Elbert R. 1963-1996
    J. Preston h/o Patricia D.; 1915-1994
    Patricia D. w/o J. Preston; 1927-1996
    Virginia L. w/o William M.; 1917-1994
Hills
    Angela Kay Sisk 6 Jun 1961- 21 Oct 1996
Hoch
    Donna R. 1903-1974
    Joseph 1888-1966
    Richard A. 1895-1976
Holbrook
    Clinton D. 1920-1986
    Estelle L. w/o Henry Edd; 1911-1996
    Henry Edd h/o Estelle L. 1922-1980
    John S. 24 Jul 1934-26 Apr 1986
Holcomb
    Comer h/o Mary E.; 1909-1997
Holcombe
    Cecil W. h/o Velma R.; 1905-1984
    John C. h/o Martha N.; 1939-1984
    Katie 1925-1998
    William E. h/o Alice W.; 1906-1990
Holder
    Madeline H. 1913-1996
Holifield
    Summer Dommica 20 Jul 1977-7 Jun 1997
Holland
    Henry W. 1913-1981
    Jerry 1936-1992
Hollis
    Charles A. 12 Feb 1956-6 Jun 1993

Holt
  Lloyd Elmo   19 Jul 1949-8 Aug 1983
Honea
  Jeffrey M.   1961-1989
  Marvin   1930-1983
Hook
  Albert C. h/o Louise F., f/o Alan & Kimberly; 1929-1997
Hope
  Joy B.   4 Jan 1928-30 Jun 1994
Horan
  Ralph R. h/o Harriette; 1916-1996
Hornsby
  Ruby B. w/o Samuel J.; 3 Jul 1913-24 May 1995
  Samuel J. h/o Ruby B.; 26 Apr 1908-11 Apr 1985
Hoskyn
  William R.   1936-1997
Howard
  Frank P.   7 Aug 1935-31 Oct 1980
  Madge C.   1905-1993
Huddleston
  Dearwood W. h/o Effie S.; 29 Aug 1895-12 Jan 1957
  Effie S. w/o Dearwood W.; 5 Jan 1896-16 Nov 1947
Hudgins
  Violet P. w/o William Lee; 1913-1989
  William Lee h/o Violet P.; 1909-1981
Huff
  John Lawrence   13 Dec 1926-24 Mar 1994
Hughes
  Mary J.   1923-1994
Hulsey
  Herman L. h/o Nettie E.   1915-1973
  Nettie E. w/o Herman L.; 1921-1984
Hunton
  Danny C.   1945-1977
Hurst
  Charlotte S..w/o Jack A.; 1935-1993
Hutton
  Ben R.   2 Dec 1928-15 Jun 1994
Ivy
  Joe Brown   23 May 1921-20 Feb 1994

Jabbour
   Jameel 1954-1992
Jackson
   Asa C. 1905-1989
   James Lewis h/o Alice M.; 20 Mar 1910-8 Aug 1992
James
   Elizabeth w/o Frank L.; 10 Aug 1923-20 Nov 1995
   Gladys K. w/o Harold W.; 1907-1995
   Harold W. h/o Gladys K.; 1903-1998
Jarrett
   Jacquelin Cobbs 1940-1976
   John Harley h/o Mariane M.; 1921-1986
   Kali Angel 30 Jul 1992-1 Aug 1992
Javo
   N. Michael h/o Deborah; 1957-1997
Jeffries
   Les A. 1953-1992
Jenkins
   Barbara J. 1932-1998
   Dorothy G. 20 Jul 1908-16 Oct 1992
   James I. 1932-1987
   James I. 25 Jan 1956-21 Mar 1989
Jerran
   Doris w/o Edward; 1907-1971
   Edward h/o Doris; 1907-1998
Jewell
   Harold G. h/o Evelyn A.; 1910-1995
Johns
   Patricia G. 1 Feb 1937-26 Jul 1993
Johnson
   Angela C. d/o Tanya T.; 1988-1989
   Florence A. w/o Billie R.; 1918-1989
   Gloria D. 6 Mar 1932-29 Jan 1983
   H. Elmer h/o Velma S.; 1904-1991
   J. Howard h/o M. Pearl; 23 Aug 1905-21 Jul 1964
   Johnny B. h/o Carolyn J.; 1937-1993
   Margaret Alicia d: 26 Mar 1985
   Maurice D. h/o Charlotte A.; 8 Dec 1933-13 Apr 1991
   M. Pearl w/o J. Howard; 29 Dec 1907-23 Sept 1979
   Neil h/o Nina R.; 1908-1980
   Nina R. w/o Neil; 1906-1995

Paul M. h/o Jettie C.; 1910-1986
Tanya T. m/o Angela C.; 1956-1989
Teresa Hagan 1952-1996
Velma S. w/o H. Elmer; 1909-1988
Jokl
Flake P. 23 Dec 1923-23 Nov 1987
Jones
Alice J. 24 Jun 1924-9 Oct 1994
Alvin Jackson 1935-1980
Charlie Jimmy 5 Nov 1931-13 Aug 1989
Mary E. 21 Jul 1898-28 Sept 1991
Theodore A. 20 Jun 1952-21 Oct 1991
William H. h/o M. Ruth; 1913-1985
Jordan
Edith 27 May 1923-6 Apr 1996
James B. 23 Mar 1923-17 Sept 1996
Jean w/o Donald E.; 1940-1999
Lewis 1952-1986
Joyner
Faye K. w/o Orbrie W.; 1919-1985
Kahl
Russell F. 6 Jan 1923-19 Jan 1993
Kane
Mary Fox 28 Feb 1913-1 Sept 1995
Kaplin
Sally 1923-1997
Karkella
Charlotte M. 1914-1992
Kato
Elizabeth 1909-1942
Kelley
Dorothy A. 1908-1994
Elder W.S. h/o Velma J.; 1909-1992
Velma J. w/o Elder W.S.; 1912-1995
Kelly
Bessie Yeargin w/o Prue Harvey; 3 Oct 1909-21 Apr 1981
Ronald 1935-1979
Kendall
M. Tain h/o Idell P.; 1904-1982
Kennedy
Fred lee 3 Apr 1926-19 Nov 1986

Lee R. 1914-1995
Mark 5 Mar 1977-3 Feb 1998
Kenny
  Lavina S. 1911-1985
Kent
  Ollie F. h/o Mary M.; 1914-1988
  Sarah C. w/o Larry F.; 1943-1998
Kerr
  Gene J. 1933-1994
Kilgore
  Joseph B. h/o Delores F.; 28 Feb 1925-2 Oct 1997
Kimbrell
  C.W. h/o Nettierene; 1930-1987
King
  Henrietta 1914-1997
Kingsolver
  John D. 19 Jun 1945-6 Mar 1997
Kirby
  Clarence 1923-1998
  Everett D. h/o Geraldine; 1917-1992
  Jane 1932-1988
  Lawrence R. 27 Jul 1932-18 Dec 1992
Kirkland
  Albert S.M. h/o Eva Elizabeth; 1919-1984
Kirkwood
  Mikeal Shirley 1969-1985
Kiser
  Herbert J.W. h/o Betty S.; 1928-1990
Klein
  Robert A. 1936-1991
Koenig
  Herman A. 1907-1979
Korenfeld
  Irina 1956-1998
Kossman
  David M. 15 May 1943-10 Dec 1997
Krakovski
  Leonid Issac 1934-1995
Kramer
  Charles M. 4 Jan 1911-7 Mar 1988
  Richard M. 1926-1996

Kreis
    Foster C.; h/o Oneta D.; 1913-1987
    Oneta D. w/o Foster C.; 1923-1990
Kshyna
    Michael h/o Helen; 1913-1986
Kuhn
    Helen A. w/o Matt W.; 1923-1994
Kyper
    Stanley M. 1943-1990
Lafon
    Gilbert h/o Harriet Thistlewood; 1915-1998
Lamalz
    Mary 1910-1986
Lamb
    Charles H. h/o Mary B. 1913-1978
    Myrtle C. w/o Robert S.; 1908-1977
    Robert S. h/o Myrtle C.; 1905- 1995
    R. Stanley h/o Laverne D.; 1939-1998
Lamond
    Yvonne E. 1922-1987
Lance
    Patricia A. w/o Lamar F.; 1940-1984
    William E. 1913-1977
Lane
    Audrey 1928-1996
    J. Gid h/o Lois F.; 1898-1977
    Lois F. w/o J. Gid; 1903-1995
Langley
    Timothy Rowe 14 Jan 1919-17 Sept 1979
Lanier
    James Jerry 20 Feb 1943-21 Mar 1991
Lauth
    Barbara Jean 1941-1988
    Elizabeth E. 1924-1997
    Noble D. 1914-1989
Lawes
    William D. 1920-1990
Lawson
    Joseph 1925-1994
    William E. 1910-1987
Laycok

John F. 1921-1990
Leake
Frank K. h/o Mildred M.; 1921-1989
Mildred M. w/o Frank K.; 1917-1989
Ledford
Wayne h/o Dot M.; 1938-1970
Lee
Jong Pal h/o Soon Nam 1943-1994
Leech
Janice B. w/o Kenneth R.; 1935-1977
Leighton
Paul S. 1961-1985
Lein
David Ray 8 Apr 1961- 18 Nov 1994
Levergood
James L. 4 Feb 1943-8 Jul 1995
Levine
Elizabeth M. w/o Bertram; 1916-1998
Lewis
Evie F. w/o William F.; 1927-1987
Laura w/o James Glenn Dudley; 1916-1994
Peggy Lee 1948-1987
William F. h/o Evie F.; 1923-1993
Liao
Charles T. W. 1915-1983
Lieberman
William 1940-1994
Lietch
Allen Eugene h/o Emily M.;; 8 Jan 1933-19 Oct 1988
Limbeck
Janice P. w/o Merle W.; 28 Aug 1923-2 Feb 1987
Merle W. h/o Janice P.; 29 May 1922- 26 Nov 1996
Lingerfelt
Perry Edward 1929-1989
Lingo
Raymond G. h/o Margie N.; 1937-1990
Linke
Florence G. w/o Harold F.; 1920-1997
Harold F. h/o Florence G.; 1914-1983
Lipsey
Wayne D. 17 Nov 1939-15 Oct 1992

Liston
  Demecia R. 1953-1992
Little
  Eloise w/o Leroy 1938-1999
Locke
  Cora M. w/o Fred R.; 1917-1982
  Fred R. h/o Cora M.; 1908-1966
Lockridge
  R.L. 1923-1998
Loner
  John 1902-1959
  Odessa M. 1920-1995
Long
  Joel R. h/o Ollie M.; 1909-1982
  Ollie M. w/o Joel R.; 1912-1978
  Willie H. h/o Inez L.; 1916-1979
Lopez
  Lourdes D. w/o Jose I.; 1926-1992
Lord
  Carrie F. 1909-1987
  Henry C. h/o Betty E.; 1931-1992
Loudermilk
  Michael h/o Dorothy V.; 1912-1979
Lowe
  Janet Lee 1953-1981
Lowry
  Randall J. h/o Dorothy F.; 1923-1970
Lucas
  James W. h/o Evelyn T.; 6 Jan 1913- 5 Jan 1995
Luke
  Vivian Sherer 30 Nov 1955-22 Aug 1996
Lummus
  John Wesley h/o Lillie Mae C.; 1898-1987
  Lillie Mae C. w/o John Wesley; 1900-1984
Lynn
  James William 1909-1990
Lyon
  Judson B. h/o Mae E.; 1912-1995
  Mae E. w/o Judson B.; 1910-1992
Lyons
  Algernon 3 Nov 1933-18 Jun 1995

Mabry
    Doyle M. h/o Sarah V.; 1931-1981
MaClellan
    Sylvia R. 13 Aug 1924-9 Feb 1996
Macrae
    Lawrence S. 1914-1993
Madden
    Annetta J. 1938-1993
Maggiore
    Rose 26 May 1908-30 Nov 1996
Mahoney
    Lucy Cecilia 1954-1994
Major
    Tony 13 Jul 1959-12 Jul 1978
Mallory
    Jason 1974-1996
Malone
    Bradley 1990-1992
Manning
    Eileen 1940-1999
    Margaret E. w/o John H.; 1924-1998
Mansell
    J. Paul h/o Ouida H.; 1913-1990
Manus
    Wesley h/o Geraldine; 1935-1993
March
    Lewis h/o Mary; 1914-1999
    Mary w/o Lewis; 1917-1993
Markham
    Peggy 1933-1982
Marks
    Robert Harold 1914-1981
Marshall
    Roxanna Leigh 1970-1988
Martin
    Charles Anthony 16 Feb 1960-17 Feb 1960
    Charles E. h/o Betty J.; 1935-1982
    Earl S. 6 Apr 1928-18 Jan 1992
    Ellie J. w/o James S.; 1908-1973
    Gordon h/o Pearl B.; 1909-1988
    James S. h/o Ellie J.; 1913-1978

Kitty L. w/o Abbie O.; 1910-1998
Myrtis 24 May 1914-17 Aug 1914
Paul K. 1936-1991
Pearl B. w/o Gordon; 1915-1991
Willie Mae 1923-1996
Mason
Albert C. h/o Nadine H.; 1910-1992
Nadine H. w/o Albert C.; 1909-1990
T. Jerry 21 Dec 1957-14 Jun 1993
Mastrangelo
Arnold h/o Angela; 9 Mar 1930- 16 Nov 1997
Nunzia 1909-1996
Matiz
Andrez Antonio 1923-1997
Mattes
Adolph h/o Theresia; 1906-1990
Theresia w/o Adolph; 1909-1994
Matthews
Jason H. h/o Pauline M.; 1894-1983
Pauline M. w/o Jason H.; 1902-1985
Mauney
Arthur L. h/o Colee; 1928-1991
Maxwell
Edgar F. h/o Mary Nell; 1920-1983
McArthur
Catherine I. 10 Aug 1918-19 Oct 1998
John B. h/o Margaret Bobo; 10 Jul 1921-27 Feb 1985
McAuley
W.H. 1922-1986
McCart
Edna Winn 1920-1995
McClure
Emma D. 1910-1998
McConnell
Mildrew W. 1918-1997
McCowan
Ruby F. 1909-1995
McCracken
Gerald A. 1907-1985
Lawrence 1939-1984

McDade
Mark R. 1959-1991
McDonald
Emmett B. h/o Lena Mai; 1885-1973
Lena Mai w/o Emmett B.; 1888-1980
McDonaugh
Charlotte H. w/o John H.; 1932-1989
Joseph 1933-1995
McFarland
Marcus D. 1930-1987
McGarity
Charles H. 1932-1991
McGilvary
Barbara Dollery 13 Aug 1956-5 Apr 1982
Michael A. 1 Feb 1945-5 Apr 1982
McGinnis
Annis N. w/o Hubert W.; 1908-1977
Hubert W. h/o Annis N.; 1908-1981
Marvin W. h/o Betty F.; 1929-1986
McHenry
Terrence J. 1954-1995
McKenna
Harry James 31 Aug 1931-10 Mar 1992
McKinney
Vicki Ruff 1936-1987
McKinstry
Dawn C. 15 Mar 1964-12 Mar 1999
McMartin
Robert W. 1923-1993
McMullen
Ray A. 1915-1983
McNaughton
Annie N. 1903-1989
McNeely
Cinda C. 14 Jul 1958-22 Sept 1990
Meacham
Claude M. h/o Ruth L.; 1907-1992
Ruth L. w/o Claude M.; 1914-1984
Metropoulos
George S. h/o Krystalia P.; 1917-1989

Michael
  Thelma R. 17 Oct 1931-8 Oct 1996
Mielke
  Jeanne D. 1914-1997
Mikola
  Robert B. h/o Allene W.; 1927-1986
Miller
  Helen H. w/o Stuart T.; 1914-1991
  Stuart T. h/o Helen H.; 1915-1998
  William F. h/o Viola C.; 1891-1978
Milsap
  Mary E. w/o Roy V.; 1934-1988
Miner
  Edna Schafer 1891-1989
Mitchell
  Aaron W. h/o Lura Mae; 1919-1997
  Lura Mae w/o Aaron W.; 1923-1992
Mitchler
  Lillian Krumm 1898-1994
Mitry
  Cleo 1911-1996
Mobbs
  Euclid L. 8 May 1920-30 Oct 1993
Moebius
  Alma F. w/o John W.; 1913-1997
Mohr
  Frederick J. 4 Apr 1916-16 Jan 1991
Monroe
  Joan J. w/o Donald A.; 1936-1992
  Shirley R. h/o Lillian B.; 1927-1994
  Walter Ivan h/o Kathleen M.; 21 Apr 1923-26 Dec 1993
Montesi
  Jacqueline Mary 1939-1994
Montgomery
  Barbara M. 1940-1997
Moon
  James F. 1956-1971
  John W. 25 Oct 1919-6 Mar 1995
Moore
  Euell R. h/o Betty ; 1928-1999
  Jean Shirley d/o Euell R. and Betty; 1946-1946

Riley W. 1917-1992
Morace
    Marie R. 23 Oct 1917-17 July 1995
Morgan
    Joe C. h/o Maggie L.; 1917-1983
    John W. 1912-1994
    Richard H. 1949-1993
Morgillo
    Pietro h/o Maria; 1931-1998
Morris
    David L. 12 Jul 1953-17 Nov 1998
    Dessie B. w/o Oliver B.; 1913-1985
    Elijah D. 30 Dec 1909-14 Oct 1993
    Flora Lee 5 Jun 1915-18 Nov 1981
    Oliver B. h/o Dessie B.; 1909-1991
    Robert W. 1969-1996
Moss
    Crawford L. h/o Lucile B.; 1914-1971
    Gary Paul 28 Apr 1947-26 Jan 1998
    Grace N. w/o Trammell T.; 1916-1972
    Kendra Lynn 28 Feb 1975-5 Mar 1975
    Paul J. 9 Apr 1917- 24 Oct 1991
    Trammell T. h/o Grace N.; 1915-1992
    Virginia Leigh 13 Feb 1985-13 Dec 1985
Mozley
    Evelyn M. w/o William G.; 1905-1998
Mueller
    Wayne L. 1941-1994
Myott
    Erme w/o Frances E.; 1897-1968
    Frances E. h/o Erme B.; 1897-1990
Natale
    Nicholas A. h/o Joyce E.; 1913-1985
Neese
    Forrest 1923-1991
Nelson
    Gus H. h/o Vanira .; 1913-1979
    Vanira w/o Gus H.; 1911-1997
Nestor
    Adeline A. 1928-1995

Neumann
 William John h/o Martha Sewell; 8 Oct 1923-17 May 1989
Newton
 Frances B. w/o Amos J.; 1929-1983
Nicholes
 David T. h/o Genevieve J.; 1909-1982
 Genevieve J. w/o David T.; 1909-1980
Nichols
 Claude E. h/o Peggy D.; 1917-1989
 Peggy D. w/o Claude E.; 1922-1997
Nicholson
 John F. h/o Loretta C.; 1906-1991
 Loretta C.; w/o John F.; 1916-1998
Nicoletti
 Carl Michael 1965-1988
Nilsson
 Birdeen 1887-1971
Nix
 Marie L. w/o Roy W.; 1923-1992
 Preston S. 30 May 1939-5 Aug 1984
 Roy W. h/o Marie L.; 1917-1993
Nixon
 Alvin D. h/o Nita Kell; 1916-1994
 Nita Kell w/o Alvin D.; 1927-1990
Norris
 Lillian w/o Robert T.; 1925-1984
Nunnally
 James W. 28 Nov 1929-9 Dec 1990
O'Brien
 Michelle Ann 27 May 1959-21 Sept 1994
 Tracy A. 6 Apr 1965-6 Aug 1998
O'Bryant
 Ricky H. 25 Jan 1956-27 Jul 1973
Oemke
 Terrance Arthur 1945-1990
Ogletree
 Brian Mitchell 15 Jun 1975-16 Jun 1975
Ohara
 Joanne w/o Warren J.; 1926-1996
 Warren J. h/o Joanne; 1925-1988

Oliver
Beatrice E. 1936-1993
Elbert W. h/o Maggie L.; 1910-1979
Maggie L. w/o Elbert W.; 1914-1989
R.L. 1944-1992
Orme
Eva H. 1912-1982
Ornduff
Anna J. 25 Sept 1949-10 Nov 1993
O'Neil
Charles W. 1907-1983
Sarah Ellen 1980-1996
Owens
John Burgess 15 Aug 1930-2 Sept 1991
Padgett
Thurston Russell h/o Beatrice M.; 14 Mar 1923-15 Aug 1997
Pagan
G. Gregory 29 Jul 1956-4 Jan 1997
Painter
Lavonia B. 1932-1983
Papineau
George C. 10 Aug 1906-29 Mar 1972
John Robert 3 May 1958-7 May 1977
Paris
Charles L. h/o Evelyn W.; 1922-1988
C. Leland h/o Lera C.; 1893-1977
Elizabeth Wright 15 Jun 1914-7 Feb 1979
Lera C. w/o C. Leland; 1894-1957
Lewie Melford 26 Jul 1901-24 Feb 1976
Park
Charles C. h/o Youn A.; 1935-1993
Parker
Ellis 1924-1995
Gertrude 14 Mar 1907- 17 Nov 1984
William 12 Jan 1924-6 Oct 1998
Pastorelli
Alfred 1920-1998
Patchell
David Wayne 12 Apr 1968-18 Feb 1981
Patterson
Clyde R. 20 Mar 1936-16 Feb 1997

M. Willene 9 Jul 1937-1 Nov 1973
Raymond C. 1935-1986
Paulk
    Aloyse 1902-1997
    George Paul 1919-1970
    Gregory Brent 1948-1994
Payne
    Allene w/o N.C.; 1915-1993
    Calvin E. h/o Pauline P.; 1938-1994
    N.C. h/o Allene; 1913-1996
Peet
    Penelope Ann 1953-1977
Pendley
    Lewis E. h/o Lucy P.; 1909-1986
Penland
    Marion R. 1925-1995
Peron
    A. Richard 27 Jan 1943-17 Jan 1987
Perry
    James E. h/o Betty S.; 1963-1985
Petterson
    Harold N. h/o Muriel A.; 1920-1997
    Muriel A. w/o Harold N.; 1916-1986
Pettit
    R.L. h/o Barbara I.; 1921-1992
Pfister
    Anita J. w/o William J.; 1931-1992
Phillips
    Cecile S. w/o Eugene A. 1907-1998
    Eugene A. h/o Cecile S.; 1894-1981
    George M. h/o Mayme H.; 1911-1985
    Nettie L. w/o Paul T.; 1903-1975
    Paul T. h/o Nettie L.; 1903-1979
    Roy 3 Feb 1931-8 Mar 1992
    Shirley 1940-1999
Phipps
    Peggy B. 1907-1971
    Walter P. 1905-1986
Pinto
    Oscar Matiz 1957-1990

Planchard
　　Charles　29 May 1975-2 Mar 1992
Polo
　　Kathryn E.　1922-1989
Polyne
　　Lemoine　1933-1997
Ponder
　　Martha W.　w/o Herman W.;　1926-1996
Port
　　Robert Ray　h/o Joan D.;　10 May 1943-28 Nov 1993
Porter
　　Alice M.　10 Mar 1916-6 Jul 1993
　　Lessie　9 Jul 1910-15 Aug 1981
　　Leslie F.　22 Mar 1896-15 Sept 1992
Poss
　　Elizabeth S.　w/o John H.;　1903-1985
　　Robert Lee　16 Apr 1925-26 Dec 1980
　　William　31 Jan 1940-14 Jun 1981
Powell
　　Betty Jane　1922-1994
　　James W.　h/o Lillie M.;　1904-1979
　　J. Carter h/o Gladys W.;　1902-1993
　　John W.　1915-1992
　　Lillie M.　w/o James W.;　1904-1975
Power
　　Cephus H.　h/o Nellie M.;　1922-1987
　　Nellie M.　w/o Cephus H.;　1921-1969
Preng
　　Ann　w/o Matthew C.;　1917-1989
Prescot
　　William Scott　1969-1991
Pressley
　　Mildred R.　w/o Robert C.;　1915-1994
　　Robert C.　h/o Mildred R.;　1914-1974
Pritchett
　　Robert Melvin h/o Ethel Rucelle;　1935-1996
Probst
　　Raymond H.　1929-1992
Prouty
　　James 1959-1974

Puckett
    Ruby M.   1901-1992
    William M. 1907-1976
Purcell
    Matthie L. h/o Veri I.; 1921-1998
Quam
    Hi Dai 1910-1992
Quay
    William H. 1922-1991
Quigg
    Agnes 1908-1999
Quinn
    Bencil L. h/o Loretta; 1934-1988
    Bettie 1917-1991
Ramsey
    Sally w/o Arlin P.; 1927-1994
Ray
    Annie L.; w/o Stephen; 1914-1995
    Stephen h/o Annie L.; 1915-1980
    Wesley Charles 1 Dec 1978-20 Jan 1982
Rayfield
    Frances H. 1928-1993
Reece
    Becky L. w/o Joe T.; 1935-1997
    Clifford L. h/o Cleo M.; 1910-1978
    Joe T. h/o Becky L.; 1934-1998
    Marvin W. h/o Barbara D.; 1941-1986
    Wade O. h/o Ella Mae; 1898-1988
Reed
    G. 1904-1990
    Pauline 1909-1998
Reese
    Hoyt F. h/o Nan M.; 1927-1981
Reeve
    Hubert h/o Mildred B.; 1913-1988
    Mildred B. w/o Hubert; 1922-1997
Rehehan
    Doris w/o George Gorden; 6 Dec 1925-21 Feb 1993
    George Gorden h/o Doris; 16 Dec 1918-11 May 1992
Resse
    Edward 1920-1998

Reyes
   Dolores C. w/o John J.; 1941-1989
   John J. h/o Dolores C.; 1934-1997
Reynolds
   Gary 29 Jun 1964-30 Jul 1997
Reyovd
   Mary C. 1931-1995
Rheingrover
   Cary W. 11 Dec 1941-21 May 1994
Rhodes
   John Michael h/o Brenda Ward; 1947-1998
Rice
   Guy h/o Ruth R.; 1904-1987
   Ruth R. w/o Guy 1913-1976
   Tennisee 23 Jan 1912-12 Jan 1981
Richards
   Betty Jo w/o John R.; 1929-1994
   Everett R. h/o Mytrice M.; 19 Apr 1919-12 Mar 1996
   John R. h/o Betty Jo; 1922-1989
   John W. h/o Margie P.; 1912-1997
Richardson
   Gladys S. 1923-1999
   Martha M. 1898-1993
Richmond
   Pauline H. 28 Jan 1925-27 Mar 1994
Riggins
   John M. 1964-1988
   Pat C. w/o John H.; 1938-1991
Ring
   Peggy 1950-1997
Roberts
   Lester E. 1915-1988
   Samuel Jack 10 Sept 1912-19 Aug 1967
Robertson
   Lori L. 15 Feb 1975-4 Jul 1996
   Ruth Fortner 1917-1994
Robinson
   Alma Adair 1905-1980
   Grace S. 1913-1985
Rockoff
   Herman Samuel 4 Sept 1920-23 Mar 1994

Roe
Robert 23 Jun 1916-12 Jul 1987
Rogers
Faye N. 1955-1991
Francesca Elizabeth 11 May 1986-20 Apr 1989
Mary E. w/o William E.; 13 Sept 1914-10 Aug 1994
Warren G. 1985-1995
Rolling
Clyde V. 1913-1997
Roman
Octavian 1914-1997
Roper
Elbert R. h/o Rosie C.; 1909-1979
Rose
Lucille W. 1914-1996
Ross
Bruce Gray h/o Mary L.; 5 Feb 1930-7 Aug 1997
Rowe
O'Neal R. h/o Helen J.; 1927-1991
Rowland
Van Gale h/o Phyllis Campbell; 1923-1993
Ruff
Lucille Glisson 1911-1997
Russell
Rennie F. 14 Nov 1901-20 Aug 1981
Ryan
Adela 16 Dec 1908-29 Jul 1984
Evelyn M. 1916-1986
Michael Patrick 1982-1992
Sabbach
George T. 15 Jan 1905-11 Apr 1994
Sams
Evelyn Ruth w/o Lee Roy; 1918-1988
Lee Roy h/o Evelyn Ruth 1912-1977
Oscar A. h/o Millie E.; 1927-1998
Sanderlin
Charles Wesley 1927-1994
Sanders
Vergie Harper Sisk 21 Jan 1917-24 Apr 1976
Saunders
George J. 19 Feb 1913-22 Aug 1922

Sayre
  Charles h/o Virginia; 23 Feb 1919-24 Nov 1994
Scheu
  Christopher F. 1960-1985
  Fawn Lee 1959-1982
  Meryl W. 1927-1982
Schilin
  Marcia Lynn 1964-1988
Schmid
  Alexandra S. 1967-1985
Schmitt
  Amanda Jane w/o Gerald E; 1921-1997
  Gerald E. h/o Amanda Jane; 1912-1998
  Stella Ann w/o Walter H.; 1928-1997
  Walter H. h/o Stella Ann; 1930-1994
Schneider
  Mildred K. w/o William F.; 1917-1979
  Norman V. 1915-1982
  William F. h/o Mildred K.; 1914-1987
Schnitzler
  Edith M. w/o William F.; 1908-1996
  William F. h/o Edith M.; 1904-1983
Scholpp
  Harry R. 1934-1990
Seawright
  Buford G. h/o Thelma H.; 1918-1972
  Thelma H. w/o Buford G.; 1933-1972
Sedor
  Susan Thomas 22 Feb 1956-22 Nov 1991
Segnitz
  Joan w/o William H.; 1938-1992
  William H. h/o Joan; 1936-1998
Sewell
  Ernest A. h/o Myrtle L.; 7 Dec 1894- 1 Nov 1958
  Myrtle L. w/o Ernest A.; 16 Jul 1893-29 Jun 1988
  W. Guy h/o Clyda M.; 1907-1988
Shanley
  Bernice B. w/o Wallace D.; 1919-1986
  Wallace D. h/o Bernice B.; 1920-1998
Sharpe
  Mary C. 1904-1995

Shea
　Robert P. 8 Nov 1958-19 Feb 1999
Sheats
　Garland H. h/o Elizabeth C.; 1905-1980
Sherman
　Barbara J. 1927-1981
Shirley
　Kenneth L. 30 Jul 1951-16 Feb 1993
　Riley F. h/o Louise H.; 1919-1979
Shou
　James Ying 1969-1998
Sierman
　William Thane h/o Shirley Lee; 1918-1996
Silvers
　Ben F. h/o Mattie L.; 1913-1986
　Earvin C. h/o Lucy N.; 1905-1994
　Lucy N. w/o Earvin C.; 1913-1996
Skeen
　William Ross 1941-1989
Skrip
　Richard J. 1937-1998
Slade
　Doris W. 1930-1998
Small
　Effie 1909-1996
Smallwood
　Carlton E. 1926-1996
Smith
　Archie C. 24 Jul 1927-6 Mar 1997
　Jack T. h/o Mildred A.; 1919-1984
　Mary Ann 22 Apr 1960-14 Oct 1995
　Ned R. h/o Jane I.; 1926-1998
　Willie E. h/o Lilian B.; 1925-1998
Snipes
　Floyd 1910-1981
　Virginia J. 1923-1999
Snyder
　John A. 14 Dec 1934-29 Aug 1998
　Sylvia M. 1936-1992
Sommers
　Dorothy E. 1918-1985

Son
    Younsu h/o Sukja 1943-1997
Soncer
    Jane 6 Apr 1936-26 Jun 1994
Sosebee
    Beulah w/o Clifford Burke; 1907-1997
    Clifford Burke h/o Beulah; 1903-1988
Spiegel
    John h/o Juliet F.; 1905-1995
    Juliet F. w/o John; 1905-1994
Spieler
    David 11 Jan 1948-18 Dec 1995
Squires
    Frank L. 1892-1988
Stair
    Donald F. h/o Carol N.; 1923-1986
Standridge
    Hubert E. h/o Wyhell S.; 1927-1997
    Joshua L. 18 Apr 1984-26 Nov 1987
Stephens
    Bertie 1910-1998
Stephenson
    James J. 1913-1979
Stevens
    Ann R. w/o Robert C.; 1920-1993
    James A. 3 Sept 1959-21 Dec 1995
Stewart
    Cora L. w/o S.B.; 1898-1991
    Elizabeth E. 9 Mar 1891-5 Dec 1975
    Frank E. h/o Ida C.; 1906-1984
    Lloyd G. h/o Laura P.; 1908-1981
    May B. 5 Feb 1890-9 Jan 1969
    S.B. h/o Cora L.; 1898-1978
St John
    Harold W. 1902-1997
Stovall
    Lana 26 Feb 1954-26 Nov 1998
Stover
    Phillip   13 May 1943-13 Nov 1994
    Thurman 1915-1982

Stowe
Everett L. 1925-1986
Strabel
Thomas H. 1940-1996
Strickland
D. Chandler h/o Nola B.; 1914-1975
George H. h/o Lorine M.; 1907-1974
Hilton G. h/o Willene H.; 1929-1980
Lorine M. w/o George H.; 1908-1993
Stromquist
George M. 1928-1991
Stroup
Elizabeth Wood 1918-1984
Stuart
William F. 1922-1989
Sulken
Harry W. 1900-1991
Margarett A. 1912-1998
Sullivan
Charles W. h/o Shirley D.; 12 Oct 1934-20 Nov 1980
Jewel M. 1903-1976
Lucile R. 1904-1979
Surts
Brian C. 10 Sept 1951-30 Nov 1995
Sutherland
James Curtis h/o Juanell Davis; 1934-1993
Sutton
Christina Marie 28 Mar 1975-19 Jun 1995
Swann
William M. 7 eb 1937-27 Sept 1996
Sweeney
Bernard E. 16 Jul 1924-12 Jul 1996
Leo J. h/o Betty J.; 1922-1997
Taylor
Matthew V. 5 Dec 1941-13 Dec 1976
Thelma 9 Sept 1911-31 Jan 1994
William Alexander 8 Sept 1990-25 Dec 1996
Tennyson
Donall Lee 1937-1983
Thaxton
H. Dean h/o Grace S.; 30 Oct 1923 22 Mar 1995

Therrel
  M.D. 1898-1975
Thomas
  Clebera M. w/o Jackson E.; 1935-1993
  Jackson E. h/o Clebera M.; 1932-1989
  Otho F. h/o Sallie E.; 1905-1984
  Ovalyne H. w/o William H.; 1923-1993
  Sallie E. w/o Otho F.; 1905-1991
Thomoff
  Jerry A. 24 Dec 1950-23 Aug 1997
Thompson
  Charles M. h/o Mildred S.; 1908-1992
  James Henry 10 Jan 1931-1 May 1993
  Jordon 23 Mar 1990-23 Mar 1990
  Lewis J. h/o Margaret D.; 1924-1996
  Lucille M. 20 Jul 1906-2 Jan 1987
  Robert Alden 1908-1992
Thorton
  Mildred C. w/o Winfred L.; 1897-1988
  Winfred L. h/o Mildred C.; 1897-1983
Todd
  J.Elmer 1900-1963
Tomassi
  Adam 1908-1984
Tomlinson
  Robert H. h/o Jane W.; 1931-1990
Tormey
  Peggy w/o Bob; 1947-1977
Toth
  Michael 29 Sept 1914-14 Oct 1998
Trachio
  Nicholas Anthony 7 Oct 1998-8 Oct 1998
Tracy
  Patricia Nickles 1962-1988
Tribble
  Joe C. 1916-1975
Turner
  James Nex h/o Mary Louise; 1931-1993
  Joseph A. h/o Ludie A; 1897-1991
  Joseph D. h/o Judy T.; 1923-1988
  Judy T. w/o Joseph D.; 1922-1984

Ludie A. w/o Joseph A.; 1902-1973
Twitty
  Frances J. 22 Mar 1926-5 Sept 1996
Tyherow
  Joe Ann 1932-1991
Tzortzis
  Konstantina K. 9 Mar 1911-19 Oct 1998
Upshaw
  Mildred B. w/o Thomas R.; 1929-1998
  Thomas R. h/o Mildred B.; 1929-1998
Upton
  Eugene h/o Violet 1905-1989
Vacca
  Charles Porter 1928-1998
Vam
  Cynthia Marie 1961-1987
Vann
  Annie Elizabeth 1918-1966
  Henry Sellie 1914-1966
Varian
  Barbara S. 1935-1992
Vaszkis
  Stephen 2 Sept 1901-8 May 1996
Vaughn
  Mozell Corbin 1907-1994
Vecchione
  Michael h/o Naomi; 1925-1989
Vereen
  Joseph M. 1938-1986
Vernoy
  Brian K. 27 Sept 1966-18 Aug 1985
  William D. h/o Bobbie D.; 1943-1991
Vicasu
  Philip J. 1923-1987
Vickery
  Faye W. 1936-1982
Wagner
  Todd 11 Aug 1970-26 Jun 1993
Waits
  Robert B. h/o Mary F.; 1919-1986

Waldrop
>
Jack L. h/o Louise K.; 1931-1996

Walker
>
Brenda S. w/o Larry A.; 1947-1982
Brian K. 7 Jul 1977-9 Sept 1981
Carl B. h/o Bertie V.; 1907-1986
Charlotte w/o Paul; 1931-1995
Edith E. w/o John H.; 1910-1995
Jimmy C. 11 Aug 1942-25 Feb 1985
John H. h/o Edith E.; 1905-1994
J. Timothy 1965-1985

Wall
>
James H. h/o Laura J.; 1929-1973

Wallace
>
Edith H. w/o Glenn G.; 1905-1990
Glenn G. h/o Edith H.; 1905-1977

Wallis
>
Bertha A. w/o Clayborn J.; 1911-1997
Bobby Eugene 1933-1983
Clayborn J. h/o Bertha A.; 1911-1997

Walsh
>
Jennifer Gwen 11 Feb 1979-9 Feb 1986

Walter
>
Robert Wade 1969-1992

Wand
>
Jennifer 1982-1982

Wann
>
Lela M. w/o Roy Lyndon; 1921-1990
Roy Lyndon h/o Lela M.; 22 Oct 1917-22 Mar 1993

Ward
>
William T. 2 Sept 1934-18 Nov 1993

Waterman
>
Constance 4 Apr 1932-1 Dec 1981

Waters
>
Helen C. w/o Ronald B.; 1923-1991
Ronald B. h/o Helen C.; 1919-1992

Weaver
>
C. Norman h/o Sarah C.; 1932-1982

Webb
>
Bessie B. 1906-1987
Connie Duchess 14 Jan 1964-17 Jan 1964

Mattie S. 1908-1984
Rennie E. 1903-1988
Welch
James L. h/o Jean D.; 17 May 1930-19 May 1998
Weldon
James T. 1908-1981
Wells
Jonathan Murray 9 Sept 1956-27 Jul 1986
West
Dorothy E. w/o Jesse J.; 16 Aug 1922-27 Apr 1993
Jesse J. h/o Dorothy E.; 11 Nov 1920-24 Oct 1997
William 1948-1996
William L. 17 Oct 1939-8 Mar 1995
Wheeler
Inez H. w/o James T.; 1924-1991
James T. h/o Inez H.; 1920-1994
White
Elizabeth 14 Sept 1891-4 Sept 1969
Evan Taylor 14 Feb 1990-15 Feb 1992
Gary Bruce 1951-1989
Whitmire
Iris 1 Jul 1947-5 May 1994
Whitmore
David 1923-1984
Wicks
Ronald 11 Aug 1939-10 Jan 1993
Wilchoiu
Pamela S. w/ Timothy R.; 1854-1993
Wiley
Bobby M. 1929-1986
Ed J. h/o Lou S.; 6 Aug 1922-7 Sept 1989
J. Edwin 1923-1994
Wilk
Frances 17 Aug 1928-3 Mar 1991
Wilkinson
Carlton D. h/o Mary E.; 1923-1993
Williams
Bertha Adair 1898-1982
David Lee 7 Jan 1950-29 Sept 1985
Gundy 19 Jun 1941- 15 Jun 1998
James S. h/o Mabelle M.; 1902-1987

Kelly R. 1967-1986
Mabelle M. w/o James S.; 1909-1998
Richard F. 1935-1988
Shirley M. w/o Douglas F.; 1928-1997
Wilson
Daniel J. 1897-1969
Janet O. 1913-1991
Lary P. 1892-1975
Robert C. h/o Loy L.; 1908-1983
Winstead
William K. 1917-1995
Winters
Joseph R. 1893-1961
Nell L. 1906-1983
Wirtz
Cynthia A. 6 Aug 1940-27 Oct 1994
Troy Lawrence 19 Jan 1963-13 Aug 1983
Wlodar
Larry M. 15 Sept 1950-14 Mar 1998
Wolak
Chelsea Paige 10 Feb 1990-21 Jun 1992
Wolfe
Mary M. 15 Aug 1902-23 Sept 1972
Woniaczek
Margarete w/o Alfred; 1911-1980
Wood
Gladys E. 1901-1972
Harry V. 25 Jul 1942-2 Aug 1976
Marie W. w/o Luther; 1910-1994
Roy E. 7 Jun 1909-11 Apr 1995
Wm. Everett h/o Martrelle M.; 1920-1979
Wm. Quincy 12 Mar 1913-16 May 1970
Woodson
Gratton C. 1890-1972
Woolf
Florence R. w/o Thomas J.; 1908-1998
Thomas J. h/o Florence R.; 1909-1993
Wright
Clayton M. 18 Aug 1952-22 Aug 1989
Hayden H. 1909-1992
John H. 1920-1994

Joseph H. 1907-1983
Randy A. 29 Mar 1956-24 Apr 1988
Robert W. 1926-1995
Wyatt
Arthur R. 4 Nov 1936-4 Oct 1983
Yi
Chong Yun 21 Mar 1946-30 Sept 1998
Yother
Dorothy Y. 1924-1998
Zauche
Sara K. 7 Sept 1961-23 Nov 1995
Zawko
Helen P. 1920-1993
Zerrener
Arthur h/o Mary A.; 1908-1984
Mary A. w/o Arthur; 1907-1985

ASHLEY, Kate 1 Robert 1
ATCHESON, Jesse 9
ATKINSON, Ora 9 Robert 9 Ruby 9
AUSTIN, Andy 126 G. Turner 126
AUTREY, Joe 55 Marsceanie 55
AUTRY, Dewey, 55 Meridethy 55
AWLINGS, Noona 9
AYERS, Emma 86 Neva 86
BACON, David 126
BAGGETT, Cyrell 9
BAGLEY, Elder 9 Sarah 9
BAGWELL, Ben 111 Carl 86 Delds 111 Ealston 9 Hewlett 86 Ida 111 J.E. 111 James 111 Jeffie 86 Lou 111 M.W. 111 Robert 111 Ruth 111 Stephen 111
BAILEY, A.L. 111 Alice 86 Cecil 77 Frances 86 Gene 126 Harry 77 Howard 126 James 77 Joseph 77 Lizzie 86 Lois 83 Mattie 126 Meek 77
BAILIFF, Alice 9 Gid 9 Harry 9
BAKER, Annie 1 Evelyn 1 Francis 1 George 126 L. Idean 112 L.W.E. 1 William 112
BALDWIN, Chester 101 Jessie 101 Sebern 101
BALL, Bascombe 9 Cora 9 Hazel 10 Howard 126 Lizzie 10 Martin 10 Namie 10 Otis 10 Sophia 10
BALLARD, Marvin
BALLEW, Charles 86 Elizabeth 116 R.M. 116 S.C. 116 Thomas 116
BANNISTER, George 10 Ivy 10 John 10 Lester 10 Maybelle 10
BARDIN, Charles 126
BARETT, Claude 86 Dewey 86 Myrtie 86 Sarah 86 Willard 86
BARKSHADT, William 126
BARLETT, Richard 127
BARNES, Dorcus 83 J. Jane 55 Nancy 10
BARNETT, Henry 127 Minnie 101 Randy 127 W. Cicero 101 William 127
BARRETT, Albert 101 Clarance 86 George 102 Howard 87 Ida 102 U. Lamar 55
BARRINGTON, Evely 1
BARRON, Christy 127 Riley 127 Ruth 127
BARTLEY, Ruth 127
BARWICK, Eugene 127
BASS, Alvin 10
BATES, Ada 116 Annie 116 Annis 10 Charlie 127 Daisy 116 Effie M. 127 Effie S. 127 Francis 116 George 116 George 102 Homer 10 J. K. 116 James 77, James 116, James W. 116 John 117 Lillie 117 Mattie 117 Minnie 117 Mrs J. K. 116 Nancy 77 Ruth 117 Sarah 117 Walter 117 William 127
BATTER, William 127
BAUM, Arthur 127
BAUMAN, Michael 127
BEAL, Elizabeth 10
BEALL, C.C. 1
BEAN, Christopher 127

BEARDEN, Lemuel 10 Sarah 102
BECKHAM, Mattie 127
BEEBOUT, Hugh 10 Kate 10 Lewis 10 Luther 10 Robert 10
BELL, Jennings 117 John 117Lola 127 Lula 177 Robert 127 Rosa 83
BELLING, Maye 127
BENCE, Richard 127
BENNETT, George 10 Hershel 127 Lois 10 Myrtle 127 Ray 87
William 127
BENNING, Karen 128
BENSON, Claude 56 Ida 56 James 56 Jeffie 56 Jerry 56 Naomi 56
Oscar 56 Tempie 56
BENTLEY, Curtis 128
BERNHARDT, Frances 10
BERRY, Charles 10 Chester 10 Henry 128 Mary 10 Roxie 102
BESS, Thomas 128
BETNER, Addie 1
BIBB, Lila 10
BIBIKAN, Setven 102
BIDDY, Carol 112
BIRCHALL, Walter 128
BIRD, Beverly 128 Charles 87 James 87 Marvin 87 Thomas 87
BIRDSONG, Grace 128 Guy 128
BISHOP, Carolyn 128 Cora 11 Horace 11 Ivalyne 128 Zola 11
BLACK, Margaret 128 Richard 128
BLACKSTON, Glenn 11 Mittie 11 William 11
BLACKWELL, Jesse 11 Lawton 83 Lawton G. 83 Lizzie 11 Maude 11
Virginia 83 Walter 11
BLAKE, Effat 56 Martha 128 Nonnie 56 W. Forrest 128 Wade 56
BLALOCK, Barbara 117 Bonnie 11 Eugen 117 Howell 117 James 11
James 117 Jerry 128 Maeoma 117
BLANKENSHIP, E. Erle 128
BLARR, Flora 128 Jesse 128
BLASSINGAME, Walter 128
BLOCKOWITZ, John 128
BLOOK, Claudie 11 Fred 11
BOBBITT, Jewell 11
BOBO, Frank 128 James 128 Sarah 128 Tom 128
BOGGS, Della 11 Mary 11
BOHANNON, David 129 Henry 129
BOOKER, B. Frank 77 Carl 11 Dalier 77 Frances 11 Hubert 77
Infant 77 Jane 112 Jason 112 Jaunita 11 Jennie 78 John 78 Nettie 78
Nolan 11 Robert 78 Ruth 129
BOTTOMS, Charles 129 Clara 11 Gussie 11 Paul 11 Zaida 11
BOUDREAU, Betty 129
BOVEN, Andrea 129
BOWDEN, Eugenia 11 William 11

BOWEN, D.P. 11 Lewis 11 Lydia 12 Mattie 87 Nancy 12 Rachel 87 Sarey 12 William 12 William 78
BOYD, Carl 129 Estelle 56 Jessie 129 Robert H. 129 Robert S. 129
BOYLAN, Claudia 129 Warren 129
BRACKETT, Elizabeth 87 J.A. 87 James 87
BRADBURY, Kay 129 Virginia 129
BRADFORD, Cooledge 129
BRADLEY, Arthur 129 Elizabeth 129 James 129
BRADY, Loyal 87 Ollie 87
BRANDEN, H.N. 129
BRANDENBURG, Harry 129
BRANNON, Carrie 129 Fannie 87 James 87 James 129 Ruth 87
BRANTLEY, Annie 12 Charles 129 James 12 Louie 12 Mildred 129 Quincy 12
BRANYON, Frances 102
BRASWELL, Bernice 129 James 129 Julia 12 Loy 130 S.S. 12
BRAZZEAL, Samuel 130
BREWER, Ella 130 G.W. 130
BREWTON, Bennie 87
BRICE, James 117
BRIDWELL, Jesse 102
BRIGGS, Aileen 130 Marion 130
BRIMER, Genie 12 Newton 12
BRINSTER, Ferdinand 130 Rose 130
BRITTON, Joseph 12 Willie 12
BROADWELL, Carrie 12 Hamelton 102 Harrison 12 James 12 Lavina 102 Leo 12 R. Hugh 12 Sarah 102 Spohrona 102 W.H. 102
BROCK, Earl 130 Frankie 87 Ignatius 12 Mary 12 Susan 12
BROODWELL, Fannie 87 Thad 87
BROOK, George 1 Jennifer 130
BROOKE, George 87 J.P. 87 Maude 87 Maude M. 87 Mildred 87
BROOKS, Charles 87 Charles 130 Harley 130 Pearl 1 Thomas 12 Wylene 1
BROWN, Annie 83 Barbara 102 Bertha 12 Catherine 102 Catherine 12 Charles 56 Clinton 78 Cowart 12 Donia 102 Emory 12 F. Lucille 56 George 12 Jannie 102 James 12 James 130 John 102 Katie M. 12 Katie T. 12 Lizzie 102 Mary 12 Mary L. 13 M. O. 78 R. B. 13 Samuel 13 Sarah 1 Shelia 130 Shirley 56 T. Larkin 12 Tammy 56 William 13
BROWNE, Frances 130
BROWNING, Phillip 130
BRUICE, Charles 117 Homer 117 Laura 117
BRUMBELOW, Charles 130 Effie D. 130 Effie O. 130 Eugene 56 Glen 130 Herbert 130 Iona 130 J. Will 130 Jimmy 56 Joe 130 Margaret 130 Maude 130 Oliver 130 Ora 130 Reps 130 Roger 130 Ruby 131 Tommy 56 Vurner 131 W. T. 131 Willene 56 William 131 Zadie 131
BRUNSON, Harold 131 James 131

BRUSCO, Charles 131
BRYANT, Don 131 Linton 131
BUCKMAN, Frank 131
BUICE, Ambry 13 Annie 13 Agnes 78 Daisy 117 Elisha 73 Fannie 73
H.L. 13 Hillard 13 J. Henry 117 James 117 Lillie 117 Olive 1 Ralph 13
Robert 102
BULLARD, Fanida 13 Mary 131 Mary 13 William A. 13 William S. 13
BULLOCK, Jane 7
BURCE, Richard 56
BURDETTE, Nallie 87 Robert 87
BURDICK, Jessie 131
BURGE, Cecil 88 Dixie 88 Guy 88 Mary 88 Steven 88
BURGER, Elizabeth 13 James 13 Louise 13 William 13
BURGESS, Christopher 56 Clara 117 Toledo 117 William 117
BURLEY, Lelia 131
BURNETT, Kellie 131 Raymond 131
BURNETTE, Annie 88 G.B. 88 Herbert 88 Kelly 131 M.C. 112
Raymond 131 Ruby 112 Wynell 88
BURNEY, James 7
BURNS, Grayson 56 Nomie 56
BURRELL, Claude 13 Dewey 13 Homer 13 Mercedes 13 Richard 131
BURTON, Martha 88
BUSCH, Harlod 88
BUSH, Annie 13 Asa 13 Asa 131 Eula 13 Frances 13 Harriet 13
Helen 131 Henry 13 Jason 13 Malinda 13 Nancy 13 Olive 13
BUSTAMANTE, German 131
BUTLER, Dorothy 131 Frances 13 Samuel 13 Thomas 131
BUTTERWORTH, William 78 Willie 78
BUZZARD, James 131
BYERS, Richrd 131
BYRD, Albert 56 Mattie 56
CABLE, Thelma 88
CAGLE, George 132 Hoyt 132 Lilliam 132
CAIN, Ethel 14 John 14 Newton 14 Ollie 14 Robert 14
CALDWELL, Addie 1 Richard 132 Thomas 1 William 1
CALLAGHAN, J.P. 132
CALLAHAN, Betty 132
CALLAWAY, Evelyn 132 Leo 132
CAMPBELL, D. Henry 56 Helen 56 Henry 56 Hulon 56 J.H. 56 John 57
Martha 57 Mary 14 Mary 132 Robert 57 Sam 57 Trenton 57
CANNON, J.C. 132 Silvia 132
CANTRELL, Raymond 14 Ruby 14 Tom 14
CANTRIL, Ernest 88
CARDEN, Henry 14
CARLAN, Rosa 57 Thomas 57
CARMON, J.C. 132
CARNES, Ethel 132 Jacob 132

CARPENTER, H. Wayne 14 Harvey 14 John J. 14 John R. 14 Lillie 14 Sylvania 14

CARPER, Howard 132

CARRUTH, Hugh 132

CARTER, William 78

CARTON, Monica 1

CARVER, Betty 78

CASH, Sam 132

CASSELMAN, Rosemary 132

CASSIDY, Charles 132

CASSIS, Michael 132

CASTILE, Vivian 132

CASTLEBERRY, Alice 102 Billy 88 Emory 88 Fred 132 Gladys 132 Harry 88 Henderson 88 Jack 88 James 88 John 88 Katherine 88 Louie 88 Martha 88 Nettie 88 Robert 88 Rosia 88 Rosie 88 Roy 88 Sarah 88 Thomas 102

CAT, Z. Hong

CATES, Hattie 88 Hubert 88

CECCHERINI, Rudolpho 133

CERRONI, Catherine 133 Foster 133

CHA, Jessica 133

CHADWICK, Cecil 117 Infant 117 Laura 117 Leland 133 Hazel 133

CHAMBERS, B. Gertrude 133 G.W. 14 Leonard 133 Mary 14

CHAMBLEE, Allies 57 Charity 133 Curtis 14 E.C. 133 Emmett 57 Georgia A 14 Georgia L. 14 Joseph 14 Sallie 102 Scott 57 William 14

CHAMPION, Jessie 84

CHANDLER, Annie 57 Juan 133

CHAPMAN, Vincent 133

CHASE, Rita 133

CHASTAIN, Cecil 14 Geanie 14 Joseph 14 Joseph V. 14 Mattie 14 Norma 57 Ralph 14 William 14

CHATAM, Beul 102 Gertrude 102 Willie 103

CHATHAM, Columbus 117 Elizabeth 117 George 117

CHATHIM, Margaret 89 Virgil 89

CHELDERS, Jackson 112

CHESHIRE, F. Hout 133 Ruth 133

CHESTER, Alta 112 Emoline 78 Ethel 14 Florence 78 George 15 Infant 89 James 133 Jesse 78 Larry 133 Mary 78

CHILDERS, Anna 15 Maggie 15 Mattie 15 Nolan 15

CHRISTIAN, Christian 89 Kenneth 133 Pearl 89

CHRISTOPHER, Homer 133 Pat 89 Ruby 133

CHURCH, Angela 133

CIANNETTI, Norma 133

CICCOSELLO, Jean 133

CIPRARI, John 134

CLANTON, Eva 15 James 15

CLARK, Annie 57 Benjamin 134 Bessie 57 D.W. 1 Geraldine 134
James 57 Macon 57 Tranquilla 1 Zora 57
CLAY, Lena 1 Robert 2
CLAYBORN, Lillie 15
CLAYTON, Diane 73 Frank 134 John 57 Peggy 57 Saacl 118 Sarah 84
Syrena 118 Thomas 57
CLEMENGER, Clinton 134
CLEMENT, Alman 15 Clara 15
CLEVELAND, Itallie 57
CLINE, Cecil 15 Duncan 15 Jefferson 15 Maggie 15
CLUTE, Tracy 134
COALSON, Clyde 89 Emmett 89 John 89
COATS, Floy 15 Howard 15
COBB, Ada 57 Annie 57 Annie 15 Annie 73 Buren 15 Carrie 73
Cecil 15 Clarence 73 Claude 134 Cora 73 Douglas 112 E. William 73
Erby 15 Ernest 15 Frances 134 H.T. 73 J. Howell 15 Hollis 134 J.T.
15 Jeanette 57 Jim 57 John 57 Little 73 Lucille 73 Mary 57 Minnie
15 O. Willie 73 Onnie 15 Sarah 73 Sim 57 Walter 57 William 73
COCHRAN, Hubert 134 J. Junior 134 Junior 134 James 118 John 118
Mary 134 Oscar 118 Quincy 118 Ronald 134 Sarah 118 Savannah 118
T.B. 118 Vivian 134 W.J. 118 Zemma 118
COGBURN, Bob 103 Eveline 103 J. Floyd 103 Lillie 103
COGGANS, James 15
COKER, Annie 15 Bessie 15 Charlie 15 Daisy 15 Edwin 15 Effie 16
Ernest 16 G.E. 16 George 16 Grady 57 H.S. 16 Homer 78 Len 16
Maggie 78 Mary 16 Maude 16 Sarah 16 William 16 Wyndell 78
COLE, Barbara 134
COLEMAN, Anna 16 Arthur 16 Bernadine 16 Bonnie 16 Bryson 134
Carolyn 134 Cecil 16 Charles R. 16 Charles W. 16 Debbie 16 E.F. 16
Effie 16 Eliza 16 Ellen 16 Elsie 16 Eva 2 F.J. 16 Fannie 16 Flora 2
Genia 16 George 16 Gladis 16 Harold 16 Harry 16 Herbert 134
Horace 16 Hosea 16 Hugh 16 Ida 16 James 16 Jesse 16 Joseph 134
Ludie 16 Mae 17 Marion 17 Martha 17 Mary 17 Maud 2 Melivna 17
N.E. 17 Nancy 17 Nancy 2 Nettie 17 Newton 17 Nona 134
Oretha 134 Phillip 134 Pleasant 2 R. Frank 17 R.M. 17 R.R. 17
Robert 134 Sarah 2 Susan 17 Thomas 17 Valentine 17 William 17
Willie 17
COLLETT, Charles 118 Jimmy 118 Melissa 103 Theresa 103
Willie 118
COLLIFF, Benjamin 134
COLLINS, Alice 2 Ata 89 Darius 134 Gale 134 James 134 Mark 2
COMBS, Lynda 134
COMER, George 135
COMERFORD, Debra 135
COMPTON, Nora 57
CONAWAY, Lillian 2 Marie 2 Nina 135

CONNER, Delphia 78 James 78 Janie 58 John 78 John 135 Marian 78
Offie 58 Wayman 78
CONRAD, Edith 135 Richard 135
CONTI, Vincent 135
CONWAY, Elizabeth 135
COOK, Andrew 58 Anne 135 Bobby 17 Brenda 17 Chester 135 Claud
103 Edward 103 Frances 58 Frank 84 General 103 Irene 17 James 135
Jammie 135 Jimmie 103 John 103 Lou 103 Mamie 103 Mana 135
Marie 84 Mattie 103 Mattie L. 103   Parthenia 84 R.L. 103 Rebecca
103 Thomas 135 WM. 135
COOLEY, John 84 Mahalie 84
COOMBS, Frances 135
COOPER, Carrie 135 Charles 89 Mamie 89 Sarah 58 Will 89
William 58
COPELAND, Robert 17 Sarah 17
CORBEE, James 118
CORBETT, Frederick 135
COREY, Archie 135
CORNETTE, Era 17
COSTLEY, Emmett 135
COSWICK, Delsie 89 Fred 89 John 89 Margaret 89 Walter 89
COTT, Agnes 58 William 58
COULY, Buddy 118 Jessie 118 William 118
COURSEY, Adelia 135
COVEY, Buddy 118 William 118
COVINGTON, Elias 2 Mary 2 Willie 2
COVONGTON, Alice 2 Ruby 2
COWARET, O.J. 17
COWART, Annie 103 Belle 89 Bessie 17 Charlie 103 Claudia 17
E.Dexter 17 Elsie 17 Ernest 89 Fannie 103 Geneva 103 Infant 103
J.H. 103 John 103 L.B. 17 Lena 18 Leo 18 Mary 103 Maurine 103
W.T. 135
COX, Alice 103 Artie 135 Ebbert 89 Ernest 58 Huiel 135
J. Denver 135 Maude 89
CRADDOCK, Lowell 136
CRAIN, Larry 136
CRANSHAW, Lenora 18
CRAWFORD, Berner 89 Elizabeth 136 Jerry 2 John 89 Ralph 136
CRISLER, Donald 136 Maude 89
CROCKER, Bertie 58 Gaines 58 J.W. 58 James 58 William 58
CRONIC, James 136
CROSBY, Kathryn 136
CROW, Clifford 136 H. Mary 18 Margaret 136
CROWE, Jack 18 James 18 Lizzie 18
CROWLEY, Elizabeth 18 Forest 18 Geroge 18 John 18 Margarette 18
S. 18 Thomas 18 William 18 Willie 18
CUFF, Howard 136

CULLEN, Ester 136 Frank 136
CUNNINGHAM, Cleo 18 Vantrice 136
CURTIS, Ernest 84 James 18 N.C. 18 Newell 18
CUSHARD, Thomas 136
CUSSON, Beatrice 136
CYPHER, Ross 18
DALE, Cornelia 136 Francis 136
DALTON, Carrie 58 Herbert 58 Martha 58 Maud 18 Pearl 58
Robert G. 58 Robert V. 58 Willie 58
DANIEL James 78
DARNELL, Mary 58 W.Fred 136
DAVIDSON, Fannie 112 Louis 89
DAVIS, Alice 18 Irene 18 James 136 Jane 18 John 18 Lonie 58
Nelson 58 Paul 78 Perry 136 Robert 188 Roger 118 W.S. 58
William 136 Winnie 136
DAY, Bennie 118 Emerson 118 J.C. 118 Margaret 118 Mary 118 Ruby
118 W. Lucene 118 WM. Louis 136
DEAN, Ivey 58 Joel 136 Johnny 58 Lillie 58
DEARDORFF, Janet 137
DEBOOR, Walter 137
DELANEY, Samuel 84
DEMPSEY, Alta 74 Bobby 18 Charles 18 Cleo 18 Cora 18
Elizabeth 74 Emma 19 Etter 19 Eulala 19 Frances 137 Genia 19
George 90 J. Miles 74 Jack 19 James D. 19 James H. 19 James T. 74
John 19 Joseph 19 Lelia 19 Lena 19 Linnie 19 Luna 90 Mattie 74
Mozella 90 Nan 19 O.C. 19 Ola 19 Paul 137 Rebecca 19 Reid 19
Robert C. 90 Robert G. 90 Robert L. 19 Robert M. 19 Roy 90 Terry 19
Tressie 19 Violet 19
DENNIS, Pauline E. 90 Pauline H. 90
DEPRIMO, Kevin 137
DEVERELL, L.R. 118
DEVORE, A.W. 103 D. Williams 103 Daisy 103 David 103 George
103 J. Elzorah 103 L.C. 103 Lawrence 103 Lillie 104 Lucinda 104
Mary E. 104 Mary L. 104 Missouria 104 Shirley 137 Roy 104
Wendele 137
DICKENS, Darryl 137
DICKERSON, Amanda 19 C.S. 137 J.J. 19 J.P. 19 Jennie 19
Mildred 19 Savilla 19 William 19
DICKEY, Myrl 19
DICKSON, Charles 137
DIEGO, Gregorio 137
DILBECK, Dean 137 Mae 104 Merrill 104 Susan 104
DILDY, Frances 90 J.S. 90 James 137 Joe 90 Joel 137 Lucille 137
Marie 90 Nancy 90
DILL, Christian 137
DIMITRIOS, Kohilis 137

DIMSDALE, A.P. 119 Lee 119 Malinda 119 Minnie 119 Robert 119 W.I. 119

DINKINS, Joseph 104

DINSMORE, A. Ford 137 Agens 104 Anner 119 Archie 104 Aubrey 104 Carl 104 Cicero 119 Glenn 104 Horace 90 Ida 104 Ina 104 J. 104 Keith 104 Lessie 104 Lessie L. 104 Louise 90 Luther 137 Martha 90 Martha 104 Mary 104 Maude 104 S.N. 104 Tracy 79 W.I. 104 Walter 104 William 104 Willis 90

DISBROW, Morgan 137

DISNEY, Mamie 137

DIXON, Virlyn 137

DOBBS, Asberry 138

DOCKERY, Lillie 138 Robert 138

DODD, Amy 90 Annie 104 Carlos 90 Earl 19 Elizabeth 19 Everett 19 Ira 90 J.D. 19 James 90 Lena 19 Leon 90 Odius 104 Sallie 90 Viola 90

DODDS, Alice 90 J.M. 90 Melvin 90 S.A. 90

DONEGAN, Betty 138 Herman 138 Lorena 138

DOOLEY, Alma 119 Ethel 138

DORMANN, Edwin 138

DORRIS, Avarilla 20 Charlie 20 Garrison 20 Joseph 20 Lillian 20 Nellie 20 Sim 20 Wallace 20

DOTSON, Beaulah 138 Eugene 138

DOUGLAS, Emma 20 Granger 138 William 20

DOW, Robert 138 Violet 138

DOWNS, J.W. 20

DRAKE, Amanda 20 Annie 2 Clifton 20 Elizabeth 59 Ella 20 Ernest 20 Henry 2 Horace 20 James 59 John 2 Lelia 20 Lellie 20 Margareta 2 Robert 59

DREAMER, Anna 20

DREW, Charles 138 Katherine 138

DUDLEES, Linda 138

DUDLEY, James 138 Jeanne 138

DUFF, Edna 74 Harry 74

DUKE, Evie 20 Sherman 20

DULTON, Travis 138

DUMONT, M.E. 138 William 138

DUNCAN, Frances 20 Infant 79 Rex 138 Robert 20 Theron 20

DUNN, Dan 138

DUNSON, Flora 79 Lewis 79

DUNWOODY, C.A. 2 Corrine 2 Edward 2 Ella 2 George 2 Henry 2 Howard 2 John 2 John 7 L.A. 2 Leila 2 Matilda 3

DUPREE, Francis 84

DURHAM, Dixie 20 George 20 Mary 20 Naomi 112 Paul 112 Roy 59

DUSSEAU, Roy 138 Vera 138

DUTTON, Emmett 139

EARLEY, Bertha 139 B.L. 139 Elizabeth 104 John 104 Viola 104

EARLY, Alice 20   Mae 20   W.H. 20

EDELMAN, Joseph 139

EDWARD, Iva 119

EDWARDS, Bobby 59   David 139

EGGERSMAN, Arthur 139   Margaret 139

EICHNER, Ronald 139

EIFERT, Donald 139

EISON, Carrye 90   D.S. 59   Jimmie 59   Mary E. 59   Mary I. 59   Mollie 59   Nancy 59   Odus 50   S.C. 59   Sarah 59   Verbia 59   Vester 90   W.S. 59

ELKINS, Mary 79

ELLER, Gus 139   Syble 139

ELLINGTON, Annie 20   Archie 21   Aquilla 21   Hartwell 21   Ida 21   James 21   John 21   Maggie 21   Mamie 21   Richard 21   Ruby 139   Thomas 21   William 21

ELLIOT, Alice 139   George 7   J. Carroll 139   Lucy 21

ELLIOTT, Lois 139   Van 139   William 139

ELLIS, Daisy 21   Eugene 21   John 21   William 21

ENGEL, Herbert 139

ENGLETT, Park 21

ENGLISH, J.D. 139

ENHULL, Alman 3

ERVIN, Amelia 139   Mary 139

ERWIN, Emma 21   Frances 74   Glady 21   Ida 21   Lilla 21   Ollie 21   P.N. 21   Sanford 21   Talmad 21   William 21   William 74   Zannie 21

ESTES, Blanche 119   Carlos 104   Charlie 104   Clyde 119   Hudson 105   Lala 112   Mollie 105   Onnie 119

ETRIS, Amanda 105   Gus 105   J.frank 105   James 105   Rolph 105   Sallie 105   William 105

EVANS, Barbara 139   Jack 139   Minnie 21   Nancy 21   Tina 21   W. Kernit 21   William 21

EVERHART, Betty 139

EVERTON, Virginia 140

EVES, Arnold 140   Jeanette 140

EZZARD, Mary 21   Thomas 21   Thomas M. 21

FALCITELLI, Joe 140

FARLAIN, Rosina 3

FARLEY, Hester 140   Raymond 140

FARMER, James 22   Rupert 140   Sarah 22

FARNES, August 105

FARR, Ethel 22   Eva 22   Fannie 22   Givins 22   H.C. 22   Ida 22   J.Jonathan 22   Luther 22   Margaret 22   Minerva 22   Nell 22   Paul 22   Samuel 22   William 22

FARRELL, James 140   Ronald 140

FAULKNER, Carlous 3   Charles 3   Henrietta 3   Ida 3   Nancy 22   Thomas 3

FAVERO, Elizabeth 140   Franco 140   Laura 140

FECKOURY, Della 3   John 3   Nancy 3   Phillip 3   Sarah 3   Michael 3

FEIGEL, Charles 140
FEIND, Emroy 140 Geraldine 140
FELL, Nelda 140 Roland 140
FENLEY, Harper 140
FERGUSON, Avie 105 John 105
FERRARI, Catherine 140
FERRELL, Bill 59 Donnis 59 Mariah 59 Reba 59 Margie 59 WM. 59
FIELDS, Edna 59
FILLINGIM, Ronald 79
FINDLEY, Mary 90 Sarah 91
FINNEY, May 22
FITCH, Estelle 119 Fannie 22 James 79 James F. 119 James R. 119
Rebecca 22 Van 119
FLATLEY, Maureen 140
FLEEMAN , Reece 59
FLOYD, Coy 91 Kendall 140 May 91 Oscar 91
FLYNN, Hattie 112 Joe 112 William 91
FOGELSON, Jack 74
FOLEY, Lauren 140 Patricia 140
FORD, Craig 141 Earnest 141 Joseph 141
FOREHAND, John 141
FORRESTER, Samuel 141
FOSTER, Barbara 22 Betty 91 Charles 22 Clifton 22 Eel 22 Era 22
Gussie 22 Joseph D. 22 Joseph H. 22 Margaret 22 Roy 141 Wilberg 141
WM. 141
FOULER, Corrine 23
FOUNDERBURG, Annie 23
FOURNIER, Calvin 141
FOUST, Floyd 141
FOUSTS, Esther 59
FOUTS, A. Pauline 59 Bessie 59 Bill 59 Clara 59 Dugan 23
Dwight 59 Edith 59   Elmer 23 Everett 59 Flora 23 Henry 59 Ida 23
Irene 60   J.C. 23 James 60 Janie 23 Jasper 23 Jerry 60 John 23
John H. 60 John J. 60 Joseph 23 Luster 60 Mark 60 Nellie 60 Paul 60
Robert 23 Stella 23 Syblee 60 Velva 60 William 60
FOWLER, Claud 23 Edward 23 Ernest 79 Frances 105 George 105
Gussie 79 Jessie 105 Julia 23 Robert 79 Telitha 105
FOX, Elizabeth 141 Mary 141
FRANCES, Jean 141
FRANCIS, Isaac 91 Mary 91 Mattie 91 W.A. 91
FRANKLIN, Louise 141 Nat 141
FRASER, Lucille 141 Nannie 23 W.E. 23
FRASIER, Earnest 23 Elizabeth 23 Harry 23 Henry 23 James 23
Jimmie 23 Lessier 23 Simon 23
FRAZIER, Carl 60 Martha 60 Ralph 60
FREDERICKS, Pearl 141
FREDINE, Rita 141

FREDRICKSON, Lindsey 141
FREEMAN, Calvin 74 W.T. 23
FRIGHT, John 141
FRISBY, Ruby 141
FRIZZELL, John 141
FROST, Herbert 141
FRY, Clair 142 Maudi 142
FULLER, Georgia 60
FULTON, Bonnie 142 Jack 142 Scott 142
FURR, Alene 142 W. Craig 142
FUTRELLE, James 60
GADDIS, John 119 Margaret 119
GALLAGHER, Heba 142 Michael 142
GALOSKY, Catherine 142
GARDENER, Addie 23 Exa 23 J. Early 23 J. Hughes 23 Norma 23
William 23
GARDNER, Dora 91 Sherman 91
GARGAL, Fred 142 Ozella 142
GARREN, Eliza 60 John 60
GARRETT, Bobbie 142 Charlie 142 E. 119 John 84 Laura 119
Ruby 142 W. Luther 60 WM. 119
GARRISON, David 142 Nancy 24 Texanna 24 William 24
GARROT, Vernon 60
GAYMON, Allen 142 Harold 142 Hilda 142
GAYNAIR, Carmen 142
GAYTON, Artie 142 Earnest 142
GAZAWAY, George 112 Mary 112 Plassie 24
GEESLIN, Marvin 142
GENTRY, Carrie 24 Geo 142 Nellie 142 William 24
GERHEIM, John 142
GERO, Alice 60
GERWIG, Arthur 143
GIARDOT, Norman 143 Ruth 143
GIBSON, Ben 60 Julian 60 Nancy 60
GILBERT, Billy 91 James 91 Jason 91 Ollie 91
GILLESPIE, C.C. 105 Nancy 105
GILLIAM, Jolantha 143
GILMORE, Marsha 143
GILSTRAP, Bascomb 112 Benjamin 91 Mary 91
GIPSON, Bobbie 60 Fannie 3 Grover 60 Hilliard 60 John 3 Rebecca 3
GLASCOCK, Maxine 143
GLEASON, Helen 143
GLESIAS, James 143
GLICKMAN, Sheree 143
GLOVER, Augustus 143 Doris 143 Ruby 24 Teasley 24 William 24
William 143
GOBB, Floyd 60

GOLDSTEIN, Barbara 143 Joseph 143
GOMES, Antoinette 143
GONZALES, F. Eugene 143
GOOD, Dorothyann 143
GOODRICH, Don 143
GOODSON, Hester 61
GOODWIN, Mary 24 Shirley 24 Warren 105 Willie 24
GORDON, Cena 143 Grace 143 Mattie 143
GORE, Alfred 24 Laura 24
GOSDEN, Charlorre 112
GOSS, Hiram 143
GRACE, James 24
GRAHAM, C. Edward 143 Drucilla 24 Eddie 24 Elizabeth 24
Hillman 24 L. Pauline 143 Lawrence 24 Willie 105
GRANT, Anthoney 105 John 144 Maude 105 Stephanie 105 Vollie 144
W.A. 105 William 105
GRAVIS, Harold 105
GRAVITT, A. Hubert 144 Alfred 144 Alice 144 Carl 119 Daniel 61
Ellen 61 Nanniet 119
GRAY, Geraldine 24 Lucille 24 Villa 24
GREEN, B. Cantrill 91 Bessie 91 Claude 91 Edsel 61 Elsie 61
Elvis 61 Erloin 91 Estelle 61 Gary 144 Henry 24 Ida 24 J.G. 91
James 144 Marvin 105 Mary 119 Mattie 24 Morris 24 Naomi 91
Paul 61 Richard 144 Rollie 24 Sandra 144 Walton 119
GREENWALT, Helen 144
GREER, Cordella 3 Elizabeth 24 Turner 3 Turner G. 3
GREVES, Alfred 144
GRICE, Pamela 144
GRIFFETH, Edith 91
GRIFFIN, B.L. 25 Carrie 25 Dora 105 J.J. 25 Jesse 105 O.J. 25
Robert 25 William 25
GRIGGS, Johnnie 84
GRILLO, Mary 144
GRIME, Eliza 25
GRIMES, Helen 144 Luther 144 Newton 25
GRIPPO, William 144
GRIZZLE, Hollis 144 Siddelle 91
GROBE, fRichard 144
GROGAN, A.J. 84 Lillie 84 Samuel 84 Willie 84
GROVER, Effie 25
GUNTER, Bessie 25 Bill 25 Camilia 106 Charlie 106 Daisy 25
Douie 106 E. Hugh 144 Ed 106 Elton 144 Ethel 25 Hart 25 Hugh 25
James 25 Jemima 25 Martha 106 Nettie 106 Pearl 106 Rebecca 25
Robert 25 Samuel 106 Sarah 106 Tony 106 Ulva 25 Zettie 25
GUTNER, Edgar 25
GUY, J.S. 79 Laura 79
GYURE, Barbara 144

HACKETT, John 25   Nancy 25   Walter 144
HAGER, Frank 144
HAGGOD , Grady 144   Herbert 91   Herbert C. 91
HAGLER, Mary 25
HALE, Clifford 145   Nelson 145
HALL, Charles 145   Frank 91   Katie 25
HALVERSON, Jacob 145
HAMIL, Arthur 61   Donald 61
HAMILTON, Ricky 61   Valeria 61
HAMM, James 145
HAMMOND, Robert 84
HAMPTON, Ethel 25   Jack 25   James 25   James C. 25   James H. 26
Mary 3   Sarah 26   Walter 26
HAMRICK, Carlton 119   Florence 26   Janice 119   Parlee 119   William 26
HANCOCK, Elizabeth 26   L.C. 145   R.H. 26   Wiley 26
HANEY, James 145
HANLEY, Repa 145   William 145
HANSARD, James 145
HANSON, Elizabeth 145   Harold 145
HARBIN, Tammy 120
HARDEMAN, B.M. 106   Lou 106   Serepty 106   T.D. 106
HARDEN, Howard 26
HARDIN, Thelma 145
HARDMAN, Hattie 61   Lester 61   T. Earnest 120
HARGROVE, Nora 84
HARLEY, James 145
HARMON, Howard 145   Jewel 61   Letha 26
HARRELL, Jack 145
HARRINGTON, Alexander 145
HARRIS, Ada 3   Allen 145   Ann 26   E.L. 61   Ettie 61   Eva 61   George
61   Hubert 61   John 3   John C. 61   John T. 61   Kathleen 145   Lillian 145
Mary 61   Rebecca 3   Robert 61
HARRISON, Audley 61   Betty 61   Linda 145   Vera 145
HARTSFIELD, Jesse 26
HARTTER, David 145
HARVEY, Margaret 146
HATCHER, Charles 26   Donald 26   Henry 146   Lillie 106
HAWKINS, A. Grady 26   Alfred 112   Amanda 26   Amy 26   Bertha 26
Betty 61   Clyde 61   Corrine 146   Emery 146   Ernest 146   Etha 61
Frank 146   Homer 26   J. Harold 146   J.M. 26   James 61   John 26   L.C. 62
Lilia 26   Margaret 146   Mattie 26   Myrtle 26   Nannie 146   Pamela 62
Ruth 62   Thomas 26
HAWREY, Margery 146   Robert 146
HAYES, Brenda 146   Grady 26   Mary 26   Robert 146   Tony 26
HAYS, Cephas 26   Cephas F. 26   Christopher 26   Clinton 27   Elizabeth 27
Lela 27   Lila 27   Lucy 27   Luiaz 27   Mary 27
HEARD, Calvin 112   Charles 112   Frances 112   Zoma 120

HEATH, Louise 146 Sydnor 146
HECHT, Loretta 146
HEINOLD, Frieda 146 Herbert 146
HEMBREE, Frona 62 G.J. 74 H.W. 74 J.L. 74 Maggie 27
Marlon 27 Missouri 27 F.M. 27 Queen 84 Retta 27 Robert 74
Sophia 74 Will 84 William 74 Willis 74
HENDERSON, Clarence 62 Fannie 146 Henry 146 John 120 L.T. 62
Louise 146 Thomas 120
HENDRIX, Rachel 146
HENSLEY, B. Gene 146
HERPIN, Joseph 146 Lola 146
HERREN, Willie 146
HESTER, Fate 62 Lizer 62 Michael 146
HICKEY, Henry 147
HICKS, Clyde 147 Ralph 147
HIGHNIGHT, Richard 147
HILL, Alice 147 Elbert 147 Evie 84 Home 27 J. Preston 147 Janie 84
Patricia 147 Virginia 147 Willie 85
HILLS, Angela 147
HINDES, Delynn 62
HOCH, Donna 147 Joseph 147 Richard 147
HODSON, Daniel 79
HOLBROOK, Byron 92 Clara 92 Clinton 147 Estelle 147 G.C. 120
Henry 147 John 147 Judson 92 Leon 92 Mary 120 Ollie 120 Rudine 92
William 92 Ralph 74
HOLCOMB, Clyde 106 Comer 147 Mary 106
HOLCOMBE, Arthur 120 Cecil 147 Fannie 106 John 147 John 106
Katie 147 Lillie 120 Martha 120 William 147
HOLDEN, Buney 106 Buren 106 Luther 106 W.D. 106 W.M. 92
HOLDER, Madeline 147
HOLIFIELD, Ada 27 Minnie 27 Summer 147 William 27
HOLLAND, Henry 147 Hoyt 147 Jerry 147 Tracy 27 Willie 27
HOLLIFIELD, Marie 27 R.H. 27 Robert 27 W.H. 27
HOLLIS, Charles 147
HOLMES, J. 27 Sable 27
HOLT, Lloyd 148 Ralph 27
HOLTON, Dora 27 Ray 27 Thomas 27 Thoams 27
HONEA, Jeffrey 148 Marvin 148
HOOD, Dora 27 J.D. 27 J.H. 92 James 27 James 28 John 28 L.E. 92
Louella 28 Marion 28 Ola 28 ollie 28 William 28
HOOK, Albert 148 Elizabeth 28 Gabriella 28 George 92 Golson 28
Linton 28 Luthera 28 Luther T. 28 Mary 28 Maurice 28 Minnie 74
Nora 92
HOPE, Joy 148
HOPKINS, Harvey 79 James 28 Louella 28 Pearl 79
HORAN, Ralph 148
HORNSBY, Ruby 148 Samuel 148

HOSKYN, William 148

HOWARD, Elizabeth 28   Elsie 28   Frank 148   Henry 28   Julia 28   Madge 148

HUDDLESTON, Adeline 92   Dearwood 148   Effie 148   J.W. 92   Mary 92   Pearl 28

HUDGINS, Violet 148   William 148

HUDLOW, Bertie 3   Thomas 3

HUDSON, Charles 28   J.M. 113   Jonny 112   William 28

HUFF, John 148

HUGGINS, Augusta 28   Everttem 28   J.P. 28   John 28   Willie 28

HUGHES, Cecil 28   Eliza 28   Essie 120   Gary 28   Henry 28   Henry 29   Jesse 62   Josephine 29   Lula 29   Mary 148   Pierce 29   Randall 29   Robert 29   WM. 120   Willie 29

HULSEY, Herman 148   J.Roland 79   Nettie 148

HUNT, Esther 29   Robert 29

HUNTER, Nancy 113   Jhonas 113

HUNTON, Danny 148

HURST, Charlotte 148

HUTCHINSON, Blanche 74   Winston 74

HUTTON, Ben 148

HYDE, D.T. 113   Martha 113

IMES, Augusta 29   James 29   Marvin 29

IVAN, Joel 120

IVY, Joe 148

JABBOUR, Jameel 149

JACKSON, Ada 29   Amanda 29   Asa 149   David 106   Eddie C. 29   Eddie F. 29   Elizabeth 29   Elizabeth 62   Era 29   Eugene 113   Eunice 29   Fannie 62   Frances 29   George 29   Howard 79   Hugh 29   James 149   James 62   Joseph 29   Lula 79   Minnie 29   Nancy 29   Nora 29   Ralph 29   Thomas 29   William C. 29   William S. 29   Willie 29   Willie 62

JAMERSON, Herbert 29   Morris 29   Nancy 29   Thomas 30

JAMES, Alfred 92   Bessie 92   Elizabeth 149   Gladys 149   Harold 149   Lily 92   Lucy 92   Nettie 92   Rueben 92   S.J. 92   William 3

JAMESON, Herbert 29   Morris 29   Nancy 29   Thomas 30

JARRETT, Jacquelin 149   Jesse 30   Joe 30   John 149   Kali 149   Katherine 30

JAVO, N. Michael 149

JEFFRIES, Les 149

JENKINS, Alice 62   Arthur 62   Barbara 149   Bernetta 74   Carl 92   Carl G. 92   Cleo 92   David 62   Dorothy 149   Edward 62   Emma 62   Fred 92   Gus 62   James 62   James 149   James I. 149   Jessie 92   Mae 62   Mamie 92   Mary 92   Mary 62   Mary J. 92   Melvin 62   Pauline 62   Thomas 62

JERKINS, Della 62   Gene 62   Walter 62

JERRAN, Doris 149   Edward 149

JETT, Adam 62   C. Harold 62   Ellen 62   James 63   John 63   Joseph 63   Julie 63   Laural 63   Mary 63   Menerril 63   Nora 30   Sarah 63   T.B. 63   Theo 63   Theodosia 63

JEWELL, Harold 149
JOHNS, Patricia 149
JOHNSON, Alice 30 Angela 149 Ann 30 Anna 79 Arthur 79 Aubry 63
Avirila 30 Beatrice 74 Christopher 120 Delia 30 Dorothy 79 Dovie 79
Eloha 30 Fannie 74 Florence 149 Gloria 149 Grady 30 H. 30 H.H. 30
H. Elmer 149 J.U. 30 J. Howard 149 Jackie 63 John 74 Johnny 149
Lela 30 Loyd 74 Luvina 79 M. Pearl 149 Margaret 149 Martha A. 30
Martha E. 30 Maurice 149 Neil 149 Nina 149 Paul 150 Sallie 30
Tanya 150 Teresa 150 Velma 150 W.B. 79 William 30
JOHNSTON, J.A. 30 L.C. 30
JOKL, Flake 150
JONES, Alexander 30 Alice 30 Alice 150 Alma 92 Alvin 150
Annie 30 Bartow 30 Brenda 75 Carra 92 Charlie 150 Clyde 30
Crawford 92 Daisy 106 Earnest 63 Emmons 30 Eugene 30 Evans 63
Evelyne 30 Felton 30 Gertrude 30 Henrietta 75 Horace 30 Ira 63 J.T.
63 James A. 75 James C. 75 Janice 93 John 75 John 106 Josephine
63 Laura 63 Lawrence 30 Lelia 31 Leonard 106 Lula 63 Mary 63
Mary 150 Mattie 93 May 93 Nancy 63 Roswell 31 Roy 31 Ruth 75
Samuel 31 Sarah 63 Susan 3 Theodore 150 Thomas 31 Trude 31
Voncile 31 William 63 William 150 William C. 93 William G. 93
Z.T. 31
JORDAN, Edith 150 Hugh 31 James 150 Jean 150 Lewis 150
JOYNER, Faye 150
KAHL, Russell 150
KANE, Mary 150
KAPLIN, Sarah 150
KARKELLA, Charlotte 150
KATO, Elizabeth 150
KAY, Effie 93 Walter 93
KEESEE, Joseph 113 Lillie 113
KELLEY, B.M. 63 Dorothy 150 Elder 150 J.M. 31 Jane 31 Jimmie 63
Joseph 31 Velma 150
KELLY, Bessie 150 Ronald 150
KELPIN, A.B. 31 Eona 31 Herbert 31 Joseph 31 Mary 31 Miranda 31
Susan 31 William 31
KENDALL, M. Tain 150
KENNEDY, Fred 150 Lee 151 Mark 151
KENNIGNTON, Samantha 106 William 106
KENNY, Lavina 151
KENT, Floyd 79 Idas 79 Leroy 70 Mable 80 Nora 80 Ollie 151
Sarah 151 T. Nelson 80 Troy 80 Willie 80 Zonie 80
KERR, Gene 151
KEYES, N. Thanetta 120
KILCORE, Willie 85
KILGORE, Calvin 113 J.E. 113 J.T. 113 James 113 Joseph 151
Mamie 113 Mary 113
KIMBRELL, Alfred 63 C.W. 151 Samuel 63

KING, Allie 63   Barrington 4   Barrington J. 4   Barrington S   Charles 4
Charles 63   Clifford 63   Frances 63   Henrietta 151   Inez 4   James 85
Margaret 4   Maria 4   Matty 4   Norman 4   Roswell 7   Thomas 4
KINGSOLVER, John 151
KIRBY, Clarence 151   Everettt 151   Jane 151   Lawrence 151
KIRK, A.M. 31   Acel 31   Annie 31   Annie M. 31   Charles 31   Cornelia 31
Daisy M. 31   Daisy R. 31   Dwight 31   Estelle 31   Ethel 31   Eva 31   Gus 31
Hattie 31   Henry 31   Henry A. 31   Henry F. 31   Horace 32   Hugh 32
James 32   Jasper F. 32   Jasper L. 32   John 32   Lewis 32   Melissa 32
Nancy 32   Nora 32   Ollie 32   Ralph 32   Robert 32   Sarah 32   Thomas 32
Viola 32
KIRKLAND, Albert 151
KIRKWOOD, Mikeal 151
KISER, Herbert 151
KLEIN, Florence 31   Frank 31   Robert 151
KNUCKLES, Gartrell 85   Samuel 85
KOENIG, Herman 151
KORENFELD, Irena 151
KOSSMAN, David 151
KRAKOVSKI, Leonid 151
KRAMER, Charles 151   Richard 151
KREIS, Foster 152   Oneta 152
KSHYNA, Michael 152
KUHN, Helen 152
KUYKENDALL, William 113
KYPER, Stanley 152
LACKEY, Clyde 32   Clyde 80   Dennis 32   Harley 80   Homer 63   Lena 32
Rose 32   Smith 32   Twin 80
LAFON, Gilbert 152
LAMALZ, Mary 152
LAMB, Charles 152   Myrtle 152   Robert 152   R. Stanley 152
LAMOND, Yvonne 152
LANAR, Mason 32
LANCE, Patricia 152   William 152
LAND, Alice 120   Bud 120   Jesse 120   Levi 120   Mamie 120   M.L. 120
S. 120
LANDERS, Rosa 32
LANDRUM, Flonnie 93   Grace 106   S. Calvin 93
LANE, Allen 32   Audrey 152   Bernice 32   Charlie 93   Don 32   J.Gid 152
Jack 32   Lillie 32   Lois 152   Paul 32   W.D. 107   Warren 32
LANG, John 4
LANGLE, Myrtle 32
LANGLEY, Dorothy 33   Frank 33   Gladys 33   Johnnie 33   Timothy 152
LANIER, Fannie 33   James 152   Jane 33   L.M. 33   Red 33   Selamer 33
LATHAM, William 33
LAUTH, Barbara 152   Elizabeth 152   Noble 152
LAWES, William 152

LAWSON, Clara 80 Cora 80 Doyle 80 Edward 80 Homer 80
Joseph 152 Homer 80 N. Bobbie 93 Nellie 93 William 152
LAYCOK, John 153
LEAKE, Frank 153 Mildred 153
LEAVELL, Carlton 80
LEDFORD, Elizabeth 120 Ernest 120 H. David 120 Hiram 120
Jewell 120 Lillie 120 Wayne 153
LEE, Fairy 107 Fannie 93 Floyd 93 Gordon 33 J.W. 63 Jong 153
Margaret 93 R.F. 113 William 33
LEECH, Janice 153
LEGG, C.T. 107 Nora 107
LEIGHTON, Paul 153
LEIN, David 153
LERON, Martha 4
LEROY, B.E. 4 Miranda 4
LETTERMAN, Rita 93
LEVERETTE, Dorothy 33
LEVERGOOD, James 153
LEVINE, Elizabeth 153
LEWIS, Clara 33 Estelle 33 Evie 153 James 33 Laura 153 Peggy 153
William 153
LIAO, Charles 153
LIEBERMAN, William 153
LIETCH, Allen 153
LIGHT, H. Stephens 93
LIMBECK, Janice 153 merle 153
LINDSEY, Edna 33 Emery 33 John 33 Mollie 33 Rosie 33
LINGEFOTT, Raymond 64
LINGERFELT, Nettie 80 Perry 80 Perry 153 Vera 80
LINGO, Raymond 153
LINKE, Florence 153 Harold 153
LIPSEY, Wayne 153
LISTON, Demecia 154
LITTLE, Bobbye 93 Eloise 154 George 113 Georgia 113 Jess 113
Paul 121 Wayne 121
LOCKE, Cora 154 Fred 154
LOCKRIDGE, R.L. 154
LOGGINS, Joe 33 Lee 33
LONAWAY, Lillian 4 Marie 4 William 4
LONER, Alter 64 Donald 64 Eva 64 Frances 64 Franklin 64
George 64 Henry 64 Henry 64 John 64 John 154 Mary 64 Odessa 154
Perry 64 Rebecca 64 Ruth 64 Tressie 64 William 64 Willie 64
LONG, Angelia 64 David 64 Elizabeth 64 Emory 64 Homer 64 Homer
33 Jamie 64 Joe; 154 Johnny 64 Larry 33 Lee 64 Mary 33 Maude 64
Nancy 64 Ollie 154 Roxie 33 Sylvia 64 William 64 Willie 33
Willie 154
LOPEZ, Lourdes 154

LORD, Carrie 154 Henry 154 Inas 64
LOUDERMILK, Duville 33 Michael 154 Vernon 33
LOVORN, Henry 34
LOWE, D.B. 64 Janet 154 Nancy 64
LOWERY, Homer 93 Stella 93
LOWRY, Adderson 64 Buran 64 Claude 34 O. 34 Mary 64
Randall 154 Robert 65 Russell 34 Sarah 24 Winnie 34
LOYD, J.D 65
LUCAS, James 154
LUKE, Vivian 154
LUMMAS, John 154 Lillie 154
LUMRY, Edna 34 Theron 34
LYNN, James 154
LYON, Ada 34 Archie 34 G.T. 34 Harry 34 Judson 154 Mae 154
Paden 34 Pat 34 Pearl 34
LYONS, Algernon 154
MABREY, Peena 34
MABRY, Doyle 155
MACLELLAN, Sylvia 155
MACRAE, Lawrence 155
MADDEN, Annetta 155
MADDOX, Blanche 93 C. Emmerson 93 C.C. Cicero 93 Elizabeth 93
Emerson 93 Eulalia 93 George 93 Joe 93 Lillian 34 Meda 94
William 34 Wynette 121
MAFFETT, Brownlow 80 Clyde 75 Eulah 75 Susan 80
MAGGIORE, Rose 155
MAGILL, Aurela 4 Helen 4
MAHONEY, Lucy 155
MAJOR, Tony 155
MAKIN, Andrew 107 Sarah 107
MALLORY, Jason 155
MALONE, Bradley 155
MALONEY, Addie 80 Charles 80 Cora 80 Ernest 34 Forrest 80 Fronie
80 Henry D. 80 Henry J. 80 J. Howard 80 Ola 34
MANDERS, Robert 65 Vera 65
MANNING, Eileen 155 Margaret 155
MANSELL, Annie 34 Arthur E. 34 Arthur G. 34 Billie 34 Etna 34
Gene 34 Gincy 107 Hannah 107 Hazel 34 J.W. 107 J. Howell 34
J. Paul 155 James 34 Mattie 34 Maude 34 Nora 34 Nora 35 Robert 35
Robert 107 Roscoe 35 William 35
MANSEN, Maude 35 Robert 35
MANUS, John 107 Wesley 155
MARCH, Lewis 155 Mary 155
MARCUS, Kenny 80
MARION, John 35
MARKHAM, Peggy 155
MARKS, Robert 155

MARLER, Eddie 35 Freddie 35 Leonora 35 William 35 William M. 35
MARSHALL, Alma 35 Avery 35 B.H. 107 Carroll 35 Claude 35
Cora 35 Ezzard 107 Flonnie 94 Henry 94 Roxanna 155 Sanford 35
Wanda 107
MARTIN, Austin 35 B.A. 113 Charles A. 155 Charles E. 155
Christine 35 Claude 35 Earl 155 Ellie 155 Flonnie 35 George 113
Georgia 65 Gordon 155 Hugh 94 Isla 35 J.H. 113 J.Z. 35 James 155
James L. 35 James T. 35 Jerry 35 John 35 John 65 John 113
John N. 94 Kitty 156 L. Newt 35 Laura 35 Lemina 35 Lucy 113
Lura 35 Martha 35 Martha 65 Martha 113 May 65 Minnie 85
Myrtis 156 Paul 156 Pearl 156 R. Dolores 35 Rayman 65 Richard 35
Robert 113 Ruth 94 Samuel 85 Sarah 35 Tomie 36 Vada 36 Viola 85
W.D. 94 W.H. 36 Welton 113 William 113 William H. 36
William Z. 36 Willie 156
MASHACK, Noah 121
MASHBURN, Edmond 107 Fred 107 Julia 107 Willie 107 Willene 36
MASK, Angie 94 Robert 94
MASON, Albert 156 Fred 36 Nadine 156 Rayford 36 T. Jerry 156
MASSEY, Amanda 65 Andrew 65 Claude 65 Edward 36 Elizabeth 36
Estelle 80 George 65 Hubert 65 James 80 L. Montez 65 Lula 65
Melanie 36
MASTRANGELO, Arnold 156 Nunzia 156
MATHEWS, Elizabeth 36 Ethel 36 John 36
MATHIS, Athelda 113 Clyde 113 Jessie 114 Lee 114 Leona 114
MATIZ, Andrez 156
MATTES, Adolph 156 Theresia 156
MATTHEWS, Jason 156 Pauline 156
MATTISON, Benjamin 36 Mary 36 Mattie 36
MAUNEY, Arthur 156
MAXWELL, Aby 75 A.C. 81 Arthur 75 Audrey 75 Carl 75 Carrie 75
Charles 75 Conway 75 Edgar 156 Emily 75 James 75 Jessie 75 John 75
John E. 75 John W. 75 Lillian 75 Mary 75 Mayrtle 75 Pearl 75
Samantha 75 Sarerta 75 Wade 75 William 75
MAYFIELD, James 36
MAYS, Frances 36 William 36
MCARDEN, Roy 36
MCARTHUR, Catherine 156 John 156
MCAULEY, W.H. 156
MCCART, Edna 156
MCCLAIN, Bessie 121 Dozier 121 J.D. 121 Nancy 36 Winton 121
MCCLESKEY, Dollie 121 Dovie 121 Estelle 121 Leo 121 Telma 121
Tom 121 Virginia 121 W.G. 121
MCCLESKY, L. E. 107 Ida 107
MCCLURE, Emma 156
MCCLUSKEY, Eura 121 Gus 121
MCCOLLUM, Ester 107 Infant 107 John 107 Sophronia 107
William 107

MCCONNELL, Barry 75 Mildred 156
MCCOWAN, Ruby 156
MCCRACKEN, Gerald 156 Lawrence 156
MCDADE, Mark 157
MCDANIEL, James 36 Joseph 94 Mary 94
MCDERMENT, Bertha 36 Henry 36
MCDERMOND, Ada 36
MCDONALD, Emmett 157 Lena 157
MCDONAUGH, Charlotte 157 Joseph 157
MCFARLAND, Jack 36 Marcus 157
MCGARITY, Charles 157
MCGEHEE, Elmer 37
MCGILVARY, Barbara 157 Michael 157
MCGINNIS, Annie 37 Annis 157 Baldy 37 Charles 75 Edna 37
Hubert 157 Kate 37 Marvin 157 Odus 37 Robert 4
MCHENRY, Terrence 157
MCKENNA, Harry 157
MCKINNEY, Harold 75 Vicki 157
MCKINSTRY, Dawn 157
MCLENDON, Alice 65 Arbyto 65
MCMARTIN, Robert 157
MCMULLEN, Ray 157
MCNAUGHTON, Annie 157
MCNEELY, Annette 37 Cinda 157 Claud 4 Claud 37 Edna 37 Frances
4 Gladys 37 Walter 37
MCPHEARSON, Hozay 65
MCWHORTER, Doyle 37 Glenn 37 Mamie 37 Rupert 37
MEACHAM, Claude 157 Ruth 157
MEDFORD, Georgia 37
MEDLEY, Fred 65
MEEKS, Betty 81 James 114
MERRILL, Arthur 4 Sarah 4
MERRITT, Allen 37 Danny 114 Fanny 37 John H. 37 Mae 37
Maurice 37 Mollie 37 Ross 37 Roy 37 S. Ethel 114 Toy 114
METROPOULOS, George 157
MICHAEL, Thelma 158
MIELKE, Jeanne 158
MIERS, Edith 94
MIKEL, Henry 65 Henry B. 65 Jemima 65 Mattie 65 Samuel 65
MIKOLA, Robert 158
MILLER, Helen 158 Stuart 158 William 158
MILSAP, Mary 158
MINER, Edna 158
MINHINNETT, Sarah 37
MINOR, Marcus 4
MINTON, Daisy 4 Edith 4 James 5 John 5 Mary D. 5 Mary W. 5

MITCHELL, Aaron 158 Bernard 37 Ethel 81 James 81 Lura 158
Maggie 37 Mary 65 Rossie 81 Thomas 81 Walter 65 William 81
MITCHEM, Roy 37
MITCHLER, Lillian 158
MITRY, Cleo 158
MOBBS, Euclid 158
MOEBIUS, Alma 158
MOHR, Frederick 158
MONROE, Joan 158 Shirley 158 Walter 158
MONTESI, Jacqueline 158
MONTGOMERY, Barbara 158
MOON, James 158 John 158
MOORE, Almeda 94 Bill 94 Bright 94 Carl 94 E.B. 107 Euell 158
Grady 94 Hollis 94 Homer 85 Jean 158 Loyd 107 Margaret 94 Mary
107 Mollie 94 Nancy 94 Nora 65 Riley 159 Robert 94 Rollin 65
Sara 37 William 94
MORACE, Marie 159
MORGAN, Ada 66 Alice 66 C.B. 66 Howard 66 James 66 Joe 159
John 159 Mildred 66 Richard 159
MORGILLO, Pietro 159
MORLAND, Lizzie 85
MORRIS, Alice 94 Annie 66 Buena 37 Cara 81 Carrie 76 Charlie 94
Cynthia 94 David 159 Dessie 159 Drew 66 Elijah 159 Essie 114
Fabian 38 Flora 159 George 66 Glenn 38 J.L. 76 Jack 38 James 94
James 76 Jeannette 38 Laura 66 Mamye 38 Odessa 76 Oliver 159
Randall 94 Robert 159 Rosa 66 T.J. 114
MOSHER, Maryann 38
MOSS, Ben 114 Crawford 159 Gary 159 Grace 159 H. Carroll 94 Ida
114 Kendra 159 Patrick 114 Paul 159 Trammell 159 Virginia 159
MOSTELLER, Ethel 38 Fred 38 J. Glenn 38 Thomas 38 Zona 38
MOULDER, Jep 76 Mattie 76 Thomas 81
MOZLEY, Evelyn 159
MUELLER, Wayne 159
MULLINS, M.F. Paul 94
MURPHEY, G. Fred 95 Hazel 95
MYOTT, Erme 159 Frances 159
NAAB, Leo 66
NALLEY, D.M. 114 Earley 114 Ethel 114 Glenn 114 Silas 66
NATALE, Nicholas 159
NEAL, David 95
NEELEY, Robert 95
NEESE, Forrest 159
NELSON, Mary 66
NESBIT, Anne 38 C.P. 66 Caroline 66 Elizabeth 38 Josephine 66 Orin
66 Robert 66 S.G. 66 William 66 Willie 95
NESTOR, Adeline 159
NEUMANN, William 160

NEWELL, Harvey 85 Mollie 85
NEWTON, Charles 5 Frances 160
NICHOLES, David 160 Genevieve 160
NICHOLS, Claude 160 George 95 Myrtle 95 Peggy 160
NICHOLSON, John 160 Loretta 160
NICOLETTI, Carl 160
NILSSON, Birdeen 160
NIX, C.Oscar 107 Charles 108 Charles S. 108 Fred 95 John 108
Lillian 108 Luther 95 Marie 160 Nelson 95 Preston 160 Roxie 108
Roy 160 Susan 95 Susan 108 Wade 108
NIXON, Alvin 160 Nita 160
NORMAN, C. Pierce 95 Clifford 95 Nancy 95 P. Elizabeth 95
NORRIS, Lillian 160
NORTHCUTT, Charles 121 John 121
NORTON, Anderson 66 Cloutilue 38 Esker 38 George 38 Henry 66
Hugh 38 Julie 38 Lillie 66 Lizzie 38 M.E. 108 Marvin 66 Ola 38
Syble 38
NUNNALLY, James 160
O'BRIEN, Michelle 160 Tracy 160
O'BRYANT, Ricky 160
O'NEIL, Charles 161 Sarah 161
OEMKE, Terrance 160
OGLETREE, Braian 160
OHARA, Joanne 160 Warren 160
OLIVER, Alice 138 Annie 81 Barbara 81 Beatrice 161 E. Orang 81
Elbert 161 Fermon 81 James 81 Johnny 81 Maggie 161 Peggy 38 R.L.
161 Ruby 81 William 81
ORME, Eva 161
ORNDUFF, Anna 161
OTWALL, Charlie 38 Charlie C. 38 Clifton 38 Paul 38
OWEN, Ada 38 Amanda 38 Julia 38 Luther 38 Thomas 38
OWENS, Ethel 39 John 161 Lena 66 Mattie 66 W.C. 39
PACK, George 81
PADDEN, Addie 39 Elija 39
PADEN, John 39 R.S. 39
PADGETT, Thurston 161
PAGAN, G. Gregory 161
PAINTER, Lavonia 161
PANNELL, Carrie 66 Charlie 66 Cora 66 Dewey 66 Eliza 66 Henry 67
Herbert 39 Lucy 39 Robert 39 William 67
PAPINEAU, George 161 John 161
PARIS, Bancy 39 C. Leland 161 Carrie 95 Charles 95 Charles 161
Elizabeth 161 Ernest 39 Jane 39 John 39 Lera 161 Lewie 161
Louella 39 Louise 39
PARK, Charles 161
PARKER, Cary 39 Ellis 161 Gertrude 161 Ira 114 J.W. 39 Levie 39
Robert 114 William 161

PARKS, Coke 39
PASTORELLI, Alfred 161
PATCHELL, David 161
PATTEN, Joe 39
PATTERSON, Clyde 161 Hubert 81 M. Willene 162 Pearle 81
Raymond 162 Roger 39
PAULK, Aloyse 162 George 162 Gregory 162
PAYNE, Allene 162 Calvin 162 N.C. 162
PEARL, M. 81
PEARSON, A.L. 121 Clarence 121 Infant 121 L.E. 121 Liler 121
Melvin 121 Virgil 121
PEET, Penelope 162
PENDLEY, Brad 121 C. Corbet 121 Dorres 121 Lewis 162 Marie 121
PENLAND, Jacob 39 Marion 39 Marion R. 162 William 39
PERKINS, Elizabeth 39 Katherine 39 Mary 39 Richard 39 Turner 39
PERON, A. Richard 162
PERRY, Franky 108 James 162 John 40 Lula 40 Mary 40 Minnie 40
William 108
PETTERSON, Harold 162 Muriel 162
PETTIT, R.L. 162
PFISTER, Anita 162
PHILLIPS, Adena 95 Alfred 40 Alma 122 Amanda 40 Catherine 76
Catherine 95 Cecil 162 Daisy 40 Edna 40 Emily 40 Eugene 162
George 162 H.E. 122 H. Ingram 40 Harriet 108 Hattie 40 Irene 40
J. Felton 122 Janis 122 John 108 Martha 122 Mary 40 Mary 122
Nettie 162 Nora 76 Ola 40 Paul 162 Phalonia 108 R. Forrest 122
Randall 40 Raymond 95 Richard 40 Richard P. 40 Roy 162 Shirley 162
Thomas 108 Walter 40 Walter 95 Walter G. 40 Will 76 Willie 108
PHIPPS, Peggy 162 Walter 162
PICKENS, Bertha 40 Harley 40
PINK, J. 81
PINTO, Oscar 162
PITTARE, Ralph 67
PITTMAN, Mamie 40 Pearl 40 Silas 40
PITTS, Dorothy 40 Frances 40 James 40 John 40 Martha 40 Mary 40
Mattie 40 Violet 40 Wayne 40 Zelma 40
PLANCHARD, Charles 163
PLANT, Forrest 41 Lee 41
POLO, Kathryn 163
POLTS, Gail 95
POLYNE, Lemoine 163
PONDER, Martha 163
POOL, Luther 108 Sarah 108 William 108
POOLE, Truman 108
POPER, Anne 41
PORT, Robert 163
PORTER, Alice 163 Leslie 163 Leslie F.

POSS, Bartow 41 Elizabeth 163 Howard 41 Robert 163 Trina 41
William 163
POTER, N.C. 41
POTTS, John 114
POWELL, Addie 41 Betty 163 Chas 41 Cora 67 Fannie 67 J.Carter
163 J.W. 67 John 67 John 163 Lillie 163 Mary 67 Octavia 95
Rhodes 67 William 41
POWER, Cephus 163 Charles 41 Elsie 41 Eva 41 George 5 Martha 5
Nellie 163 Robert 5
PRAT, Catherine 5 Nathaniel 5 Frances 5 Frances L. 5 Horace 5
Lilias 5 Sarah 5
PRATER, George 67 Lelar 67 Leonard 67 William 67
PRENG, Ann 163
PRESCOT, William 163
PRESSLEY, Mildred 163 Robert 163
PRESTON, E. 41
PRICE, Mary 5 Price 41
PRICHARD, Emmett 41 Gussie 41 Harold 41 Marjorie 41 Mary 41
Ruby 41 Thelma 41
PRITCHETT, Charles 67 Robert 163
PROBST, Raymond 163
PROUDFOOT, Elizabeth 41 Euphemia 41 Hugh 41 Rebecca 41
PROUTY, James 163
PRUETT, Herbert 41 Robert 41 Robert E. 41 Thanie 41
PRUITT, Beatrice 108 Cliff 41 Cliff E. 41 James 108 Lollie 41
Louie 41 Robert 41
PRUITTE, Amelia 5
PUCKETT, Ruby 164 William 164
PURCELL, Matthie 164 Theora 95
PURSLEY, James 42 Minnie 42
QUAM, Hi Dai 164
QUAY, William 164
QUIGG, Agnes 164
QUINN, Bencil 164 Bettie 164
RABERN, Jeff 42 Minnie 42
RAILEY, Vickie 108
RAINEY, Floyd 42 Glen 42 Hattie 42 James 42 Lena 42
RAINWATER, C. 42 Charles 95 Guy 42 J. Byron 42 Jimmy 95
Lessie 42 Lonnie 95 Luther 42 Nannie 95 Robert 42 Victor 42
Wesley 85 Willie 42
RAKESTRAW, Neal 81
RAMSEY, Edith 42 Estelle 96 John 96 Mildred 42 Seaborn 42
Sally 164 Shirley 114 Wilda 42
RANDALL, Frederick 96
RANSBY, Bertha 85
RANSOM, Cocia 81 W.A. 81
RAPP, William 108

RAY, Annie 164 Billie 42 Elsie 42 Linda 42 Stephen 164 Wesley 164
RAYFIELD, Frances 164
RAYFORD, Mark 122
RAYNER, Glen 96 Glen R. 96 Kate 96 Noah 96 Paul 96 Robert 96
REDD, John 108 Lee 108 Luther 122 Martha 108 Rilliat 108
William 108
REECE, A.L. 108 Becky 164 Clifford 164 D.W. 108 E.A. 108
E.M. 109 Eli 109 Emma 109 J.L. 109 Joe 164 Marvin 164 Wade 164
REED, Charles 42 Ferbia 42 G. 164 Hubert 42 Pauline 164 Posey 42
REESE, Clara 43 Clarence 43 Hoyt 164
REEVE, Cussie 67 Hubert 164 Mary 67 Mildred 164 Sister 67
W.N.N. 67
REEVES, Ardilla 43 Bessie 43 Charlie 43 Dora 43 Estelle 43 Eva 43
Fannie 43 Georgia 43 Harry 43 Henry 43 Irene 43 J.T. 43 Julia 43
Lewis 43 Louella 43 Mathew 43 Montgomery 43 Pearl 43 Posey 43
Posey D. 43 Ruth 43 thomas 43 Todd 43 William 43 Willis 43
REHEHAN, Doris 164 George 164
RENLAND, Anna 5
RESSE, Hoyt 164
REXROADE, Noel 43
REYES, Dolores 165 John 165
REYNOLDS, Gary 165
REYOVD, Mary 165
RHEINGROVER, Cary 165
RHODES, Mary 43
RICE, Guy 165 Ruth 165 Tennisee 165
RICHARDS, Betty 165 Everett 165 John R. 165 John W. 165 M.J. 81
Michael 43 Roberta 81
RICHARDSON, Fonnie 43 Gladys 165 Lucy 43 Martha 165
RICHMOND, Pauline 165
RIGGINS, John 165 Pat 165
RILEY, Arthur 43 Jesse 43 John 44 Lena 44 Margaret 44 Thomas 44
Virgil 44
RING, Peggy 165
ROBERTS, Isaac 5 Jessie 76 Lester 165 Nannie 5 Samuel 165 Sarah 5
Valpha 67 Virgil 67
ROBERTSON, Alsey 44 Elvira 44 Frances 44 Lori 165 Mamie 44
Margaret 44 Mary 44 N.L. 44 Nancy 44 Ruth 165
ROBINSON Alma 165 Grace 165
ROCKOFF, Herman 165
ROE , Albert 96 Flossie 96 Jeppie 96 Julius 96 Lillan 96 Noima 96
Robert 166
ROGERS, Earl 67 Edward 67 Faye 166 Francesca 166 John 5 Marie 67
Mary 166 Neomie 5 R.C. (Mrs) 122 Warren 166
ROLLING, Clyde 166
ROLLINS, Belle 44 John 5 John B. 44 Letha 44 M.L. 44 R.B. 44
ROMAN, Octavian 166

ROPER, Charles 67   Elbert 44   Elbert R. 166
ROSE, Lucille 166
ROSS, Bruce 166
ROWE, Lottie 44   Mary 44   O'Neal 166   Walter 44
ROWLAND, Van Gale 166
RUCKER, Edith 5   Florence 96   George 5   George 96   Horace 122
Ida 44   Jessie 82   John 44   Naomi 44   Von Teasley 96
RUDASSIL, Don 96   Katherine 96   W.L. 96
RUDOLPH, Edwin 44   Josephine 44
RUFF, Lucille 166
RUSHIN, Emmett 5
RUSK, Lula 44   William 109
RUSSELL, Della 67   Rennie 166   William C. 67   William N. 67
RUTH, E. Turner 96
RYAN, Adela 166   Evelyn 166   Michael 166
RYDASILL, Elizabeth 122
SABBACH, George 166
SAMPLER, Emily 44   Thomas 45   Willie 45
SAMPLES, Clarence 114   Daniel 114   Danny 76   Elbert 45   F. Mittie 82
G. Cleveland 114   Jennifer 109   L. Olen 82   Mary 76   Mattie 114   Noah 114
Norama 114   Victor 114
SAMS, Evelyn 166   Lee 166   Oscar 166
SANDERLIN, Charles 166
SANDERS, Bertie 82   John 96   Mary 45   Vergie 166
SARGENT, Anne 45   James 45
SAUNDERS, George 166
SAYRE, Charles 167
SCHEU, Christopher 167   Fawn 167   Meryl 167
SCHILIN, Marcia 167
SCHMID, Alexandra 167
SCHMITT, Amanda 167   Gerald 167   Stella 167   Walter 167
SCHNEIDER, Mildred 167   Norman 167   William 167
SCHNITZLER, Edith 167   William 167
SCHOLPP, Harry 167
SCOGGINS, Charles 82   Charles 45   Chester 45   James 82   Joseph 82
Robert 82   Verdie 82
SCOTT, A.J. 67   Alma 67   Ann 67   Calvin 68   Calvin M. 68   Carrie 68
Carter 68   Chandler 68   Claud 68   Cora 68   Dan 68   Emma 68   Eugene 68
Evia 68   Frances 68   Gary 68   Glenn 68   Homer 68   J. Michael 68
James 68   James G. 68   James H. 68   John 68   John 45   John T. 68
Johnnie 68   Leara 68   Lelia 45   Lois 45   Luna 68   Marion 68   Mary 68
Mary M. 68   Mary S. 68   Mattie 68   Myrtie 68   Obeen 68   Oscar 68   R.M.
68   Rachel 68   Robert 68   Robert 45   Robert J. 45   Robert L. 68   Rosa 68
Rosette 68   Ruby 68   Ruby H. 68   Vertice 69   W. Claud 69   W.G. 69
W.L. 45   William 69   William C. 69   William F. 69
SEAWRIGHT, Buford 167   Thelma 167
SEAY, Callie 69   John 45   John 69   Mamie 45   Samantha 69   Veston 69

SEDOR, Susan 167
SEGNITZ, Joan 167 William 167
SEGY, Lewis 69 Octavia 69
SEWELL, Ben 45 Ernest 167 Myrtle 167 Odessa 45 Penny 122
W. Guy 167
SHANLEY, Bernice 167 Wallace 167
SHARPE, Maury 167
SHAW, C. Warren 96 John 96 John R. 96 Mary 96 Nettie 96 R.B. 69
W.I. 96 William 69
SHEA, Robert 168
SHEATS, Garland 168
SHEFFIELD, Thomas 97
SHELTON, Curtis 109 Felix 97 Lessie 97 Ruby 109
SHERMAN, Barbara 168 Bessie 5 Ellen 6 Frances 45 John 6 John 45
N.L.S. 45 Susan 45 W.E. 45
SHIRLEY, Amanda 69 B.N. 97 Carlos 97 Chase 76 Dara 114
Edward 114 Effie 114 Fannie 114 Fannie 114 Horace 115 Infant 115
James 115 James W. 115 Jennie 115 John 115 John R. 115
Kenneth 168 Lille 115 Mamie 115 Mary 115 Mary G. 115
Mary H. 115 Riley 168 Sarah 115 Shirley 115 Tribble 115 Wilburn 115
SHOU, James 168
SHUFELT, Lynn 45
SHULER, John 109 Nellie 109
SHUTLEY, Robert 69
SIERMAN, William 168
SILTON, Sara 45 Thomas 45
SILVERS, Ben 168 Earvin 168 Lucy 168
SIMMONS, Elizabeth 45 Thomas 45
SIMS, Amanda 97 Faye 97 J.R. 97
SKEEN, William 168
SKELTON, Jule 45 Sybil 45
SKINNER, Beverly 69 Ralph 69
SKRIP, Richard 168
SLADE, Doris 168
SLAUGHTER, Robert 46
SLEEVENHOEK, Dirk 46 Homer 46 Marcia 46 Minnie 46 Villian 46
SLOAN, Lucius 46 Marylou 97 R.L. 97
SMALL, Effie 168
SMALLWOOD, Carlton 168
SMITH, A.F. 46 Albert 69 Alpha 115 Amanda 46 Angus 69
Archie 168 Aubrey 46 Carrie 69 Chester 46 Chris 46 Cleo 46 Clyde 82
Delora 46 Dolores 97 Edna 97 Effie 46 Elizabeth 69 Emerson 97
Ernest 97 Estelle 122 Fannie 82 Fannie 109 Farrel 46 George 69
George 122 Gilbert 46 Harold 6 Hartwell 109 Henry 69 Herbert 82
Ida 69 J. Clifford 97 J. Edwin 82 Jack 168 James 46 James 69
James P. 69 James T. 46 John 46 Julie 46 L.E. 46 Launia 122
Lavell 46 Lola 97 Lonzo 109 Loy 46 Lucy 46 Maggie 97 Malaney 82

Mamie 46   Mary 46   Mary 115   Mary 168   Mary S. 46   Maude 46
Myrtle 82   Nancy 109   Ned 168   Nettie 46   Ollie 46   Phillip 97
Philip E. 97   Richard 69   Roy 46   Roy 97   Rufus 97   Samuel 46
Sarah 69   W.A. 69   W.M. 122   Willie 168   William 46   Zollie 97
SNEED, Charles 46
SNIPES, Floyd 168   Virginia 168
SNYDER, John 168   Sylvia 168
SOMMERS, Dorothy 168
SON, Younsu 169
SONCER, Jane 169
SOSEBEE, Beulah 169   Clifford 169   Jack 97
SOUTHERN, Marshall 47
SPARKS, Austin 69
SPENCE, Aytch 109   Cecil 97   E, Dewitt 97   Hattie 109   Jeff 109
Mary 97   Stacy 97   Tracy 97   William 109
SPIEGEL, John 169   Juliet 169
SPOENEMANN, Lillian 47
SPRUILL, Alice 70   Charlie 70   Lucile 70   Mary 70   William 70
SQUIRES, Frank 169
ST JOHN, Harold 169
STAHL, Elbert 47
STAIR, Donald 169
STANDRIDGE, Andy 70   Annie 47   B. 70   Emma 70   Hubert 169
James 70   Joe 70   Jolly 47   Joshua 169   Nettie 70
STANFORD, Horace 47   Paul 47
STARK, P.J. 47
STEIN, Auguste 47   Helene 47
STEPHENS, Arthur 82   Bertie 169   C.O. 82   David 82   Edith 82   Essie
47   Etna 47   F.E. 82   Fannie 97   Flossie 82   Frank 47   Henry 82   James
82   Jessie 82   Jewell 82   Lou 70   Louise 82   Luna 97   Manda 82   Nola 82
Paralee 82   Robert 98   Rossie 82
STEPHENSON, James 169
STEPHINS, Betty 70   W.P. 70
STEVENS, Ann 169   James 169
STEWART, Cora 169   Elizabeth 169   Frank 169   Jackie 82   James 47
John 70   Lloyd 169   Mary 47   May 169   S.B. 169   Vaughan 82
STICKLAND David 98   Elizabeth 85   Florence 98   Mat 115   Ollie 98
STILL, Evelyn 47   Ronald 47
STONE, Eva 115   Susan 115   Suvilla 47   Thomas 115   William 47
STOREY, Estelle 47   Frances 47   Otis 47   Steve 47
STOVALL, Lana 169
STOVER, Buchie 109   George 109   Phillip 169   Sam 47   Thurman 169
STOW, Frances 47   Walter 47
STOWE, Everett 170
STOZIER, Henry 98   Henry M. 98   Joel 98   Ola 98   William 98
William A. 98   Winnie 98
STRABEL, Thomas 170

STRAPLER, Grady 70
STRAYHORN, Bessie 70
STRIBLING, Asa 48   Nannie 48   Paul 48   Paul O. 48
STRICKLAN, William 48
STRICKLAND, Alvin 48   Anna 115   Arlinta 115   B.F. 48   Burean 48
Carl 115   Cecil 48   Charlie 48   Clementine 48   D. Chandler 170   Effie 115
Eva 48   Florence 48   George 170   Harold 48   Harold 115   Hilton 170
I.J. 115   Jerry 48   John 48   Joseph 48   Lorine 170   Luke 115   Maltha 48
Mary 48   Mathew 115   Nancy 115   R.A. 115   Riley 48   Robert 48
Sarah 48
STROMQUIST, George 170
STROUP, Charlie 48   Elizabeth 170   Fannie 48
STUART, William 170
SUDDUTH, Charlie 48
SULKEN, William 170
SULLIVAN, B. Irene 48   Charles 48   Charles 170   David 48   Frederick 48
George 48   Ida 48   Ira 48   Jean 48   Jewel 170   Lucile 170   Marie 48
Martha 48   Ollie 49   Rosa 49   Susie 49   Tillman 49   William 49
SUMMERALL, Hubert 49
SURTS, Brian 170
SUTHERLAND, James 170
SUTTON, Arthur 98   Christina 170   John 98   Ollie 98
SWAFFORD, Elena 98
SWANN, William 170
SWEATMAN, Sarah 115
SWEENEY, Bernard 170   Leo 170
TAI, Juanita 70
TALLEY, Ella 49   Ella M. 49   Joseph 49   Lelia 49   J.T. 49   Martha 49
TATUM, John 98   Willie 70
TAYLOR, Carolyn 49   Florence 49   Matthew 170   Prince 85   Simeon 49
Thelma 170   William 170
TEASLEY, Isham 76
TEDDER, Amanda 49   Arminda 49   Elsie 49   Georgia 49   John 49
Lula 49   Nada 49   Pearl 49   Ransoms 49
TENCH, Betty 70   Gregory 70
TENNYSON, Donall 170
TERREL, Len 98
THAXTON, H. Dean 170
THERREL, M.D. 171
THOMAS, B. Clinton 49   Clebera 171   Elias 49   Florence 98   George 49
Jackson 171   Louise 49   Mary 49   Otella 76   Otho 171   Ovalyne 171   Packs
49   Polly 98   Sallie 171
THOMASON, Addie 70   Emma 49   Henry 70   James 70   John 70
Lucille 49   Marion 49   Mittie 70   Steve 49   Warren 50   Warren G. 50
THOMOFF, Jerry 171
THOMPSON, Agnes 98   Albert 109   Ambry 50   Annie 122   C.J. 115
Charles 171   Cora 83   Esther 109   Fannie 98   Isaac 98   James 115

James 171   James H. 122   Jordon 171   Lewis 83   Lewis 171   Lucille 171
Mamie 50   Martha 109   Robert 171   T.G. 50   William 109
THOMSON, Alex 6
THORTON, Mildred 171   Winfred 171
TILTON, Eller 70
TINNEY, John 50   Lena 50   Louie 50   Maud 50   Mattie 76
TIPPENS, Daryl 109   Richard 109   Samantha 50
TODD, J. Elmer 171
TOLLISON, Clifford 98   James 98   Myrtle 98
TOMASSI, Adam 171
TOMLINSON, Robert 171
TORMEY, Peggy 171
TOTH, Michael 171
TRACHIO, Nicholas 171
TRACY, Patricia 171
TRAMMELL, James 98   Mary 98   Maude 76   Montiner 76
TREADWAY, Barbara 71   David 71   Fannie 71   Hugh 71   Mary 71
Nora 71
TREADWELL, Eli 109   Mary 109
TRIBBLE, Elizabeth 71   Eva 98   Herman 98   Homer 99   J.W. 116
Jack 50   James 71   Joe 171   Maggie 71
TUCKER, Beulah 110   Delia 110   Dialphia 110   Howell 122   J.W. 110
Julia 110   Martha 6   Octava 110   W. Rollin 110   Willis 110
TUGGLE, Kennith 71   William 71
TUMLIN, George 50   Leona 50   Sarah 50
TUNNELL, Katherine 6
TURNER, Annie 71   Bessie 76   Bessie M. 76   Caroline 76   Conley 76
E. 71   Elizabeth 76   Fern 99   George 76   George T. 76   Guy 76   Harold 76
Harrison 99   Hazel 99   James 71   James 171   James A. 71   Jane 76
Jessie 50   John 76   John 71   John 99   Joseph 171   Joseph D. 171
Judy 171   Katherine 6   Lela 77   Lisa 77   Lizzie 99   Ludie 172   Martha 77
Mathew 77   Maudie 99   Minnie 77   Nancy 77   Pierce 77   Ronnie 99
Scott 77   W.J. 71   William 71   William 77   William H. 77
TWITTY, Frances 172
TYHEROW, Joe 172
TZORTZIS, Konstantina 172
UPSHAW, Arah 99   Charlie 110   Clarenda 110   Dora 99   Florence 99
J.M. 110   Mildred 172   S.C. 110   Thomas 172   William 99
UPTON, Eugene 172
VACCA, Charles 172
VAM, Cynthia 172
VANN, Annie 172   Henry 172
VARIAN, Barbara 172
VASZKIS, Stephen 172
VAUGHAN, Cliff 50   Daisy 50   Eliza 71   Emmett 122   G.B. 71   G.M. 71
Harry 122   Harsey 50   Louise 77   Lucile 50   N.E. 71   Roy 50   Willie 50
VAUGHN, Eliza 110   Mozell 172

VECCHIONE, Michael 172
VEREEN, Joseph 172
VERNOY, Brian 172 William 172
VICASU, Phillip 172
VICKERY, Chris 50 Faye 172 Floyd 50 Lottie 50 William 50
VILLYARD, Grover 116
VINSON, Addie 50 Elijah 50 K.T. 50 Martha 50
VOSS, Nancy 50 P.M. 51
VOYLES, Lester 83 Norman 83 Vellar 83
WADE, Collins 116 David 116 James 99 James E. 99 Ruby V. 99
WAGNER, Todd 172
WAITES, Warren 71
WAITS, Eula 71 R. Earl 71 Robert 172
WALDROP, Chessie 51 George 122 Jack 173 John 51 Pauline 122
WALKER, A.A. 110 Brenda 173 Brian 173 Carl 173 Charlotte 173
Edith 173 Fred 99 Ina 99 J.W. 122 J. Timothy 173 Jane 110
Janelle 122 Jimmy 173 John 173 John 99 Joseph 110 Julia 99 Laura 99
Pamela 51 R. Mack 99 Robert 99 Sallie 110 Teddy 99 V. Ernest 110
W.A. 99
WALL, James 173 John 51 Mary 6
WALLACE, Edith 173 Glenn 173 Julie 51 Mary 51
WALLIS, Bertha 173 Bobby 173 Clayborn 173
WALRAVEN, Joe 51 John 51 Linnie 51 Mae 51
WALSH, Jennifer 173
WALTER, Robert 173
WAND, Jennifer 173
WANN, Lela 173 Roy 173
WARD, William 173
WARNER, Harold 51
WARREN, Andrew 110 Louise 116 Thomas 71
WATERMAN, Constance 173
WATERS, Agnes 99 Almesta 71 A.M. 50 Charles 71 Chasbert 71
Claudine 71 Cleo 99 David 99 Denise 51 Dora E. 99 E. Marion 99
Edward 71 Edwin 99 Glenon 99 Helen 173 Henry 71 Henry 99 J.C. 72
J. Arvil 99 Josephine 99 Lula 72 Luna 72 Mary 72 Mary E. 72
Ralph 99 Ronald 173 William 99
WATKINS, Eppie 100 Louis 100 Lyman 51 R.D. 100 Ruby 100
Ruth 100 Velma 100 Verna 51
WATSON, Alma 122 Galie 6 Julius 123 Pashant 6
WEATHERFORD, Nora 100
WEATHERS, Dewey 72 Jerry 72
WEAVER, C. Norman 173 Floyd 51 Mettie 51
WEBB, A. Thomas 51 Bertha 51 Bessie 173 C.C. 72 C.M. 51
C. Byron 100 Casandra 51 Charles 100 Claude 51 Clinton 51 Connie
173 Curtis 100 Edward 51 Eonalula 51 Frank 72 Hattie 51 Hubert 100
Jack 51 Joel 116 Johne 51 Joseph 100 Mary 100 Mattie 174
Mollie 100 Morgan 85 Odessa 100 Quilton 100 R.O. 100 Ralph 51

Reath 100   Rennie 174   Robert 100   Robert 116   Roy 51   Ruth 72
S. Gober 52   Samantha 100   Susan 116   Thomas 52   Virginia 100
William 100
WEBSTER, Beulah 72   Herbert 72
WELCH, James 174
WELDON, James 174   Ribert 52
WELLS, Jonathan 174   Mary 85   Otis 85
WEST, Dorothy 174   Jesse 174   Joyce 123   William 174   William L. 174
WESTBROOK,   Amanda 100   Annie 52   Brenda 52   C. Paul 110
Cora 72   Cora 123   Ella 52   Ellen 110   G.R. 52   Gertrude 110
James 123   John 100   John 123   Junnie 72   L.T. 52   Luther 123
Marion 100   Maude 100   Opal 123   Ophelia 123   Patricia 100   Ruby 123
Thomas 100   Thomas 123   Wiley 72   William 110
WESTBROOKS, Berlene 100
WETT, Betty 52
WHATLEY, Aughney 52   Margaret 52   Mary 52   Robert 52   Wilson 52
WHEELER, Buford 52   Eliza 52   Inez 154   James 174   Levis 52
Lillie 52   Mary 110   Rovanna 52   William 52
WHITE, Elizabeth 174   Era 123   Eura 123   Evan 174   Gary 174   J.C. 123
J.T. 110   J. Vesta 123   James 123   Maggie 123   R.E. 123   T.M. 123
WHITEN , Carolyn 52
WHITFIELD, C.C. 83   Carl 83   Clarence 83   Cleo 83   Clyde 83
Lucile 52   Mattie 83   Peggy 83
WHITING, Ada 100   Thomas 100
WHITLEY, Annie 52   Ella 52   Henry 52   Ina 52   J.H. 52   Lula 52
Ola 52   Robert 52   Roy 52   William 52
WHITMIRE,   Frances 6   Iris 174
WHITMORE, David 174   Frances 6
WHITT, Ethel 100
WICKS, Ronald 174
WILBANKS, Franklin 72   Richard 72   Rosa 72   Rosa A. 72   Ross 72
WILCHOIU, Pamela 174
WILEY, A.C. 53   Bobby 174   D.T. 53   Ed 174   Guy 53   Helen 53
Herman 53   J. Edwin   J. Huford 53   Mae 53   Marvin 53   Mary 53
Odessa 53   Odessa A. 53   Olary 53   Robert 53   Rosa 53   Sarah 53
William 53   William O. 53
WILK, Frances 174
WILKE, Doyle 123
WILKENS, H.B. 72   Hattie 72   Lewis 72
WILKINS, Betty 72   Carrie 72   Herman 72
WILKINSON, Carlton 174
WILL, J. 72
WILLIAMS,   Bertha 85   Bertha 174   Cory 100   David 174   Dellar 53
Elizabeth 85   Gundy 174   Hugh 83   James 174   Jessie 85   Joann 53
John 53   Kelly 175   Mabelle 175   Naomi 72   Oma 83   Richard 175
Shirley 175   Taylor 83
WILLINGHAM, Alma 72

WILSON, Alice 72 Celia 123 Daniel 175 Elijah 123 Emerson 123
Infant 123 Irene 73 J.L. 53 Janet 175 John 123 Lary 175 Laura 123
Mamie 123 Robert 175 Savannah 123 Susan 53 Susan S. 53 Woodrow 73
WING, Ada 6 Cecile 6 Eliza 6 Geroge 6 George W. 6 Hattie 6 Jehile
6 Mary 6 Nicholson 6 Olive 6
WINGO, Almond 53 Claude 53 Lavada 53
WINKLER, Catherine 53 Flonnie 110 John 53 Julia 53 Thomas 53
Wilbur 110
WINSTEAD, William 175
WINTERS, Joseph 175 Nell 175
WIRTZ, Cynthia 175 Troy 175
WLODAR, Larry 175
WOLAK, Chelsea 175
WOLFE, Mary 175
WOMAD, James 53
WONIACZEK, Margarete 175
WOOD, Alline 110 Annie 6 B.B. 123 Boyd 110 Chas 53 Celia 123
Cicero 101 Clarence 123 Colline 101 E. Glen 111 Eugene 6 Fannie 111
Frances 111 G.W. 123 General 101 General 111 George 111 George 123
Gladys 175 H.P. 53 Harold 101 Harry 123 Harry 175 Howard 111
Howard 123 Ida 111 Ila 124 Irene 101 Isham 101 J. Will 101 James
111 Jason 6 John 111 John M. 111 Josephine 6 Julia 53 Linda 123
Lizzie 123 Lola 111 Louanna 54 Luster 111 M.W. 111 Mamie 101
Marie 175 Mark 111 Mary 101 Mary 111 Mattie 111 Mattie L. 111
Mollie 111 O.W. 101 Paul 111 Roy 175 Ruby 101 Sally 101 Savilla
111 Twigs 123 Vennie 124 W.B. 124 W.M.E. 175 W.M.Q. 175
Wilborn 124 William 101 Willie 111
WOODALL, Belle 73 James 73 Martha 73
WOODSON, Gratton 175 Scarlet 83
WOOLF, Florence 175 Thomas 175
WORAKE, John 6
WORD, Susan 54
WORSHAM, George 54
WRIGHT, Alice 54 Amanda 54 Carlton 73 Charles 124
Charles E. 124 Clayton 175 Clyde 54 Elizabeth 124 Ellene 124
Gladys 54 Hayden 175 Henry 54 Henry 124 Henry F. 124 I.O. 124
Isabell 7 J.I. 54 James 54 James H. 54 Jewell 124 John 124 John 175
Joseph 176 Julia 54 Kate 54 Laler 54 Larry 124 Lena 124 Mary 54
Minnie 124 Nettie 54 Nettie 124 Odessa 124 Olive 54 Ralph 54
Randy 176 Robert 54 Robert 124 Robert 176 Thelma 73 Thomas 124
Thomas W. 124 Virgil 124 WM. 124 William 124 William T. 124
WYATT, Arthur 176
YARBROUGH, Henry 54 L.H. 54 Oma 54
YEARWOOD, Hannah 73
YI, Chong 176
YORK, Joann 101
YOTHER, Dorothy 176

YOUNG. Cliff 54   Dillard 54   Flora 54   Julia 54   Lucy 73   Michael 54
Palmer 73   Thomas 54   William 54   William 73
ZAUCHE, Sara 176
ZAWKO, Helen 176
ZERRENER, Arthur 176   Mary 176